THEN & NOW

STOCKTON

OPPOSITE: The intersection of Main and El Dorado Streets was an essential crossroads for Stockton citizens during the transitional decades from 1849 to 1950. In January 1916, a rare snowstorm passed through Stockton. Using a handheld camera, Stockton photographer Van Covert Martin captured Stocktonians reveling in this unique moment for the San Joaquin Valley. (Courtesy of University of the Pacific Archives.)

THEN & NOW

STOCKTON

Daniel Kasser and
Amanda Zimmerman

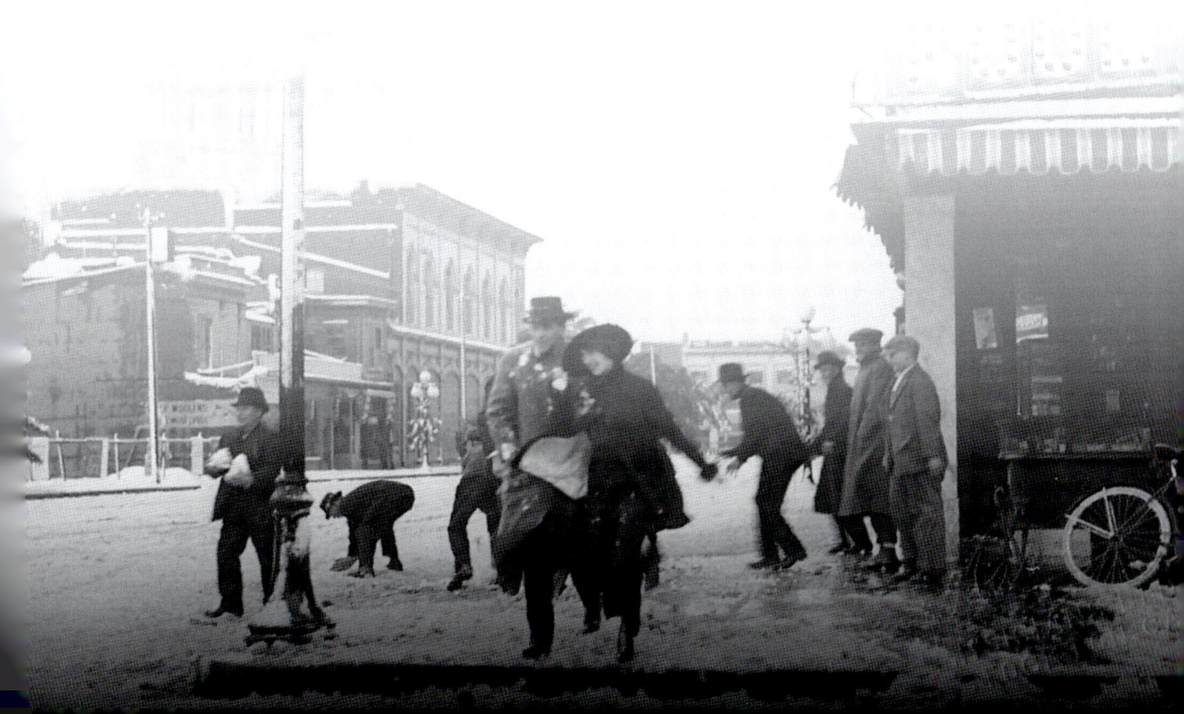

To my husband, Rob, my family—who always supports me, and my son Aidan, who spent hours sitting quietly in the archives while we immersed ourselves in Stockton history

—*Amanda Zimmerman*

To my wife, Lucinda, who contributed her editing finesse, provided continuity on the home front while I chased down site locations, read Stockton history, worked at the computer, and neglected the yard

—*Daniel Kasser*

We jointly dedicate this book to the people of Stockton who have remained gracious while Stockton has been misrepresented. Stockton is a quintessentially American city, with all that implies. Those of us who live here know how to live well with the rewards that good land and good work have provided us.

ISBN 978-0-7385-8888-9

Library of Congress Control Number: 2011935793

Published by Arcadia Publishing
Charleston, South Carolina

Printed in the United States of America

For all general information, please contact Arcadia Publishing:
Telephone 843-853-2070
Fax 843-853-0044
E-mail sales@arcadiapublishing.com
For customer service and orders:
Toll-Free 1-888-313-2665

Visit us on the Internet at www.arcadiapublishing.com

On the Front Cover: A patriotic Stockton public gathers at the Head of Navigation to tour a military barge in this photograph from around 1923. The Hotel Stockton, prominently featured in the middle ground, was constructed in 1910. The hotel was a focal point for interurban rail and water transportation. Today, the hotel is an integral part of Stockton's urban redevelopment. (Then image, courtesy of University of the Pacific Special Collections; Now image, courtesy of Stockton Re-Photographic Survey.)

On the Back Cover: Between 1912 and 1931, the passenger steamship *Fort Sutter* routinely ported at the Head of Navigation, located directly across the street from the Hotel Stockton. Today, this is the site of DeCarli Plaza. (Courtesy of Special Collections Library, University of the Pacific.)

Contents

Acknowledgments vii
Introduction ix

1. Encampment to Metropolis 11

2. Stockton's Portal to the World 31

3. All Roads Lead to Stockton 47

4. Subdivision and Suburbanization 63

5. The Urban Life Cycle 81

Bibliography 95

Acknowledgments

First, we would like to acknowledge the archivists and directors of regional archives who graciously gave us access to their vast collections of photographs and manuscripts. Without their enthusiasm and trust, this book would not have been possible. Our heartfelt thanks to the following: Roger Barnett, professor emeritus, University of the Pacific, and his work on the history of Stockton, which was critical to understanding Stockton's development and writing this book; Bill Maxwell and Angela Brusa from the Bank of Stockton Archives; Kimberly Bray and Todd Ruhstaler from the Haggin Museum, Stockton; Leigh Johnsen and the staff at the San Joaquin Historical Society in Lodi; Shan Sutton, Michael Wurtz, and Trish Richards from the University of the Pacific's Holt-Atherton Special Collections Library, Stockton Campus; *The Record* newspaper; Judy Baumann from the Port of Stockton Archives, and all of the University of the Pacific students who have contributed to the Stockton Re-Photographic Survey archives since 1987.

We also encountered many generous, spirited individuals and businesses that helped us at critical moments in the development of this publication. The support of the Stockton community was essential in the re-photographic portion of the book. We hope that sharing their leads to interesting places and stories will shed a positive light and bring insight to our city's history and affirmation to a community rapidly reinventing itself for the 21st century. The community members are as follows: Mahala Burns and Dan Cort of the Cort Companies; Susan de Polo and her family's long history and dedication to the community; Debbie Morris, Anna Sass, Janelle Meyers, Mari Tripp, Lincoln Center Marketing; Jeffery Miller, Stockton Metropolitan Airport; Sam V., Sass Bar and Grill Downtown Stockton; Thomas Reeves, San Joaquin Regional Rail Commission; Gabe Karam, San Joaquin County General Services Department; Kristopher Johnson and Ed Ferrell, BLR Commercial; Larry Gaines, for his insight and access to his family archive; Dave Kirsten, for his dedication and sense of adventure; Taige Ramey, for his unknowing contribution on airport history; Arnold Chin, Fritz Chin Photography; Geiger Manufacturing; Kate Post, Stockton Asparagus Festival; Kevin Hubert, Grupe Company; David Worfolk and Beth Stoeder; Robin Knowlton and Stefan Sekula; Ort and Sylvia Lofthus; Robert Mentelos, Penny Newman Bulk Cargo Facilities; Tricia Wilkalis and Cathy Grebe, Stone Brothers Management; Marci Blower, marketing director, Weberstown Mall; Julie Garcia, Weber Point Event Center; and Brent Hipp, University Plaza Waterfront Hotel.

All "now" images included in this book are courtesy of the authors.

Introduction

This book encourages a careful consideration of Stockton's remarkable history. It responds to public questions entertained while sharing my work for the Stockton Re Photographic Survey (1987 to the present) and authoring *Downtown Stockton* (Arcadia Publishing, 2005). *Stockton:* Then & Now picks up where *Downtown Stockton* ended, extending my desire to identify themes useful to understanding Stockton and perceptions of it. The sum of this book should reveal that "then & now" is a synonym for urban renewal. I no longer accept urban renewal as big government and big machines wrecking godforsaken neighborhoods. Urban renewal occurs daily through good intent and bad luck. Working with Stockton and students at the University of the Pacific, I understand what urban geographer David Lowenthal identified as the "dilemmas of appreciation"—the potential obstacles that nostalgia and uncompromising historical designation present to old cities and younger generations, each desiring to engage the future with optimism and yield a positive outcome.

Stockton city planners from 1849 to 1920 had a different set of obstacles to overcome than those of today. Stockton was newly organized on a grid overlaying an arabesque system of tidal sloughs and rivulets responsive to daily and seasonal conditions. Despite its idyllic resources, Stockton was challenged by natural and human activity we find intolerable today. Stockton grew from an encampment to a metropolis out of a need to secure itself against devastating fire and flood, crime and disease. The Stockton public encouraged the progress from canvas to concrete; they were the repeated victims of disaster.

From 1870 to 1930, Stockton experienced significant growth reflecting changing community values and fortunes. A time-lapse film of Stockton would illustrate a city spreading in all directions from the Stockton Channel, replacing a village-like atmosphere of civic, residential, and mercantile structures with large-scale government, corporate buildings, and nationally franchised stores. Residential architecture embraced orthodox and derivative examples of Gothic, Victorian, Queen Anne, Arts and Crafts, and Art Deco styles. Large-scale civic and commercial buildings embraced the eclectic Beaux-Arts palette, a hallmark of the American metropolis during the transitional decades of the 19th and 20th centuries. Several examples still contribute a powerful presence in downtown Stockton.

A century later, the challenge to later Stockton city planners is acutely defined. How will they successfully manage the complex physical and sociological challenges to redeveloping Stockton? How will they manage historic buildings, adapting to current standards for energy, communication, health, and safety? How will the public reconcile its desire to create a future Stockton with balancing impassioned and good arguments for preserving civic and cultural heritage represented in Stockton's historical architecture? Several solutions have already appeared.

The San Joaquin River and Stockton Channel were Stockton's raisons d'être and its portals to the world. They sustained Native Americans for centuries and French fur-traders for a decade. The waterways were Stockton's most reliable access during high water in the 19th century. After permanent settlement and the 1849 Gold Rush, the Stockton waterfront experienced continuous redevelopment to accommodate the extraordinary ship traffic and merchandise supplying the city and eastward to the Mother Lode.

The Stockton waterfront of the 19th century was profoundly different from anything visible today. The Mormon Slough, once a vital tributary to Stockton Channel, has become a weed-filled depression. It once supported a thriving grain exchange, connecting smaller communities along the delta's river system such as Graysonville, New Hope, and Crescent City. The slough was slowly sacrificed to achieve flood control after 1910 and the Deep Water Port constructed farther west in 1932. Stockton's early reputation as a "manufacturing city" was exported from the waterfront; shipbuilders, tanneries, foundries, and flouring mills manufactured and traded there. Eventually, 100 years of intensive and largely unregulated use severely impacted water and air quality and exhausted the landscape surrounding McLeod Lake and Weber Point. Pollution prompted the residential community to migrate upwind, to the north and west. Interpreting the waterfront landscape provides a large Stockton history lesson.

Stockton became a regional transportation nexus through its fortunate geography and early location as a supply and manufacturing center. In 1850, nine roads intersected Stockton, supporting overland passenger and freight service between San Francisco, Sacramento, and the goldfields. The Good Roads Movement (1870s–1920s) eventually produced the 1921 Federal Highway Act and a standardized highway-numbering system in 1925. These developments enhanced Stockton's overland connectivity via the short-lived Lincoln Highway and later Highway 50 and the Golden State Highway (US 99). During the 1970s, Stockton resident/business owner Ort Lofthus inspired a grassroots campaign protesting a complacent city and state government's inability to complete the modernization plans for Stockton's highway transportation systems. In 1993, Interstate 5 and the Crosstown Freeway were finally completed, and an embarrassing era in Stockton history ended.

The era of steamship passenger and freight service (1848–1931) is one of Stockton's most picturesque and storied. The steamers produced an expedient, reliable, year-round system to connect Stockton to Sacramento–San Joaquin River Delta and San Francisco Bay terminals. The system collapsed in an explosion of unscrupulous rivalry and competition from trucks, buses, and automobiles after 1920.

In 1869, America's Transcontinental Railroad was completed and Western Pacific Railroad opened its Stockton terminal. Multiple intra- and interurban passenger companies operated in Stockton between 1875 and 1941. Today, eight railroads converge in Stockton, conducting passenger and freight service, and intra- and interurban transportation is experiencing a revival.

The city of Stockton was platted in 1849 to accommodate a population of 20,000, a number achieved in 1905. Charles Weber, Stockton's founder and largest landowner, foresaw growth and planned for land reserves. Weber envisioned a concentric city with a vital residential/commercial core buffered by a land reserve and encircled by agricultural land. Stockton expanded its city limits in 1871, igniting three speculative land booms between 1880 and 1930. Subdivision and redivision during this period produced smaller lots, opened ownership to lower-income buyers, and occasionally incurred the long-term consequences of poor civil engineering and/or zoning changes. Several proposals were aborted and later restarted. Local landholders conducted the most successful developments in Stockton. The northwestern sector of the city, platted as the "Colony Tracts," represents well-planned, paced, and long-lived communities.

Three suburban tracts—Weber Tract (Stockton Acres), Smith Tract (Ideal Garden Farms, Tuxedo Country Club Farms, and Pacific Gardens), and Bours Park—were developed between 1890 and 1930, igniting the northern suburbanization of Stockton. Tuxedo Park (1913) became an exemplary upscale suburb, coordinating extensions of public transportation into these neighborhoods and attracting College of the Pacific to Stockton. Tuxedo Park's second phase included the development of the Miracle Mile and made modern utilities, automobile ownership, and strip-mall shopping convenience integral components of residential living in Stockton.

Today, Stockton is experiencing lessons in urban life cycles. Local understanding of urban renewal conjures the large-scale removal of a nine-block area southwest of Courthouse Square. The epicenter and catalyst for renewal was the replacement of the county courthouse in 1962. Many Stocktonians considered this impulsive, and there is evidence that alternatives were offered and rejected. But, I began this discussion with the idea that sentiments invoked by urban renewal are potential obstacles to the next generation completing its work—building a future Stockton. The following images reaffirm that each generation brings change, mostly because some things outlast their meaningfulness, practicality, and ability to adapt to new social mandates. A pragmatic spirit produced Stockton's dynamic development and its golden age. Viewing these photographs, more importantly because of extraordinary people and time spent with these locations, I feel Stockton will once again fulfill its promise during the 21st century.

CHAPTER 1

Encampment to Metropolis

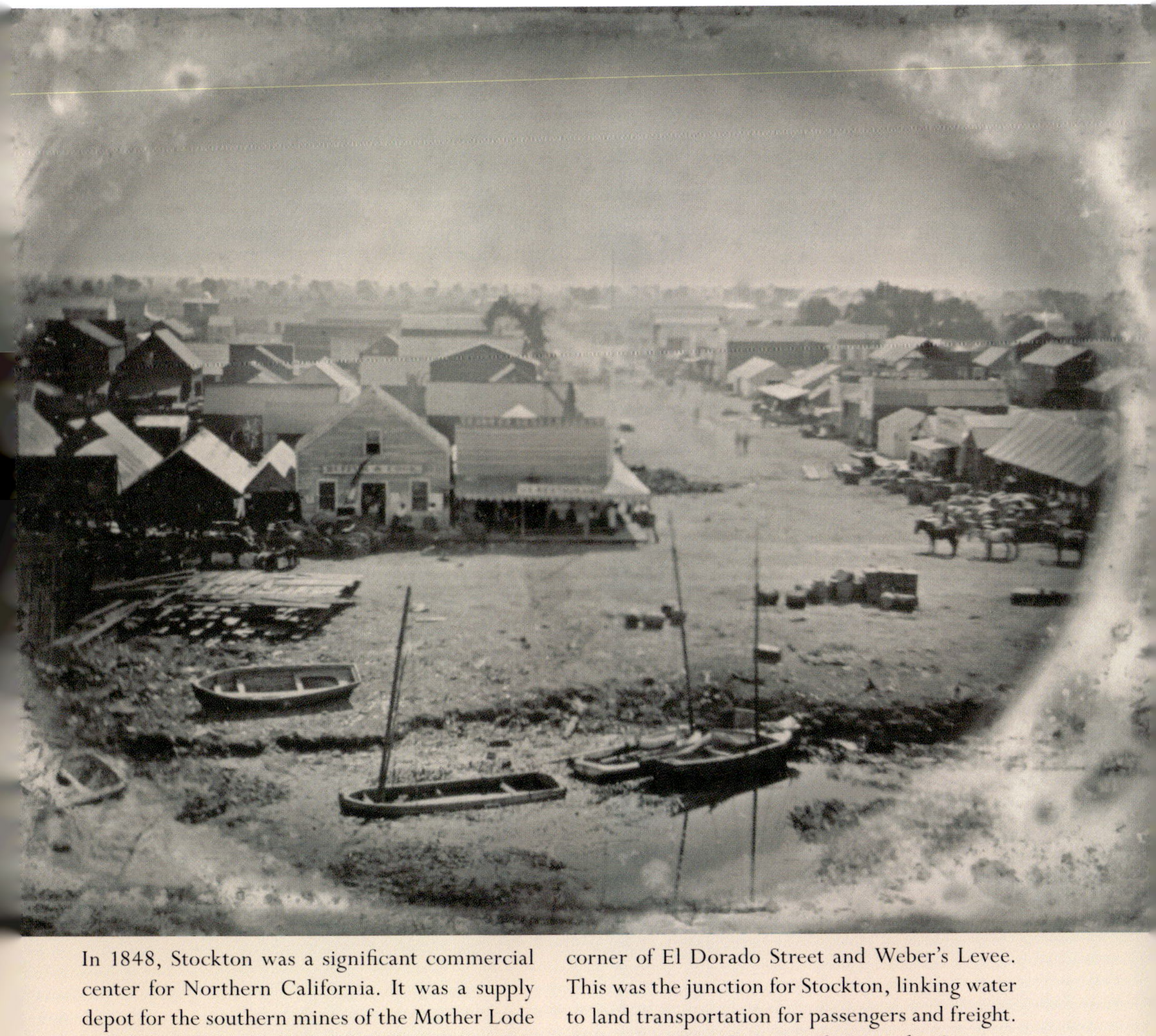

In 1848, Stockton was a significant commercial center for Northern California. It was a supply depot for the southern mines of the Mother Lode and the heart of a budding agricultural empire. The hub of commercial life was located near the corner of El Dorado Street and Weber's Levee. This was the junction for Stockton, linking water to land transportation for passengers and freight. (Courtesy of Stockton Re-Photographic Survey.)

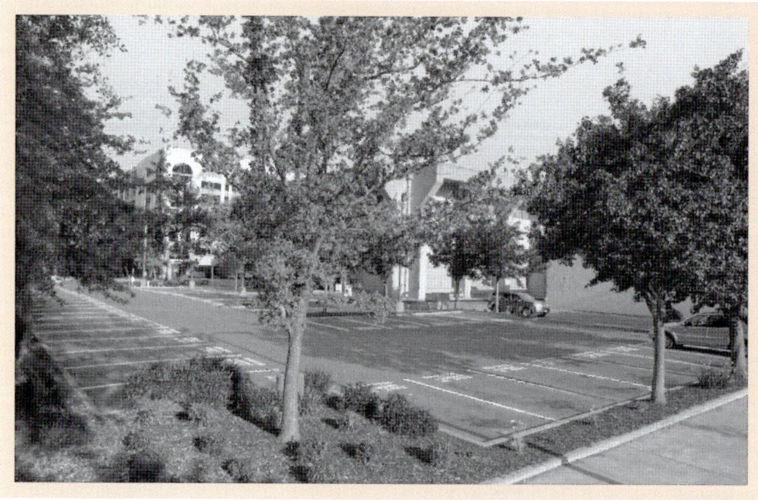

Stockton pioneer Henry Hewlett was a successful businessman and banker. His first store, established in 1851, was a frame building located on the northwest corner of Main and Hunter Streets. In the 1860s, a more fireproof building was constructed on the same location. This was part of a trend to prevent fires, which devastated life, property, and the commercial core of Stockton. Today, this location is known as Courthouse Plaza and is the planned site for a third-generation county courthouse. (Courtesy of University of the Pacific Special Collections.)

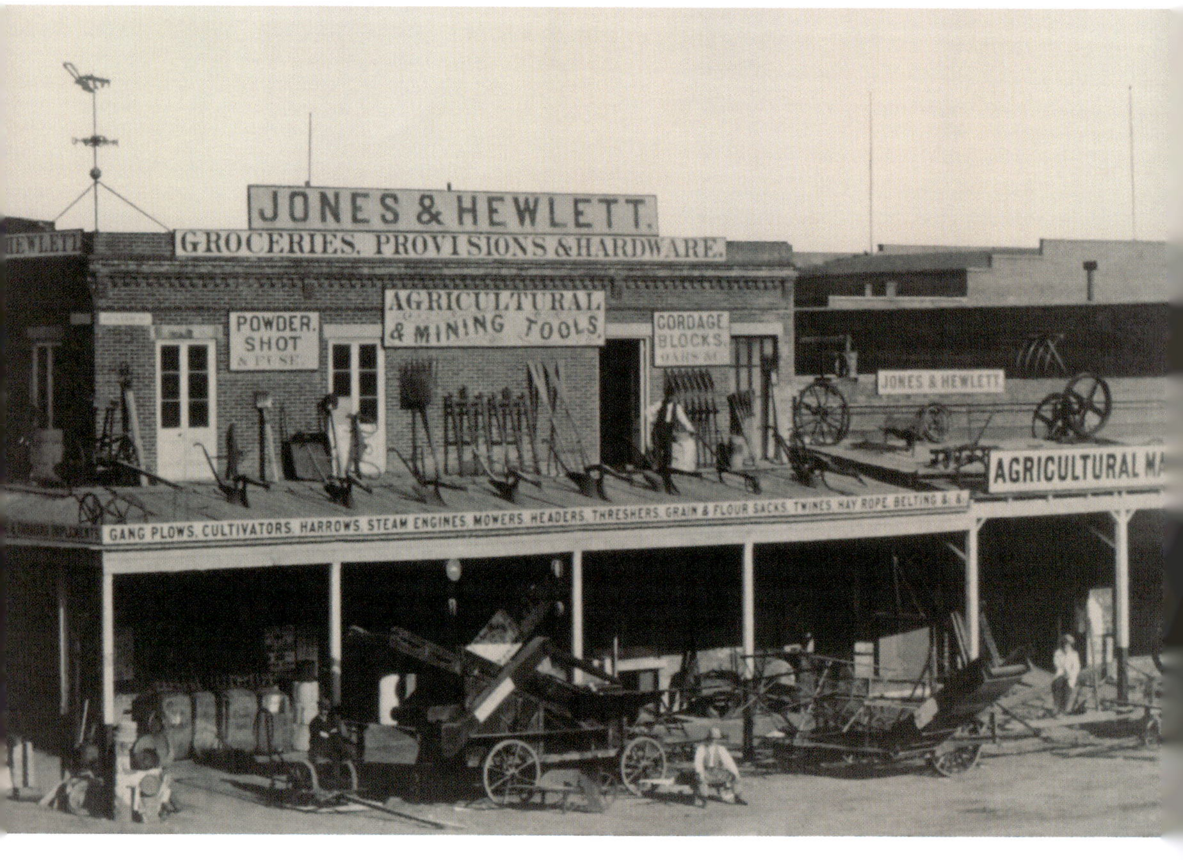

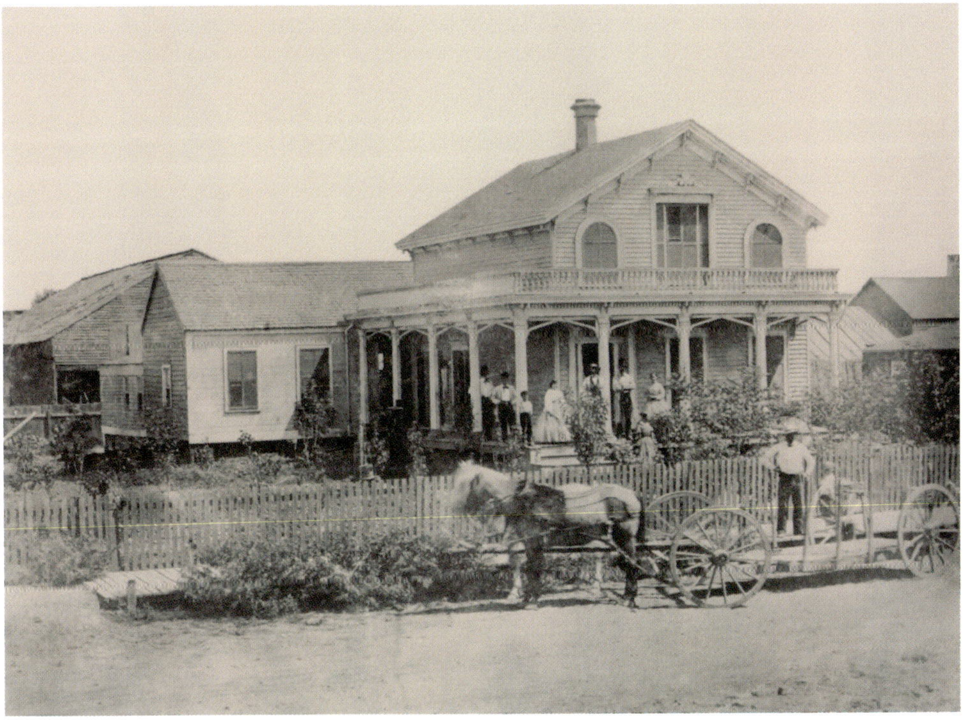

Raised high to minimize the inconveniences of flooding, the Rider home was a typical frame residential building in early Stockton. The home was located on Sutter Street, north of Main Street, in proximity to church, school, mercantile, and a variety of farming and industrial activities. Commercial life on Main Street prompted the owners of most homes and cultural institutions to move north. The Kress Department Store was built in 1929 and was remodeled in 2006 as the Kress Legal Center. (Courtesy of Haggin Museum Archives.)

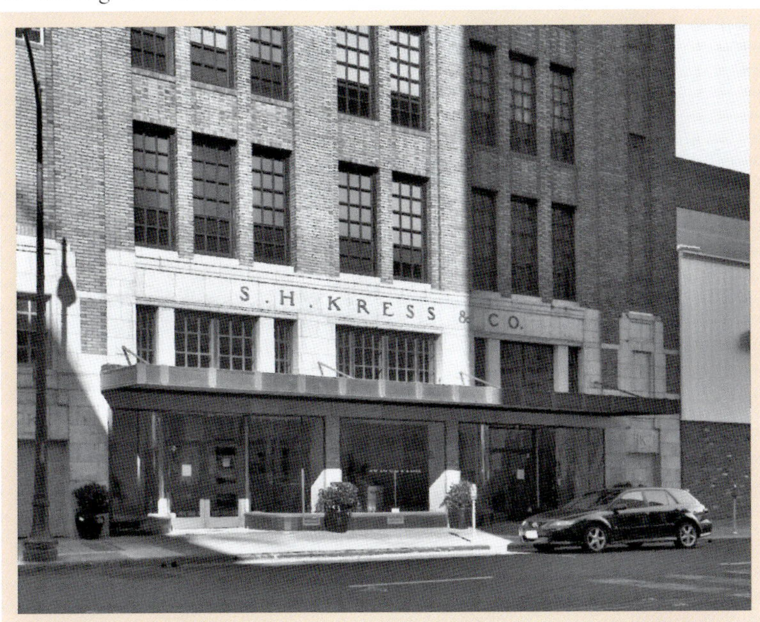

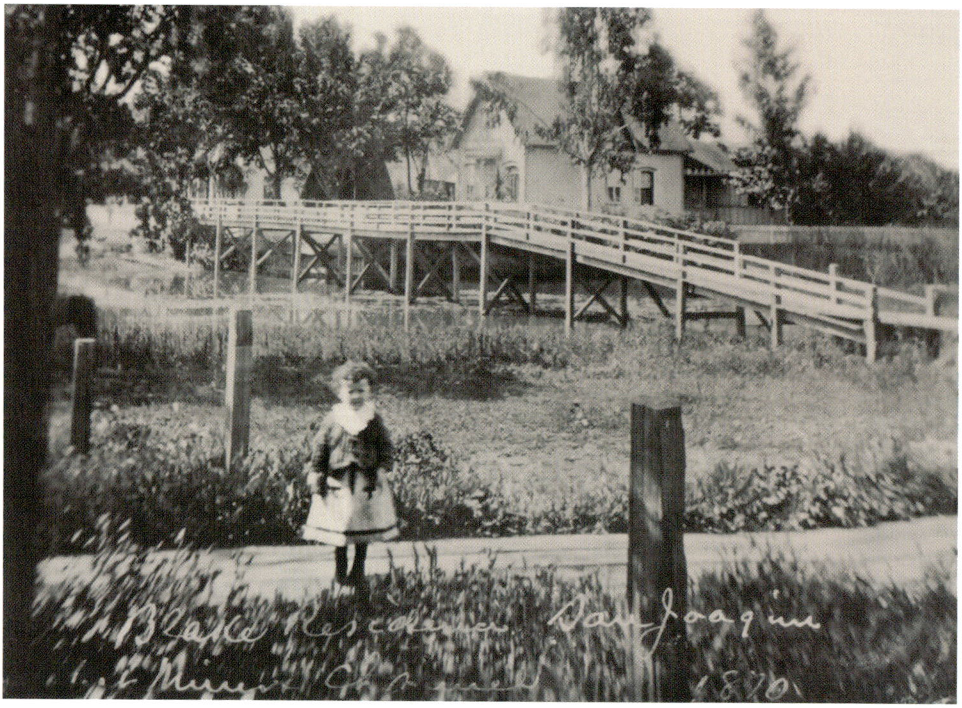

Stockton's city plan was imposed upon a natural system of sloughs and lakes that perennially flooded, causing significant hardship to residents. The Blake home was located on a small lot southwest of Miner Slough, near Hunter and Channel Streets. Between seasons, this Venice-like environment was verdant, although frequently plagued by mosquitoes. The slough was tiled for drainage and filled as the city grew to the north, and Miner Avenue became a thriving commercial artery to the waterfront. (Courtesy of Haggin Museum Archives.)

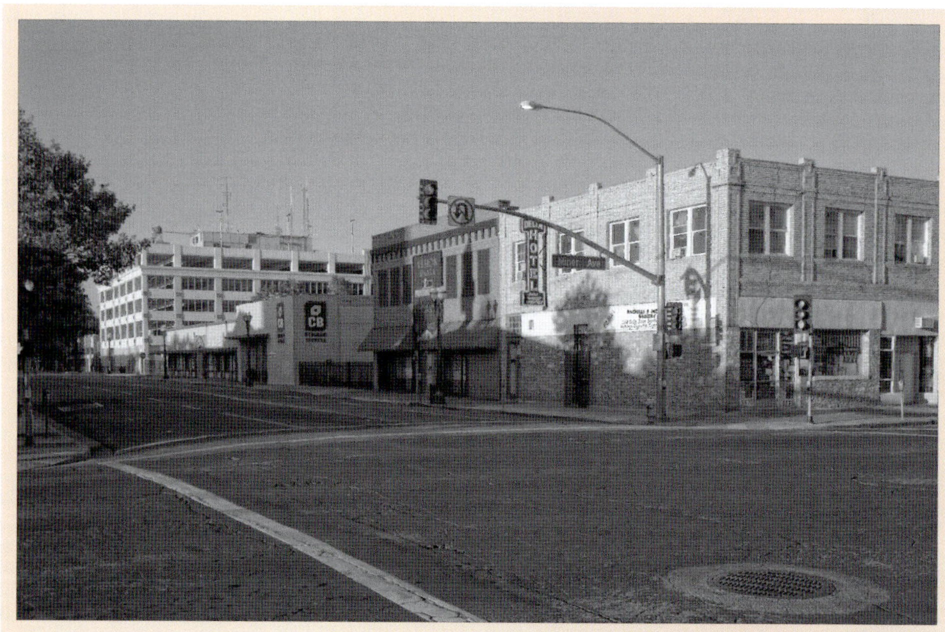

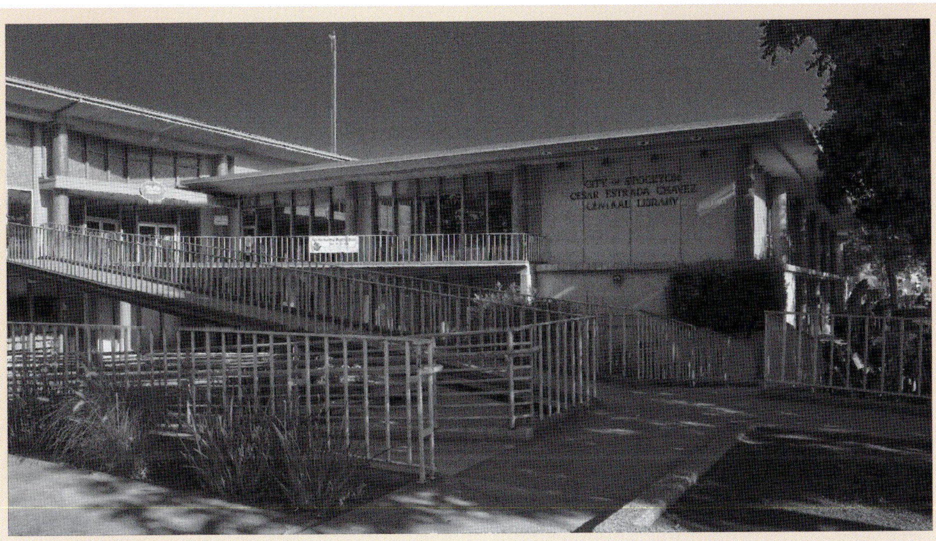

The Andrew W. Simpson home stood on the northwest corner of Oak and El Dorado Streets. The house was built in 1863 for Simpson's bride, Augusta, and their eventual six children. Simpson, a Gold Rush–era pioneer, joined his brothers in the lumber business. Andrew formed a partnership with George Gray to establish Simpson and Gray Lumber Company. In 1950, the Simpson property was envisioned as a future library site. The Chavez Central Library was dedicated in September 1964. (Courtesy of Stockton Re-Photographic Survey.)

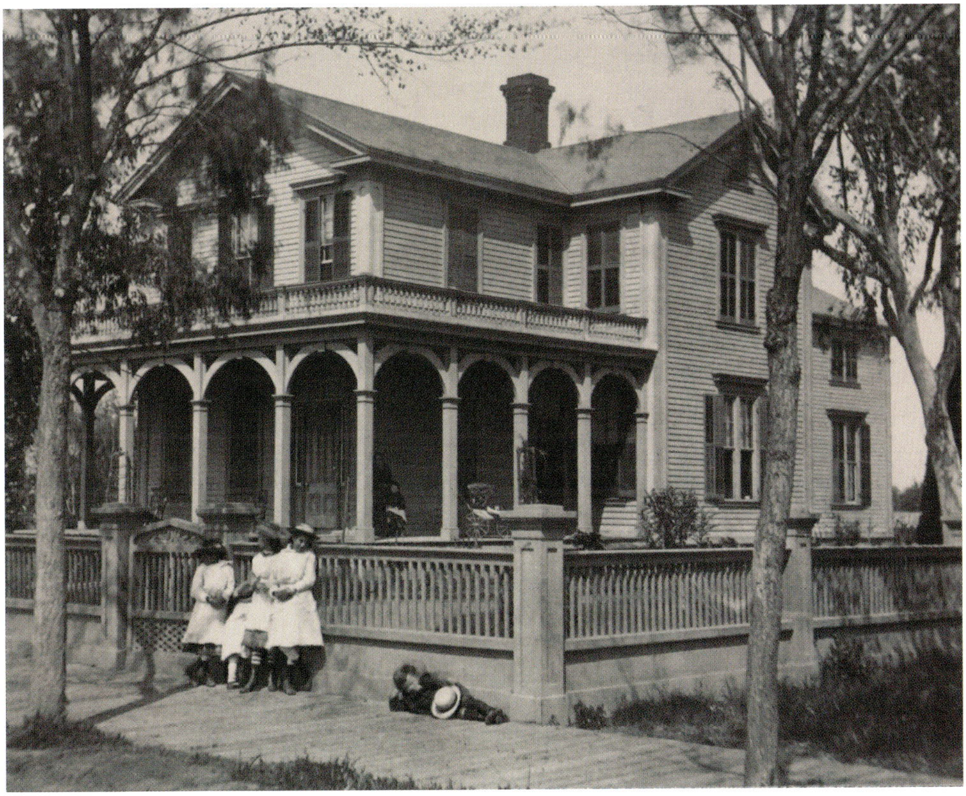

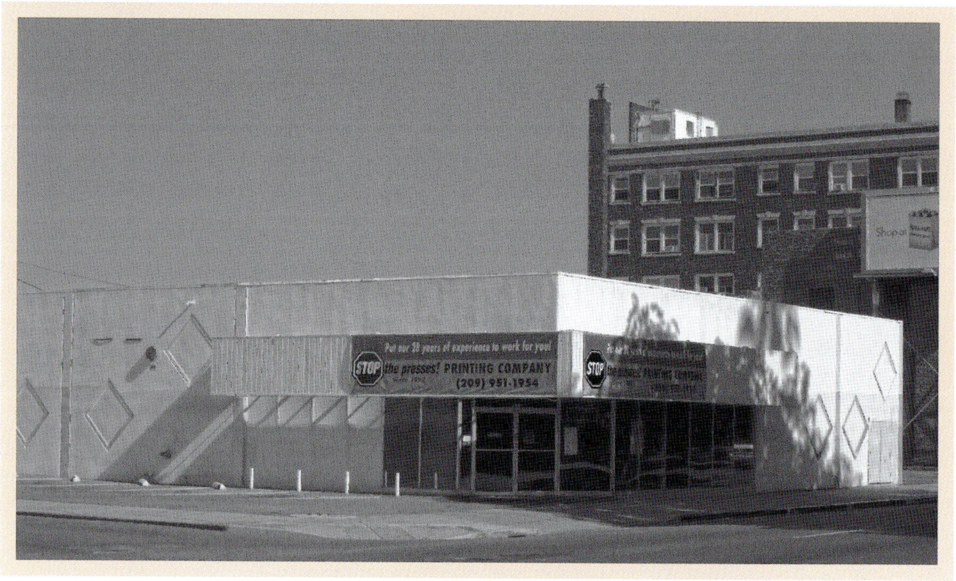

The Welsh mansion was located on the northwest corner of El Dorado and Poplar Streets. A native of Scotland, James M. Welsh came to Stockton in 1882 and engaged in diverse business interests, including the Stockton Milling Company; Alta Fire Insurance Company; Stockton Land, Loan and Building Association; San Joaquin County Valley Bank; and Samson Iron Works. The mansion ultimately succumbed to the strip-mall phenomenon and incursion of a mixed-use business district into North El Dorado Street during the 1950s and 1960s. (Courtesy of University of the Pacific Special Collections.)

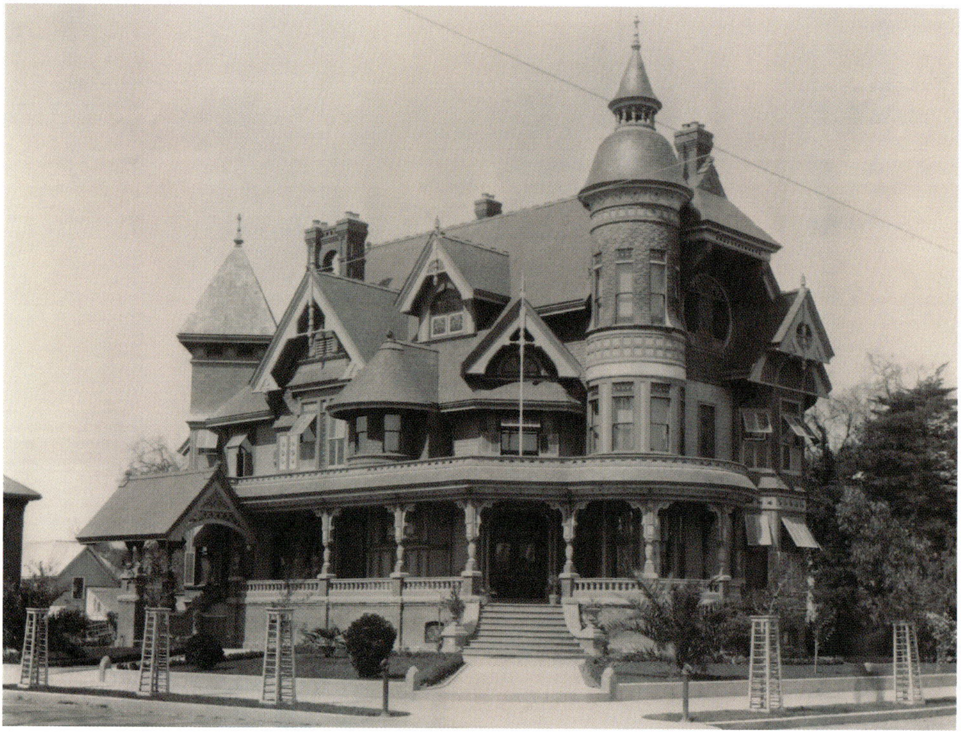

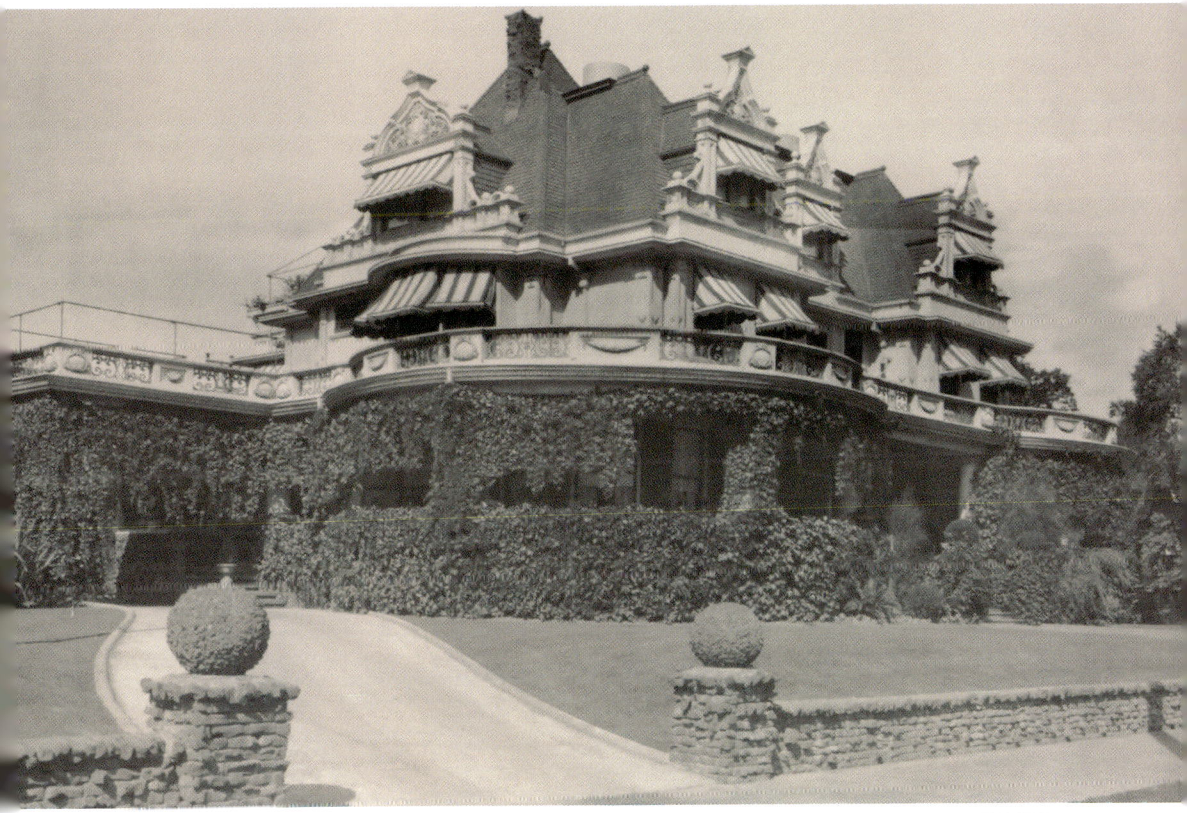

The Hillman-Rindge (aka Daisy Barnhart-Hillman) Mansion, one of grandest homes ever built in Stockton, was located on the southwest corner of El Dorado and North Streets (Harding Way). In 1905, it was built at the northern city limits at a reputed construction cost of $25,000. Daisy was an heir to the Henry and Elizabeth Barnhart fortune amassed through land speculation and development in San Joaquin, Solano, and Yolo Counties. The home became shrouded in mystery and was eventually demolished, replaced by a strip mall. (Courtesy of University of the Pacific Special Collections.)

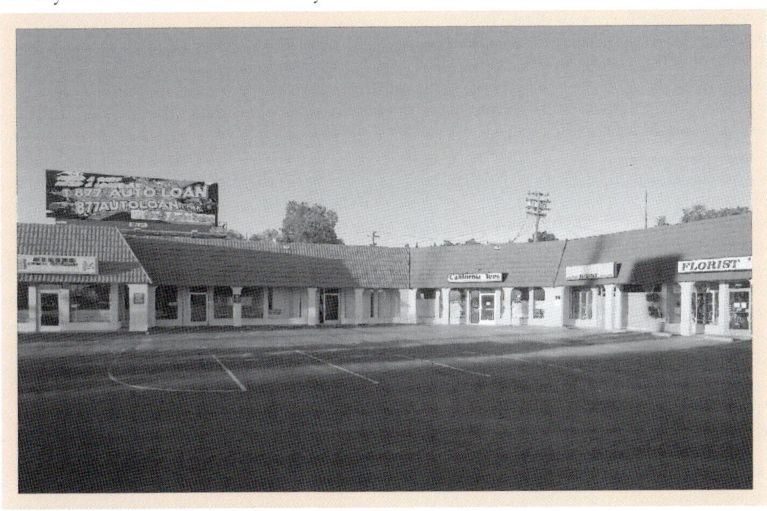

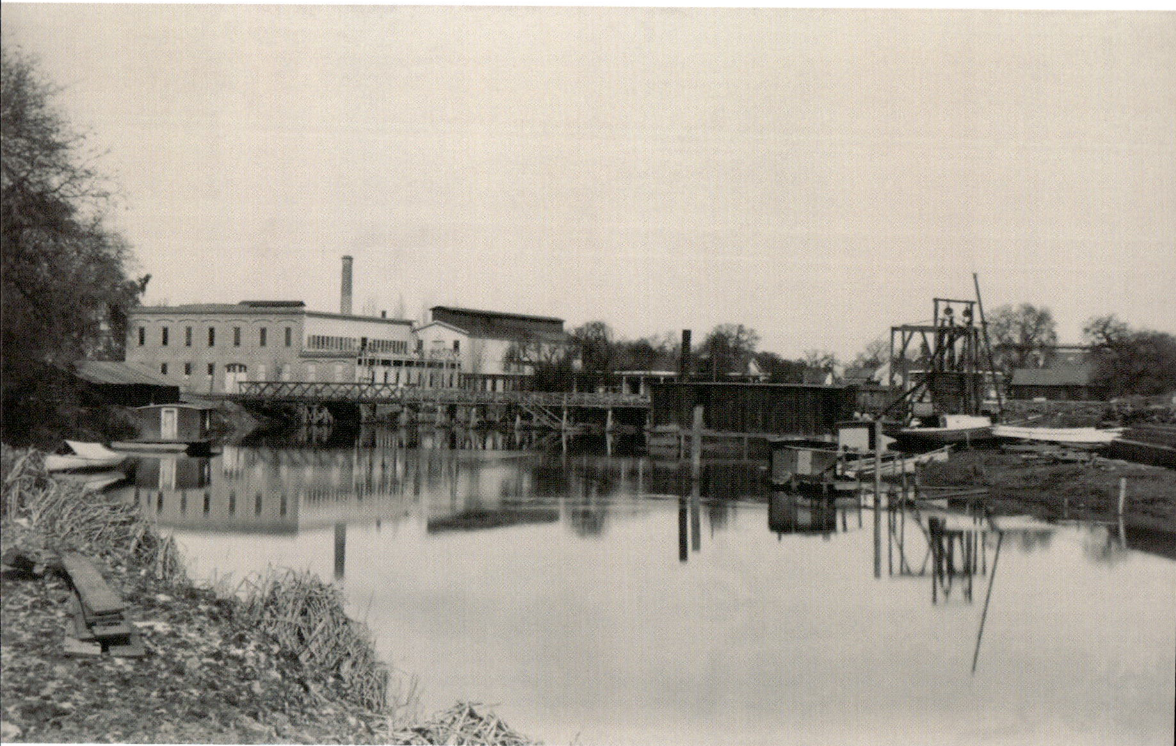

The Pacific Tannery was located between Oak Street and Miner Slough, east of El Dorado Street. Charles and Jacob Wagner established the tannery in 1856 and developed an international market for their leather. The company name was changed to Wagner Leather Company in 1895. Discouraged by tariffs, competition, and degradation to residential living in the vicinity, the tannery closed in 1928, and the family interests were reinvested. Bank of the West recently opened a new branch on the old tannery site. (Courtesy of University of the Pacific Special Collections.)

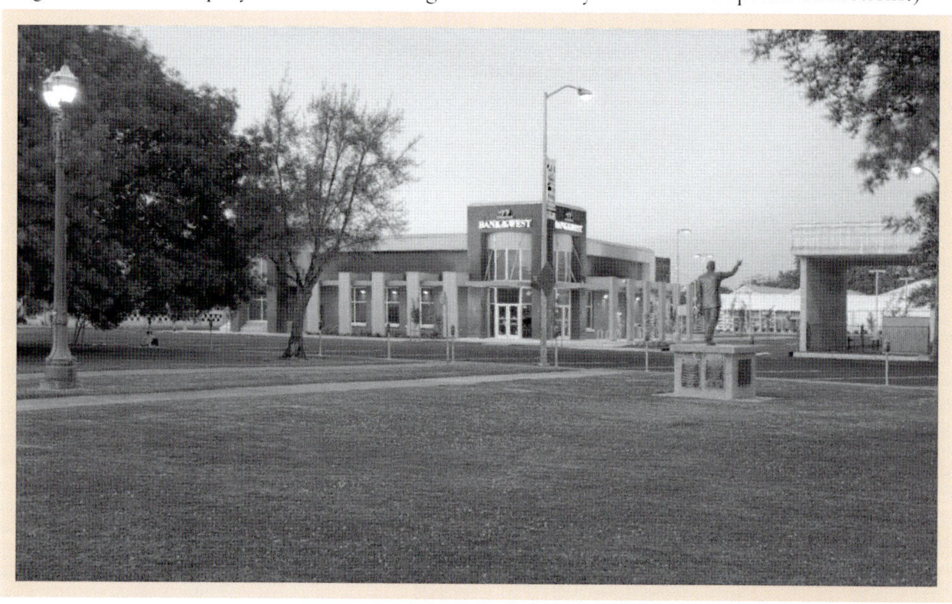

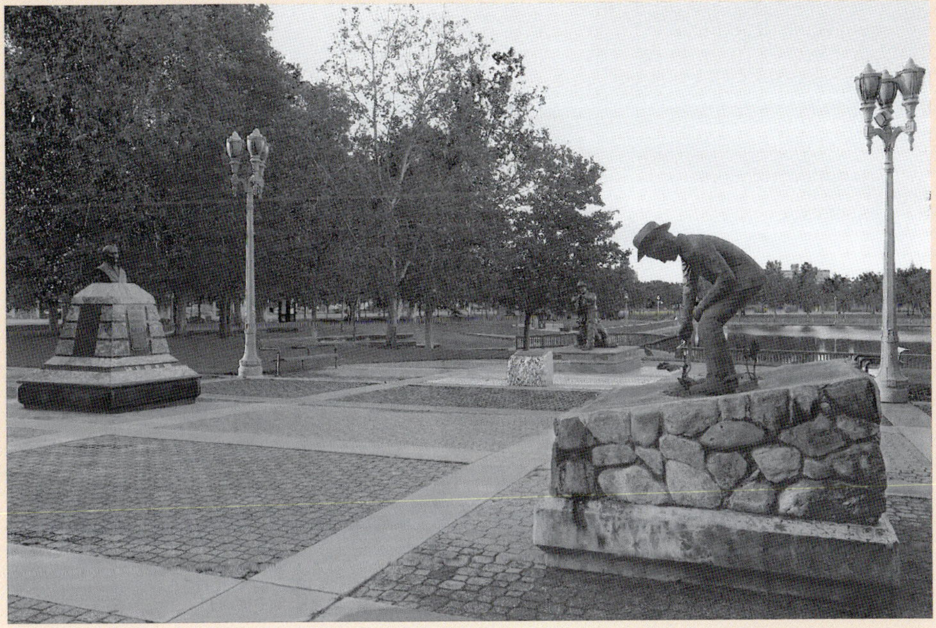

Fremont Channel is a northern branch of the Stockton Channel that drains a network of seasonal sloughs running west. French trappers, lured by the beaver populations, once frequented the channel and McLeod Lake, to the south. By the 1880s, the channel supported diverse residential, commercial, and recreational activities. The lake's scale and shape have been progressively reengineered, and today Cesar Chavez Square features memorial sculptures and plaques honoring Stocktonians who have made notable contributions to and sacrifices for the community. (Courtesy of Haggin Museum Archives.)

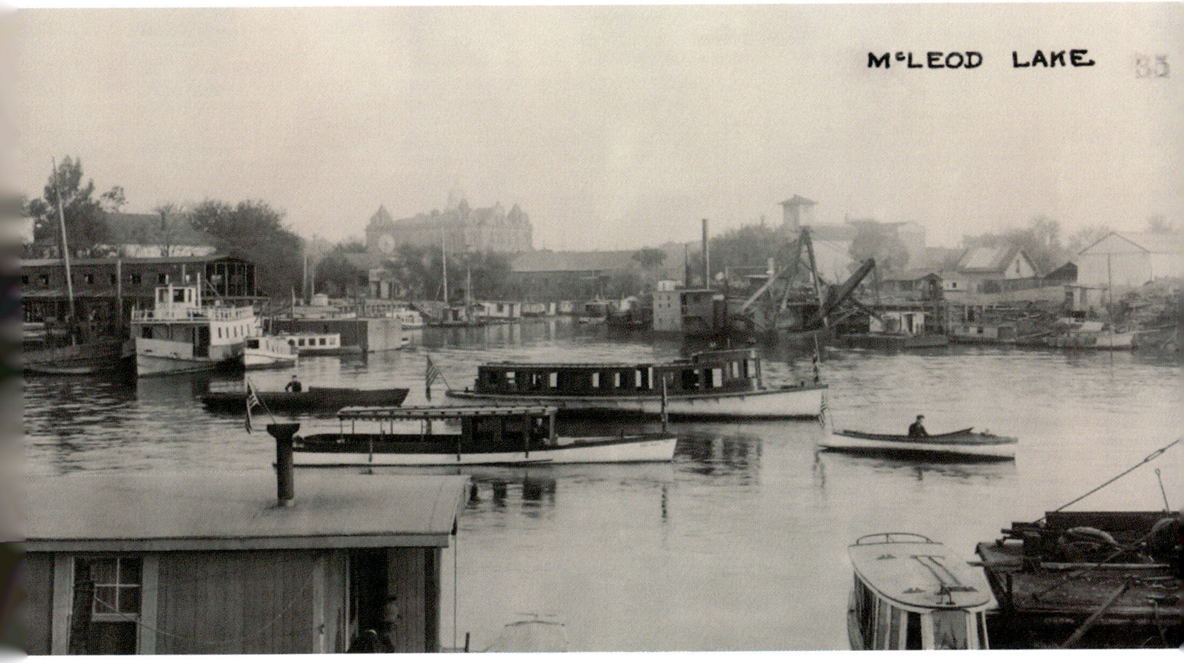

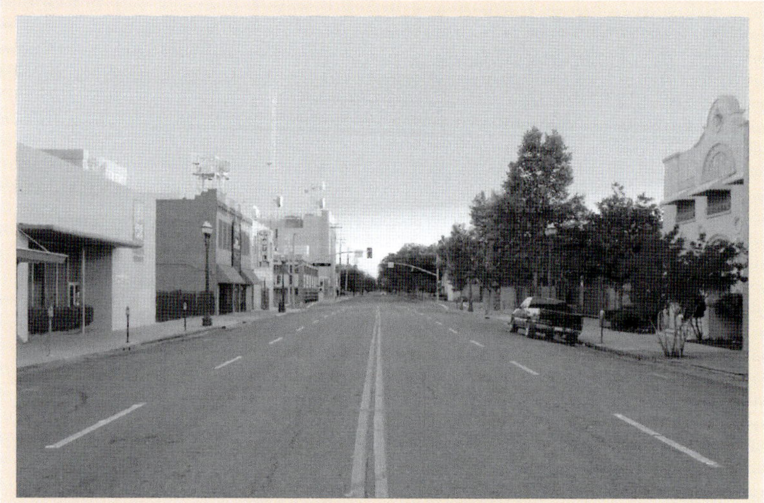

This was the view looking north on San Joaquin Street from Channel Street in 1897. Recurring floods cut off most communication and trade between communities until the water receded and the black mud hardened enough to resume daily routines. Graveling and cobbling the streets, along with new diversion canals north of the city, stopped regular flooding and changed Stockton's prospects. Today, with flood control, this threat to business and property is mostly forgotten, a photographic memory. (Courtesy of University of the Pacific Special Collections.)

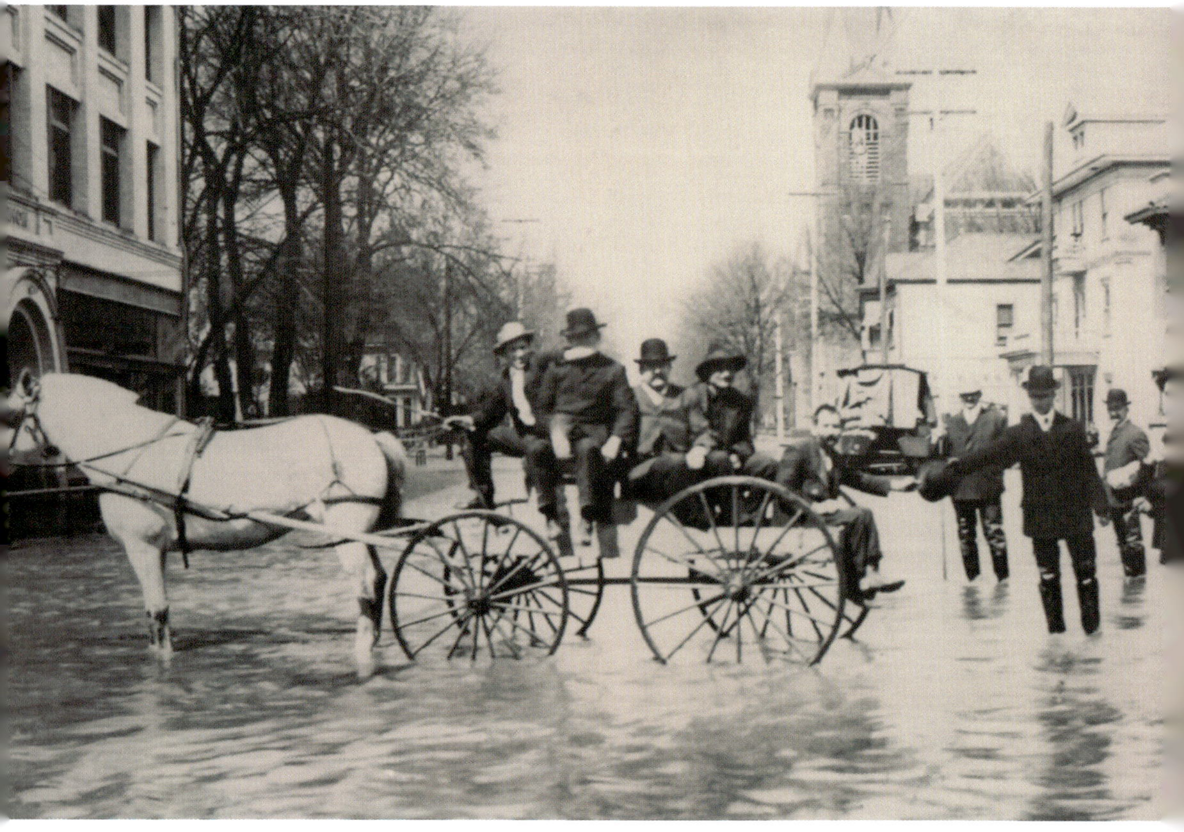

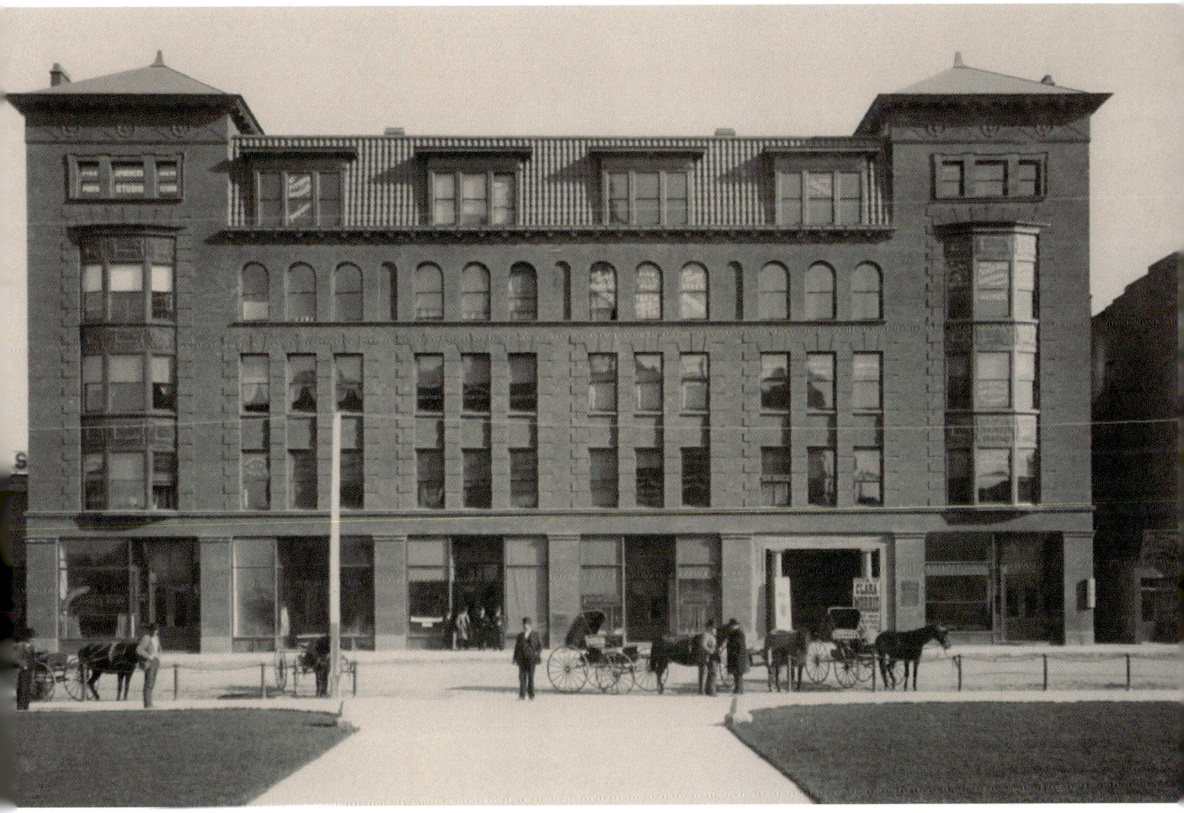

The Yosemite Theatre, opened in July 1892, was located on San Joaquin Street, north of Main Street. Five buildings have occupied this site since 1850. Stockton's first Agricultural Pavilion and a Methodist church made notable appearances. The Yosemite Building was a multiuse facility: office space on the street front, theater at the rear. The San Joaquin County Services building was constructed and opened in 2008–2009. On the ground floor, the Freedom Coffee shop offers a relaxing respite among the towers of administration. (Courtesy of University of the Pacific Special Collections.)

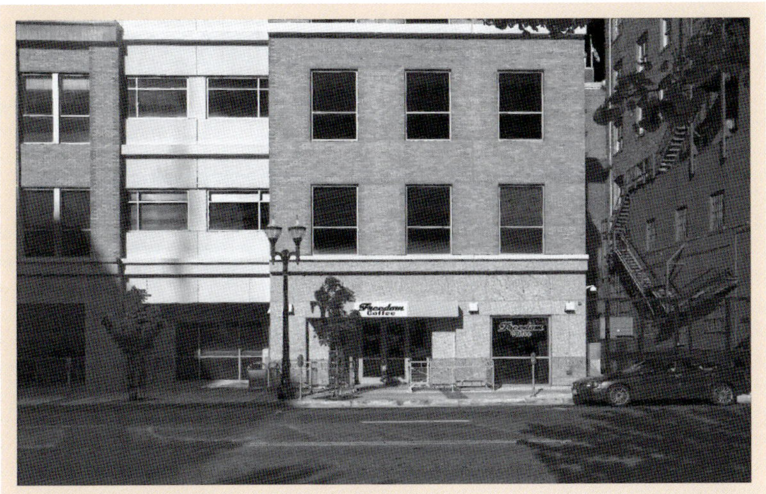

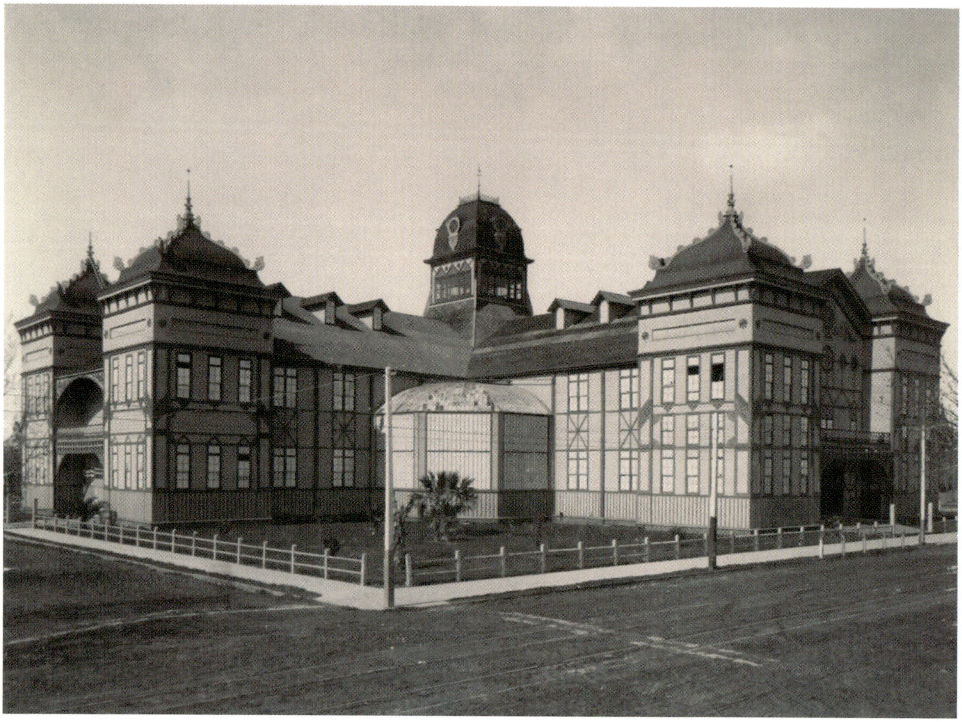

Stockton's second Agricultural Pavilion was located at Washington Street and San Joaquin Street. Constructed for the California State Fair, hosted by Stockton, it was a grand (38,000 square feet) wood-and-glass structure. The pavilion was reduced to ashes in 1902, and Washington Square Park was developed in its wake. In 1987, the last phase of the Crosstown Freeway was completed. Today, a thriving farmers' market convenes each week under the shade of the expressway. (Courtesy of University of the Pacific Special Collections.)

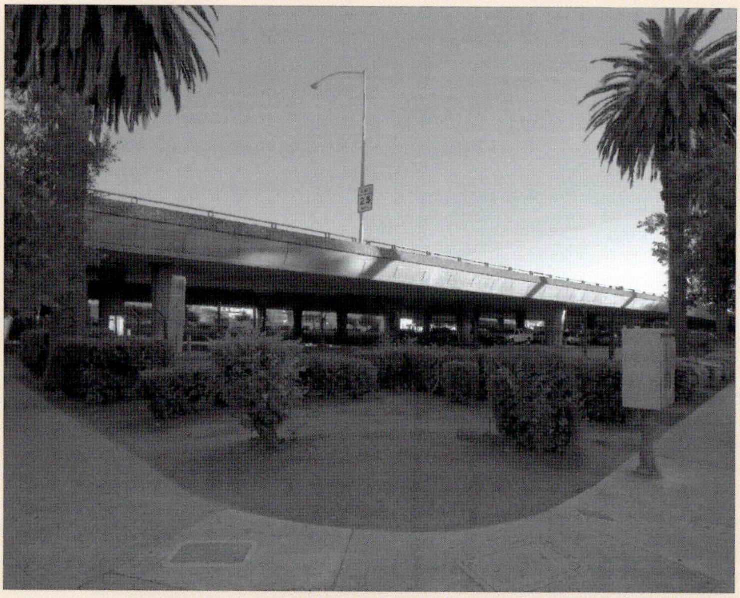

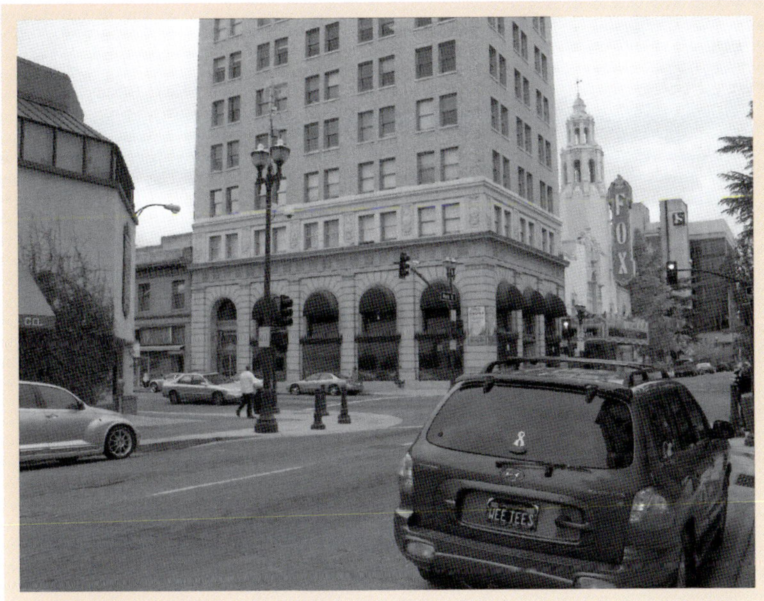

Demolition of the Rosenblum and Crawford Building occurred on June 13, 1916. The California Building (1917), distinguished by its stately Greek Revival style, became the city's third skyscraper. This furthered the evolution of the business district on Main Street during the first decades of the 20th century. The Farmers and Merchants Bank was its first occupant. The structure remains well integrated in Stockton's central downtown, surrounded by the courthouse, coffee shops, and diners. (Courtesy of University of the Pacific Special Collections.)

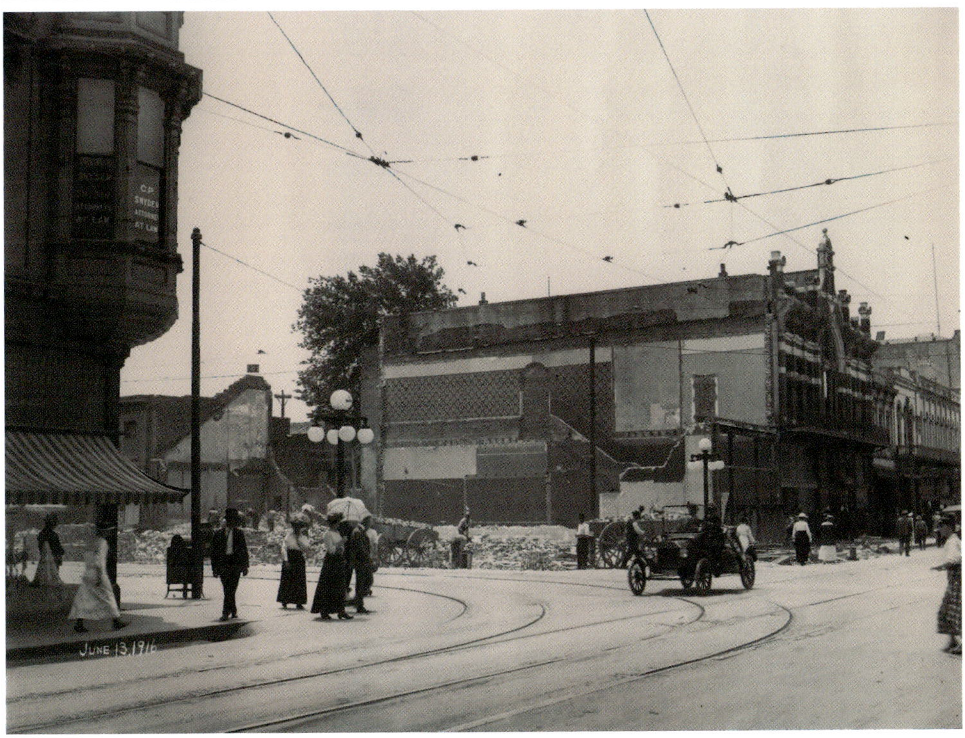

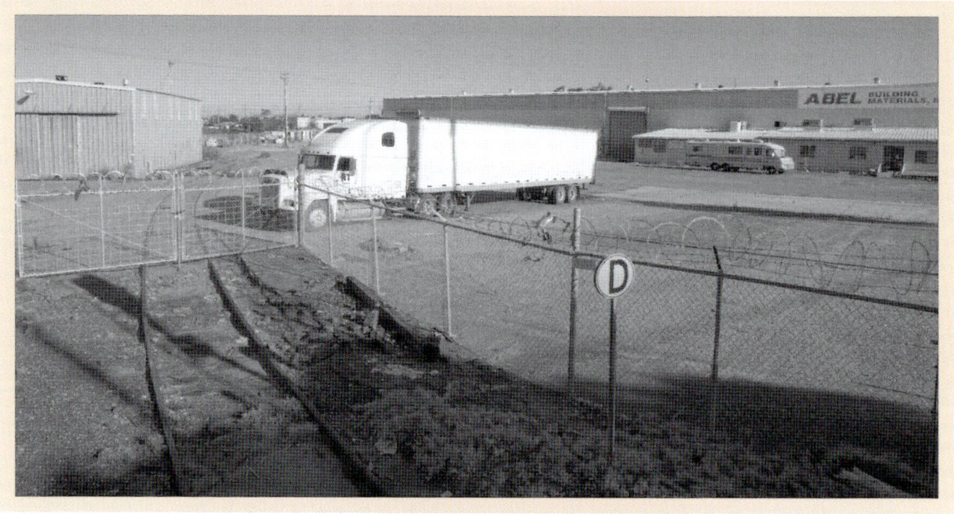

Stockton's early reputation as a manufacturing city was confirmed by the achievements of the Holt Manufacturing Company, which began operations in 1883 as the Stockton Wheel Company. The innovative Holt brothers recognized the need for efficient harvesting equipment, an enterprise that attracted international buyers. Stockton's proximity to agriculture, manufacturing resources, and shipping made it ideal for the company's headquarters. Market conditions and litigation during the 1920s contributed to Holt's move from Stockton to Peoria, Illinois, and the formation of the Caterpillar Company. (Courtesy of University of the Pacific Special Collections.)

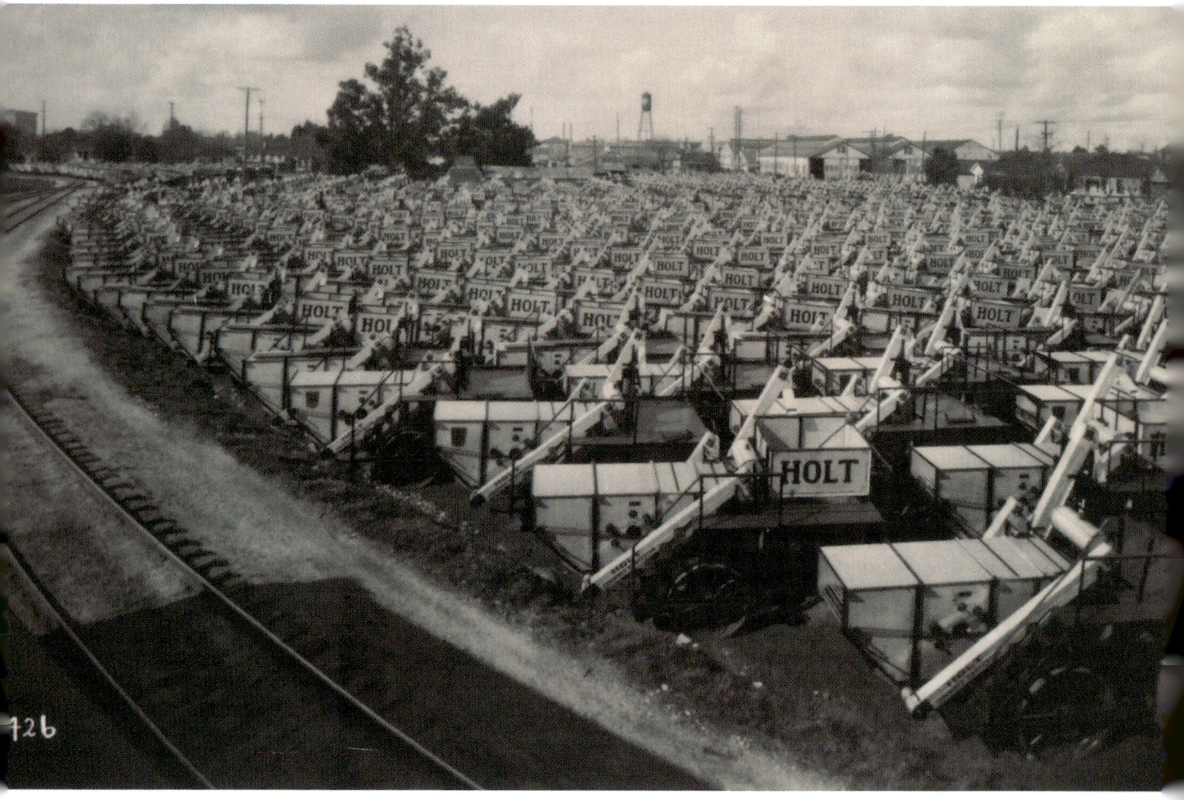

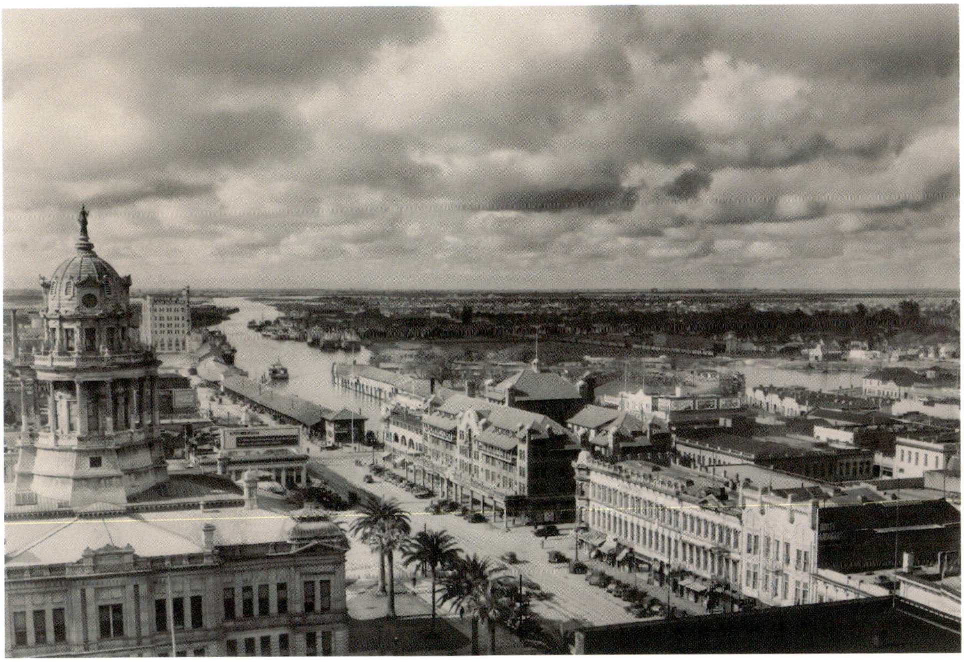

This 1920 northwest view of Stockton (above) illustrates its transition from encampment to metropolis. The community had strategically overcome many of the challenges to its prosperity. An urban design envisioned by Charles Weber in the 19th century was realized. A city banded by world-class agriculture, a second-generation county courthouse, and a strong economy with roads, rails, and a port connected to international markets poised Stockton for suburbanization. The design of the new County Services Building (view from boardroom below) was inspired by Stockton's agricultural terrain. (Courtesy of University of the Pacific Special Collections.)

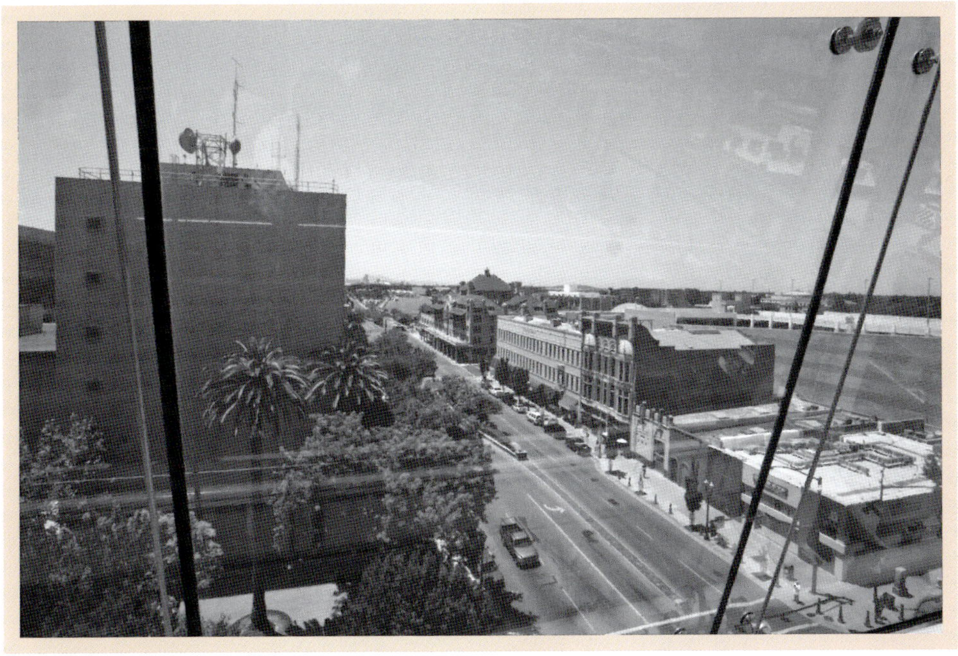

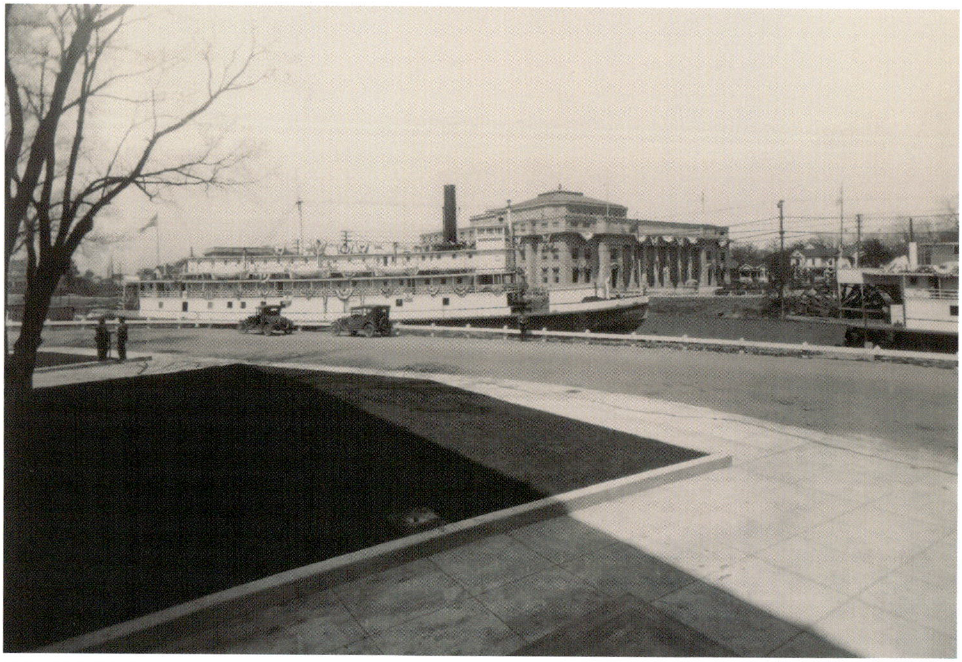

Stockton's Civic Center was developed between 1925 and 1930. The Stockton Civic Memorial Auditorium, a public monument to casualties and veterans of World War I, also fulfilled the city's need for more space for community business and entertainment. In the 1920s, the Fremont Slough extended to El Dorado Street, allowing passenger and recreational boating into this formerly residential region. The slough was filled in the 1950s, and Center Street became the uninterrupted corridor of today. (Courtesy of University of the Pacific Special Collections.)

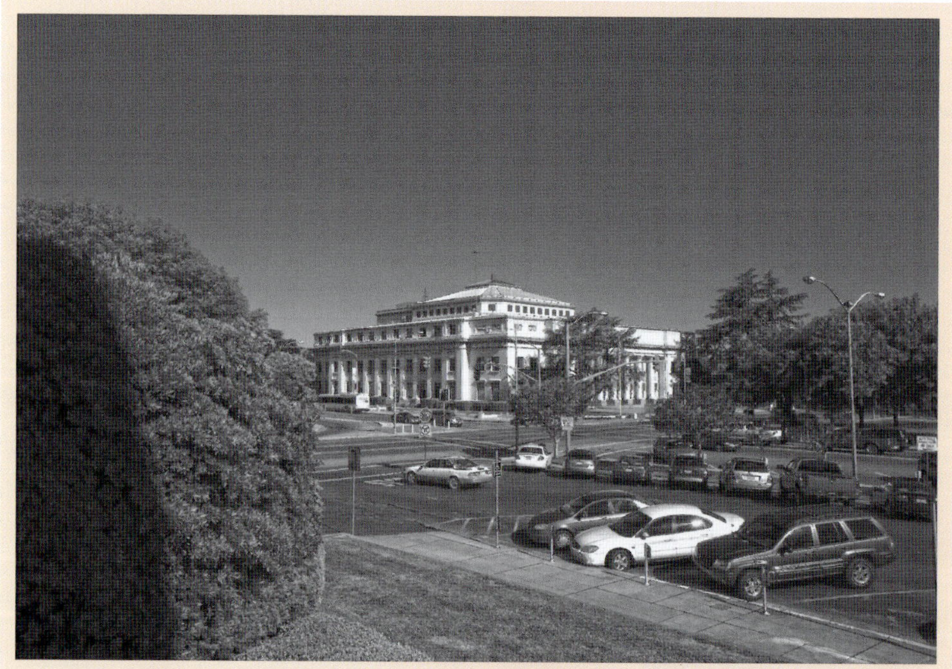

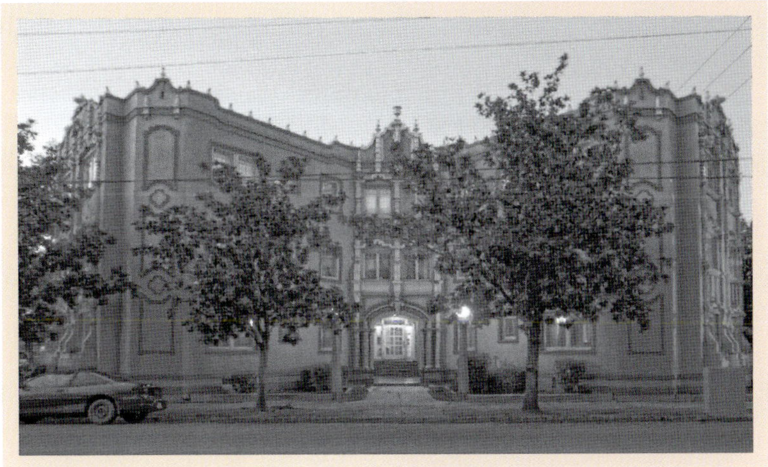

In 1919, architect Ralph P. Morrell adapted the popular Spanish Colonial Revival style to his vision for the Bennett Apartments. The apartment building and its neighbors are fine examples of architectural expression in Stockton residences between 1880 and 1930. The Bennett was designed for maximum privacy and to last centuries. It has aged well, becoming a jewel in Stockton's Magnolia Historic District, a residential zone within the city's larger midtown region that offers a mixture of residential and commercial activities. (Courtesy of University of the Pacific Special Collections.)

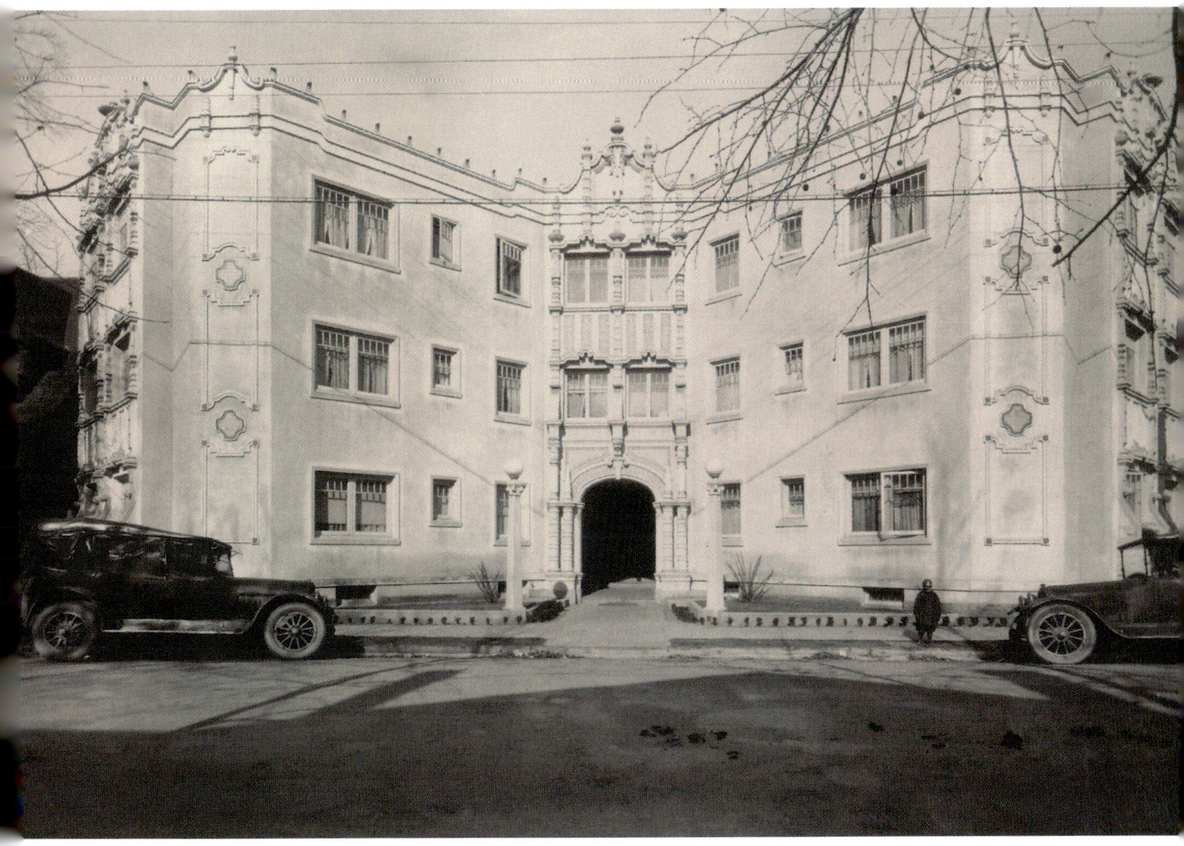

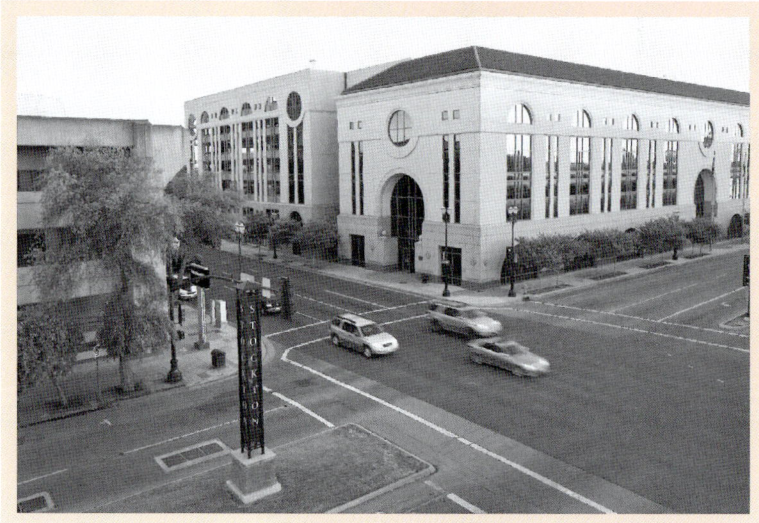

The intersection of El Dorado Street and Weber Avenue is a barometer of Stockton's changing urban landscape. This 1942 view from the rooftop gardens of the Hotel Stockton shows the Harbor Market. Both concerns were strategically located near the busy passenger depots along the waterfront and Weber Point. This region slipped into urban decay by the late 1950s and was demolished as part of urban renewal efforts in the mid-1960s. Today, the city manages office and parking facilities on this corner. (Courtesy of University of the Pacific Special Collections.)

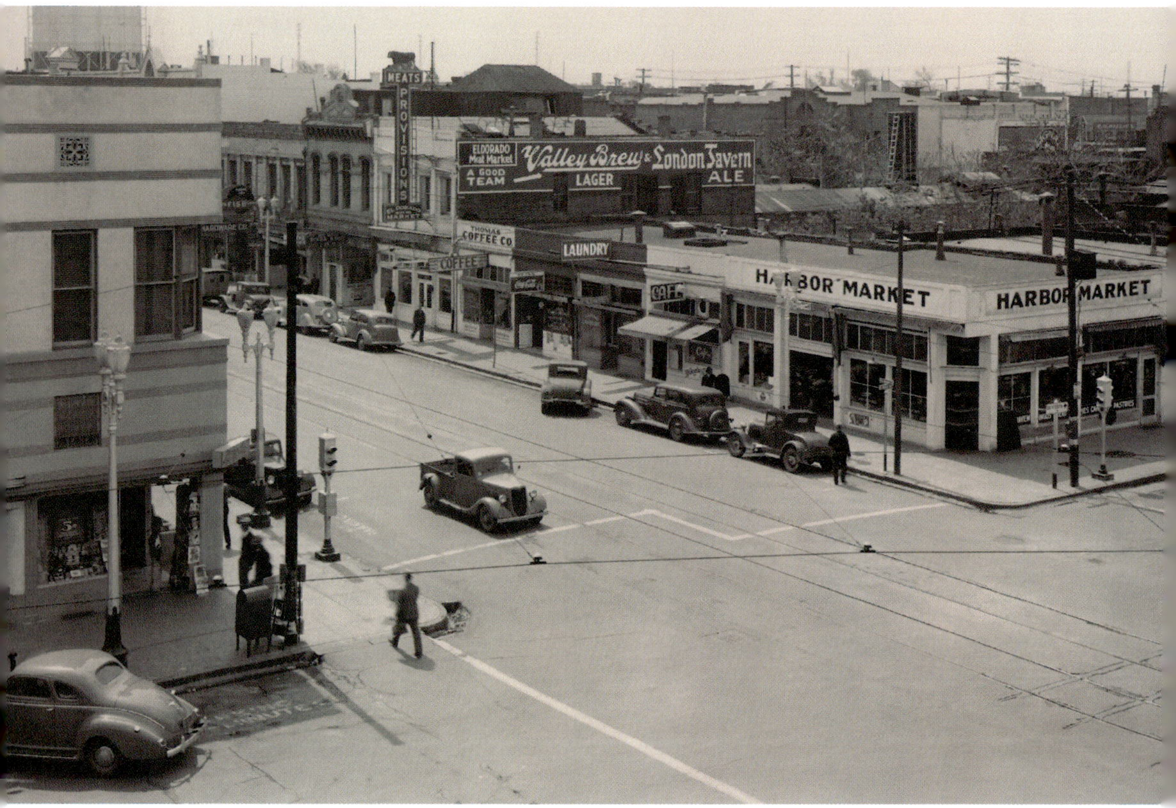

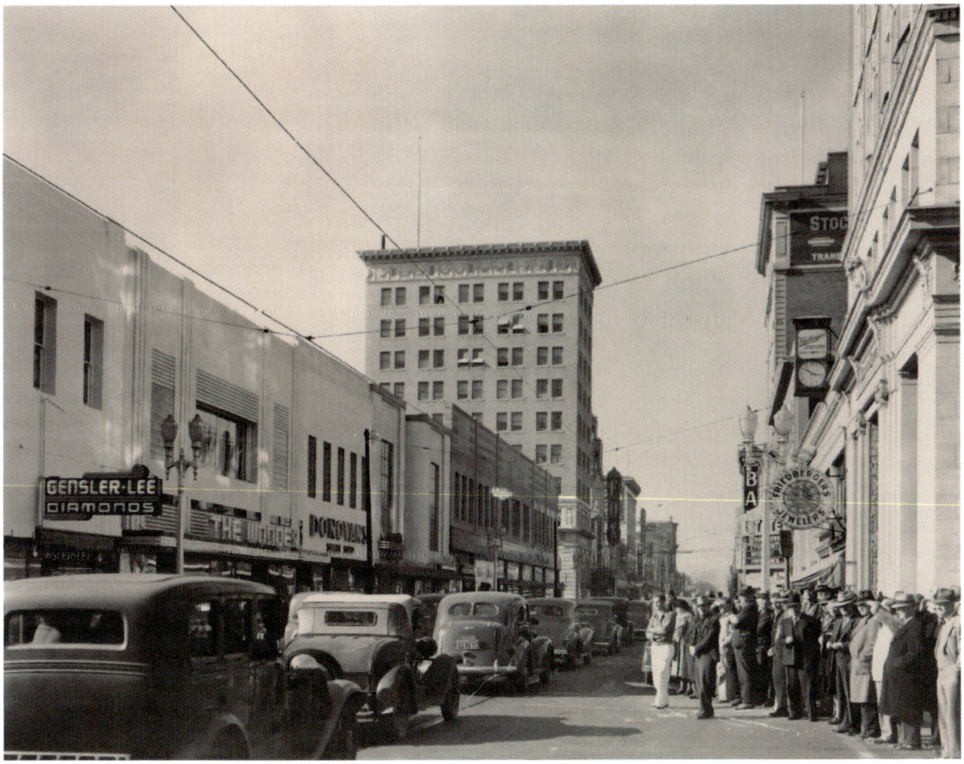

Celebrity parades to Main Street's Fox Theatre were routine in the 1940s. At its zenith, the theater drew the finest big bands of the era. Today, this stretch of Main Street is primarily a corridor for legal and county administration, accented by coffee breaks and the lunch rush. Early evening performances at the Bob Hope Theatre (the old Fox, rededicated) or early-morning foraging through the Farmers Market (on Fridays) have become the new routines for downtown. (Courtesy of University of the Pacific Special Collections.)

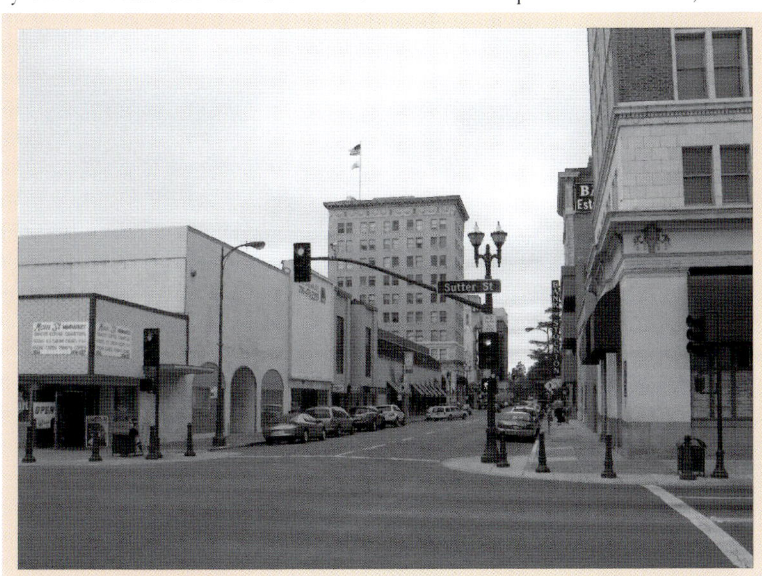

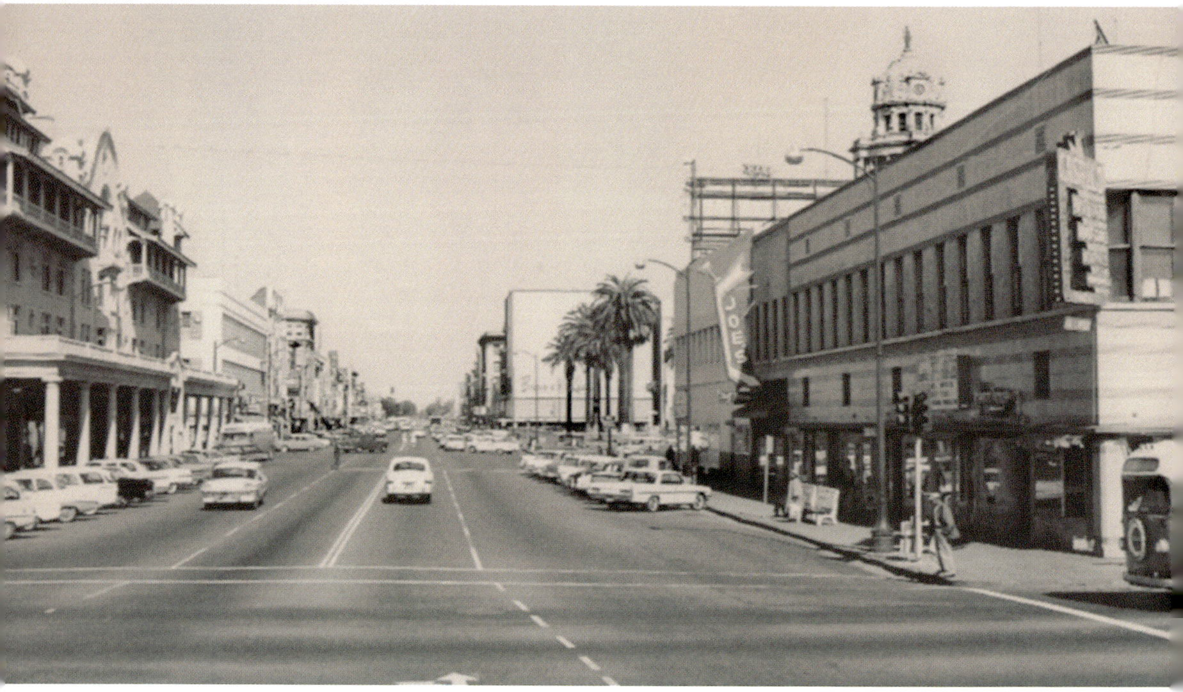

By the mid-1960s, Weber Avenue contained a collection of late-19th- and early-20th-century architecture, with some bland attempts to face-lift some old-timers as mid-century moderns. Behind the photographer, skid row threatened downtown, becoming an incentive for northern sprawl. The remaining signs of Stockton's golden age had become painful to the older generation and invisible to the young. Prompted by small civic organizations, such as Stockton Beautiful, Weber Avenue near El Dorado Street is being transformed into a well-appointed urban corridor. (Courtesy of Bank of Stockton Archives.)

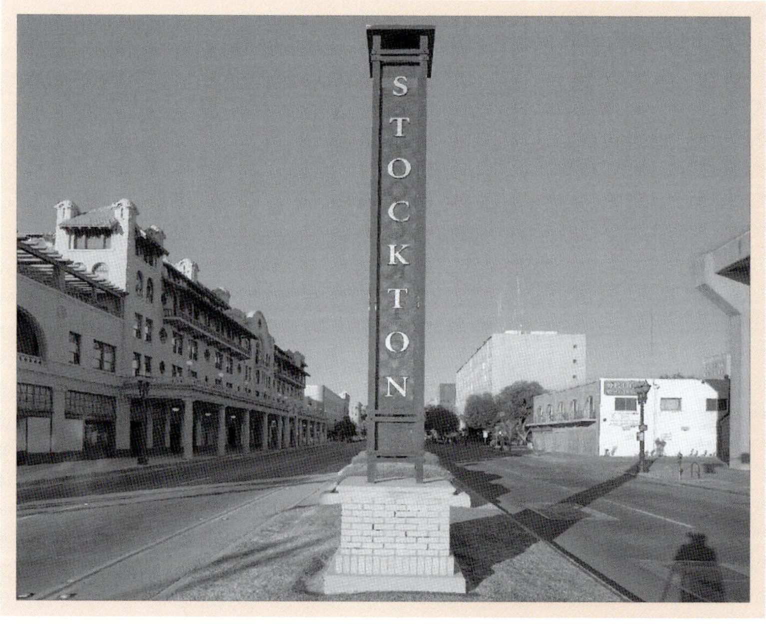

CHAPTER 2

Stockton's Portal to the World

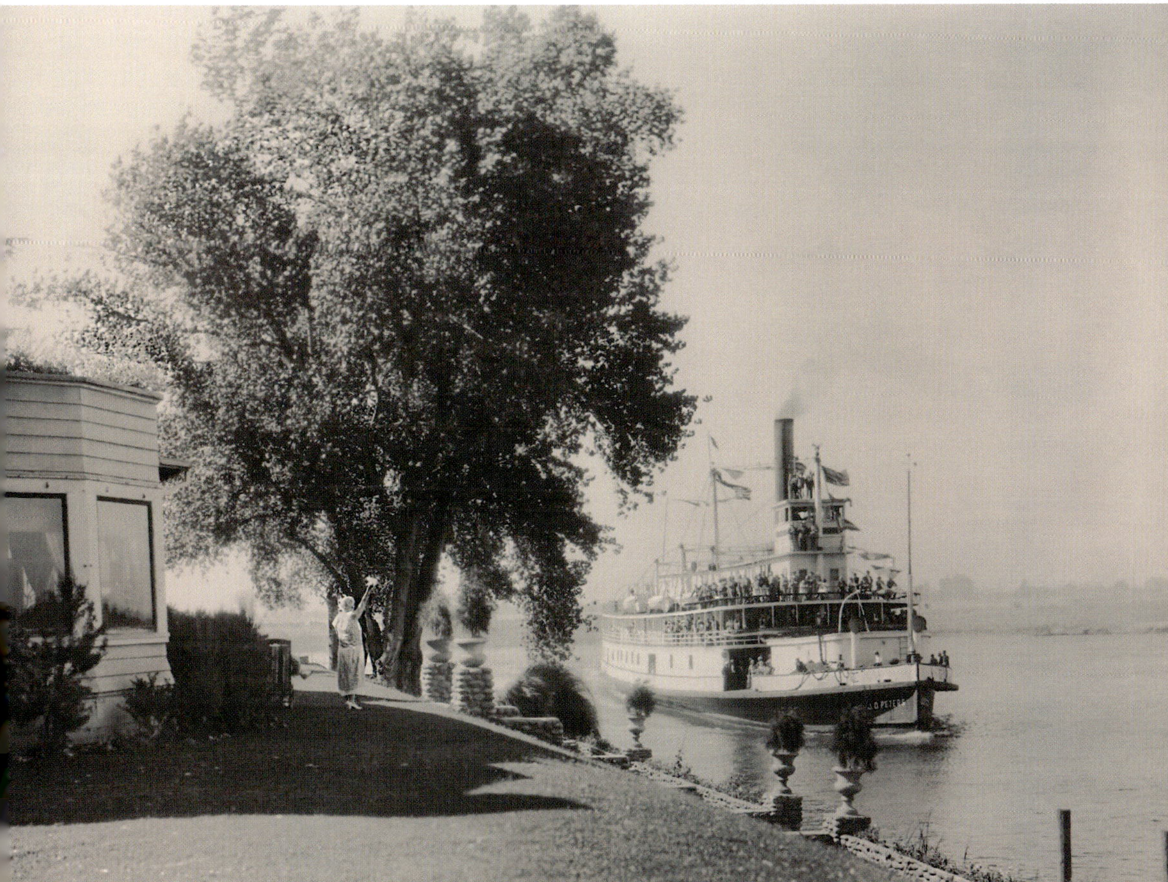

Stockton's fortunes began on the waterfront, and Stockton residents once celebrated this and the delta's abundance and contributions to the city. In the 1920s, Stockton's chamber of commerce made an excursion into the 1,000-mile waterway on the steamer *JD Peters*. (Courtesy of University of the Pacific Special Collections.)

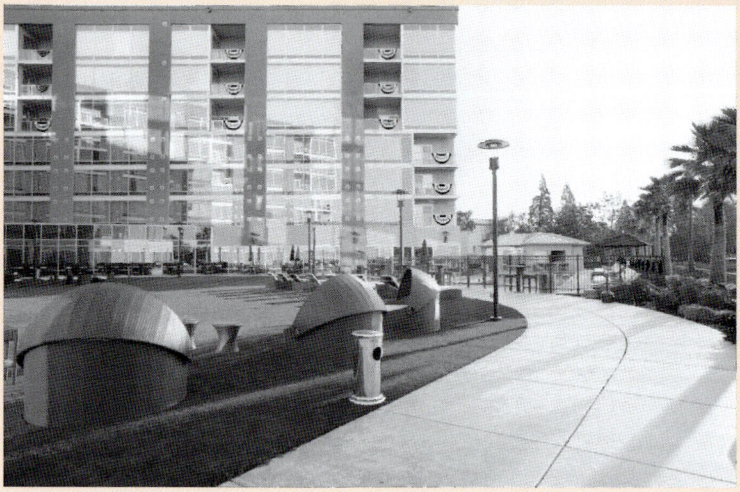

The waterfront of today was a very different space throughout the 19th and 20th centuries. The region surrounding Weber Point has been radically reengineered (reclaimed) to produce real estate, accommodate commerce, and control floods. In 1929, when the Civic Memorial Auditorium was under construction, the Fremont Slough reached northeast through the Civic Center to El Dorado and Oak Streets. Steamboat Levee provided access along the north shore. Today, the University Plaza Hotel sits above the old levee and shoreline. (Courtesy of University of the Pacific Special Collections.)

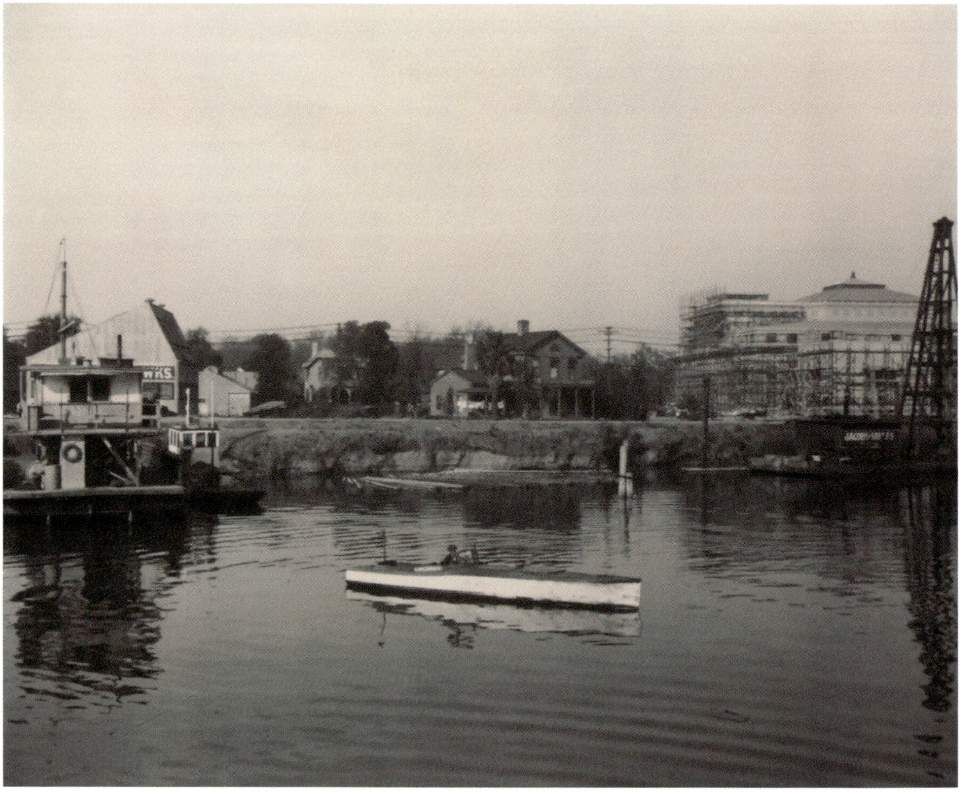

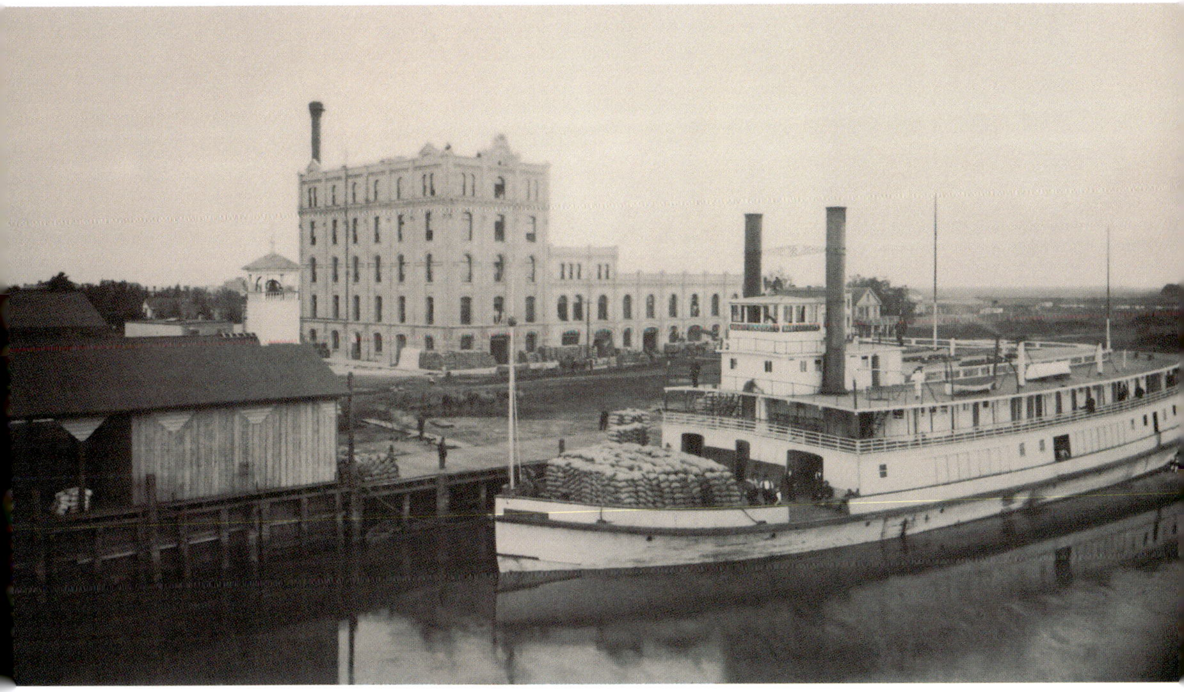

Built in Stockton by the Old Line Ship Building Company, the *Mary Garratt* operated primarily as a freighter, transporting grains and flour from Stockton to San Francisco. Pictured here in 1890, she is docked at the Sperry Flour Mill, located on the southwest corner of West Weber Avenue and Madison Street. Today, there is little evidence of the grain and milling trade that once existed along the east end of the Stockton Channel. The old Sperry office is all that remains of that era. (Courtesy of University of the Pacific Special Collections.)

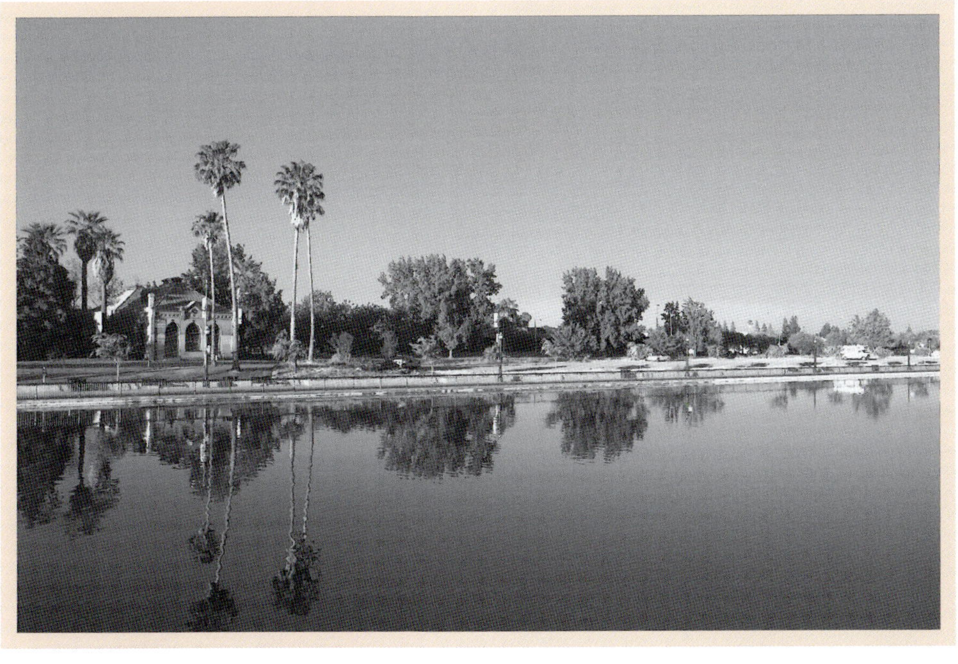

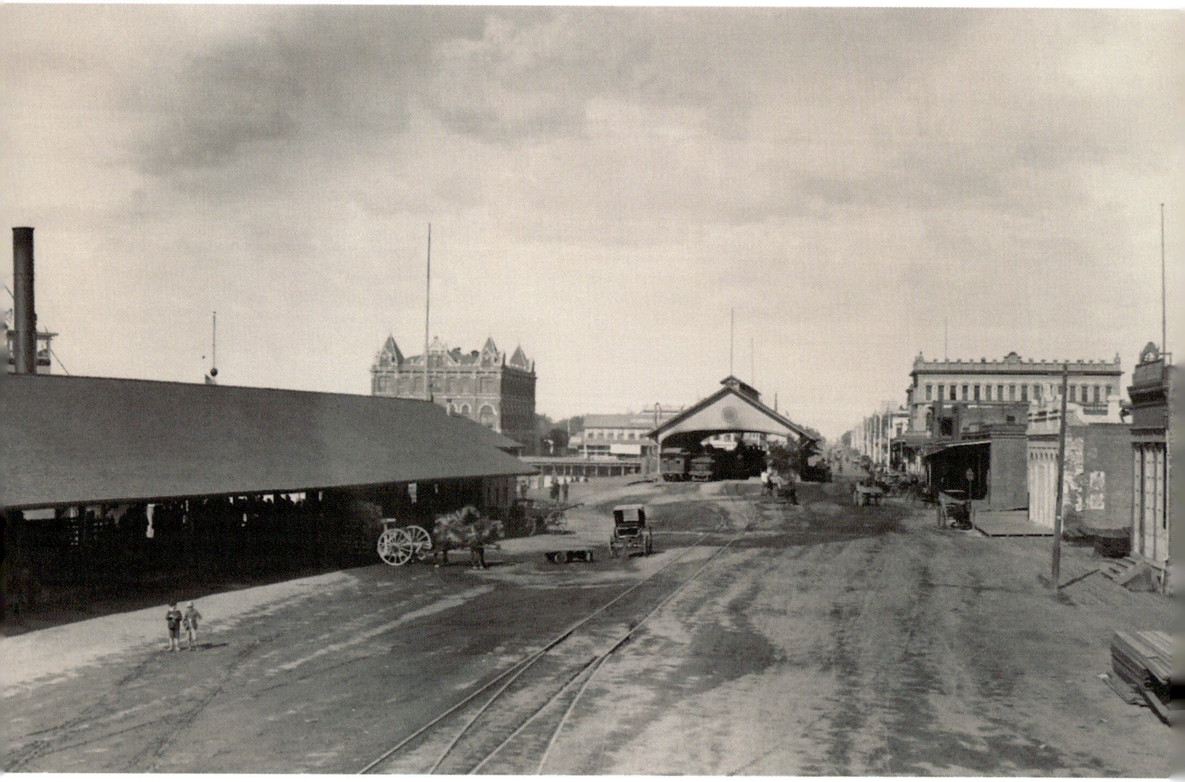

In the 19th century, West Weber Avenue was Stockton's embarcadero. It was the front side of a commercial and manufacturing landscape extending south beyond the Mormon Slough. The Stockton and Copperopolis Railroad and Terminal were constructed in 1869 to bring copper ore from the Sierra Foothills, but it arrived to a depressed market and failed. The region declined after World War II and was sentenced to urban renewal. Today, Weber Avenue points west to the modern Port of Stockton. (Courtesy of University of the Pacific Special Collections.)

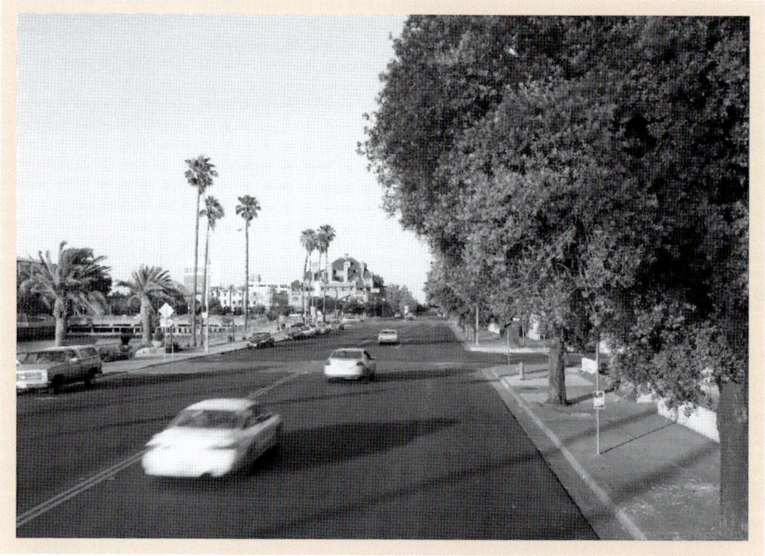

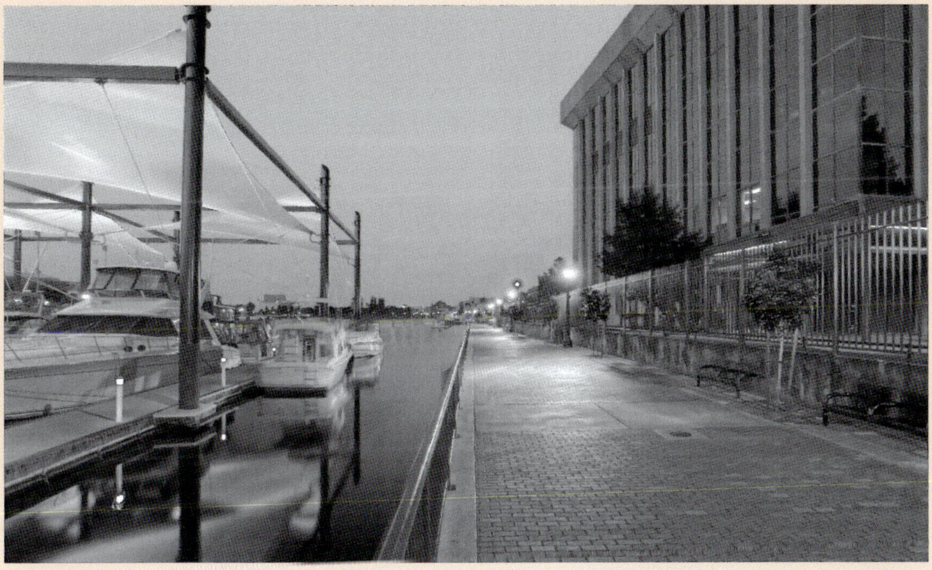

In the 1890s, the lumber, ceramic, and agricultural manufacturing trades conducted a robust business exporting from Stockton to international ports. Today, the waterfront is a recreational destination and gateway to the Sacramento–San Joaquin Delta. The Joan Darrah Promenade follows the south shore of the Stockton Channel, connecting the City Center (east) with the Morelli Park and public boat launch (west). Midway along the promenade, the Waterfront Warehouse and Stockton Marina have become popular dining, entertainment, and recreation destinations. (Courtesy of University of the Pacific Special Collections.)

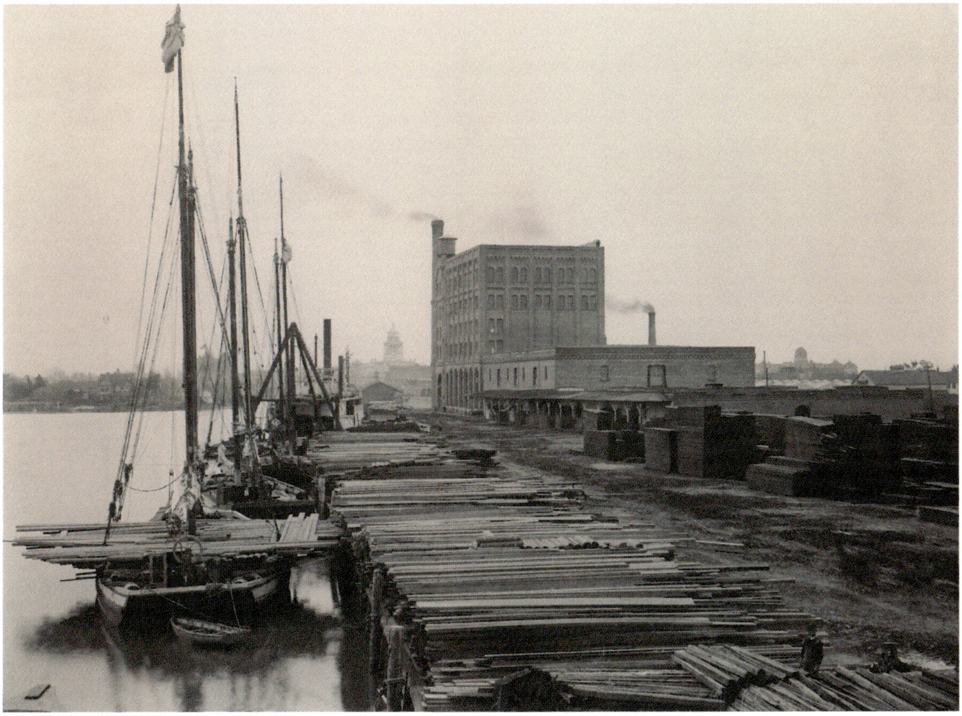

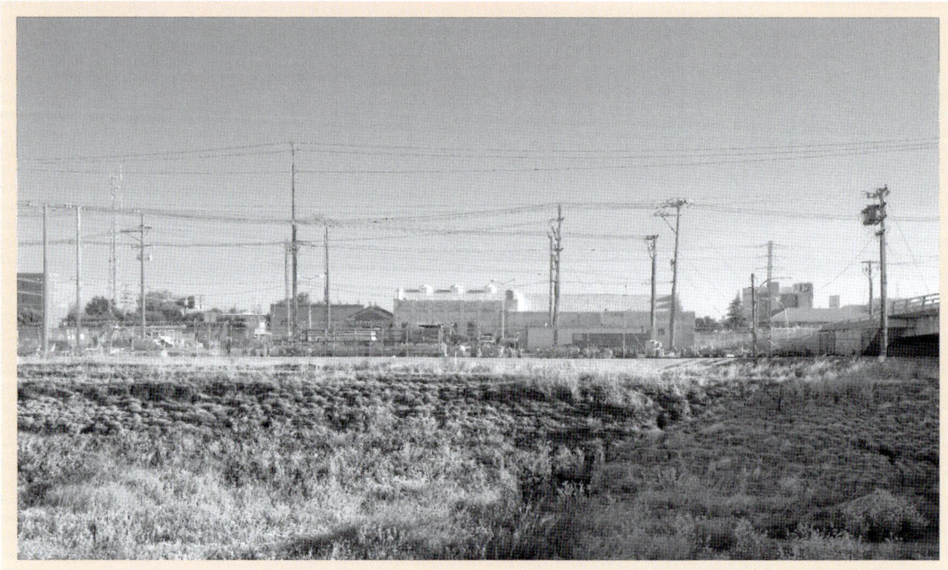

The Mormon Slough was once a prosperous branch of the Stockton Channel, serving the south side of the manufacturing district. After the construction of the Diversion Canal in 1910 to prevent flooding, the completion of dredging for the Deep Water Channel in 1933, and the addition of a new port facility to the west, the Mormon Slough rapidly declined. Today, it is a largely forgotten part of Stockton with a variety of native plants and wildflowers thriving among less attractive things. (Courtesy of Port of Stockton Archives.)

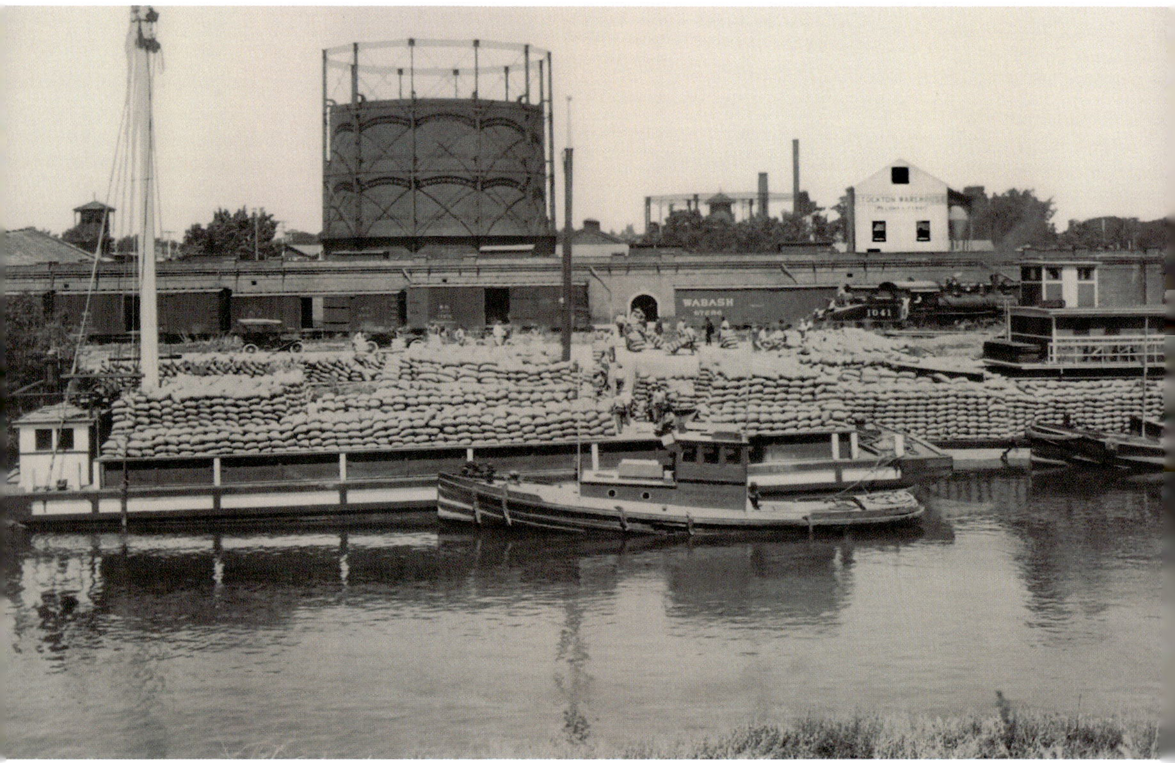

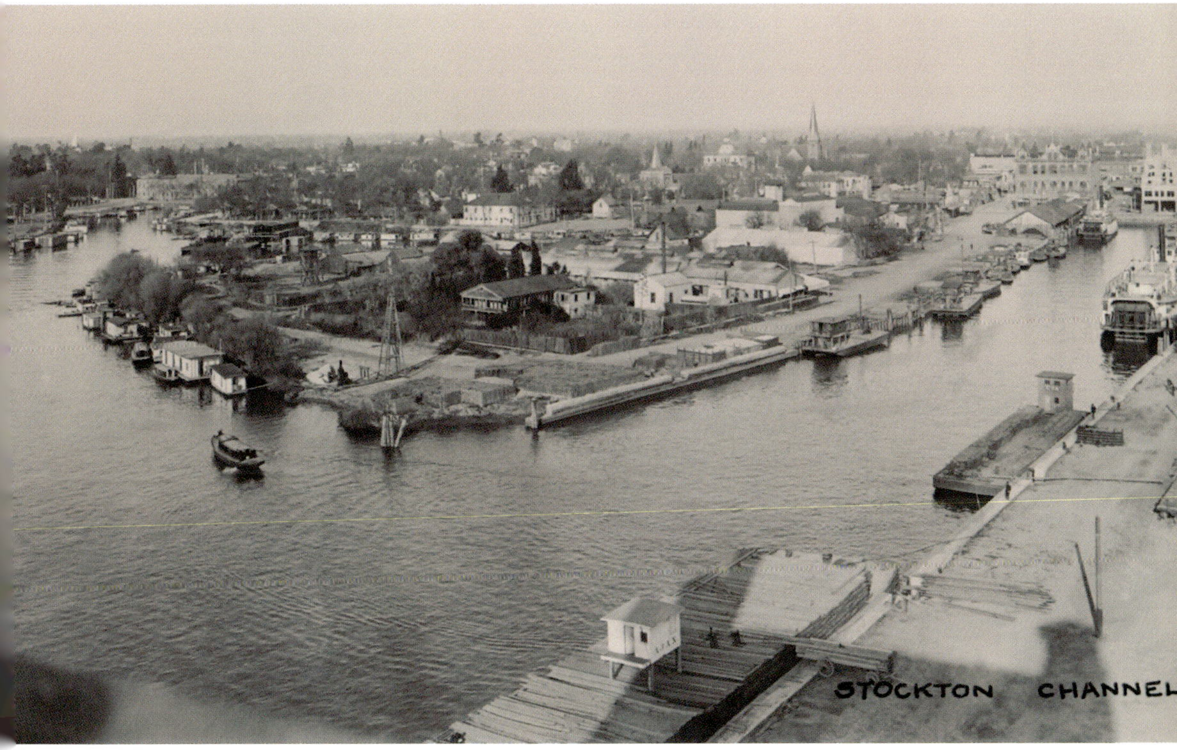

Weber Point is the historic epicenter of Stockton. It was progressively industrialized between 1860 and 1945. Unregulated use severely degraded the environment and blemished the heart of a maturing metropolis. A short-lived attempt to reestablish Weber Point with a hotel and restaurant in the 1960s did not last. By 1985, the point had become dangerous and a source of civic embarrassment. In 1997, a campaign was launched to revive Weber Point. The Weber Point Event Center opened to the public on July 3, 1999. (Courtesy of Haggin Museum Archives.)

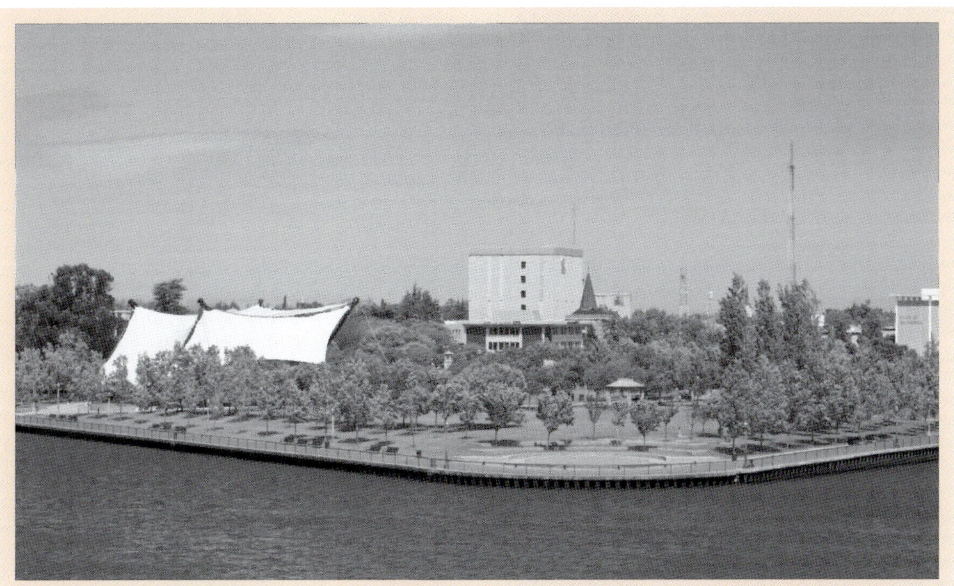

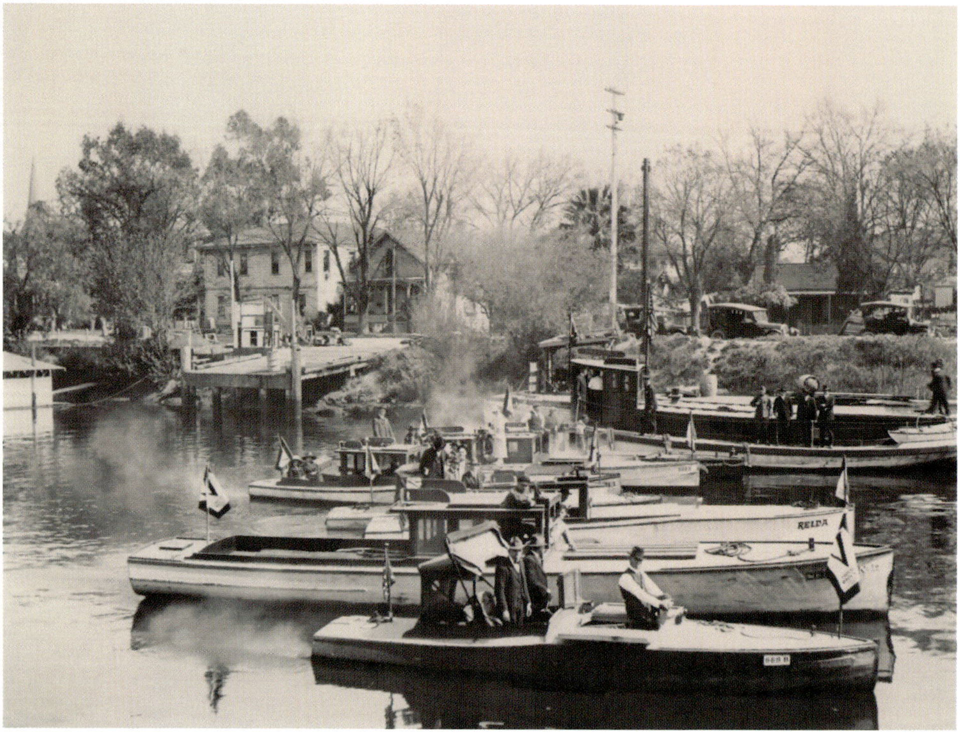

McLeod Lake, near Center and Lindsay Streets, offered a public pier for boating parties. The Stephens Brothers boats became a distinctive feature on the Stockton Channel. This photograph records a 1926 rally of Runabouts, manufactured by the Stephens Brothers Boat Builders of Stockton; Ennis Brown, Walter Perry, Dunbar Hansen, and R. M. Dixon are among the identifiable boaters. Today, McLeod Lake has been reduced and absorbed by a public park with monuments to Stockton's history. (Courtesy of University of the Pacific Special Collections.)

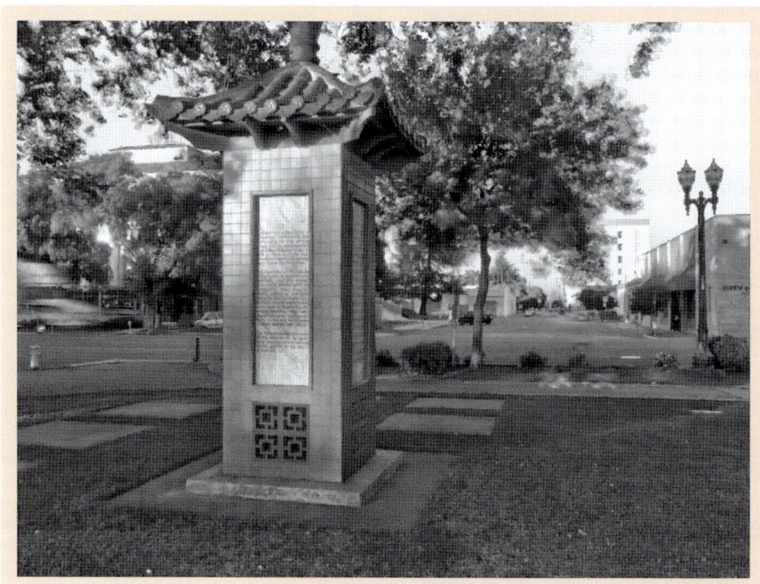

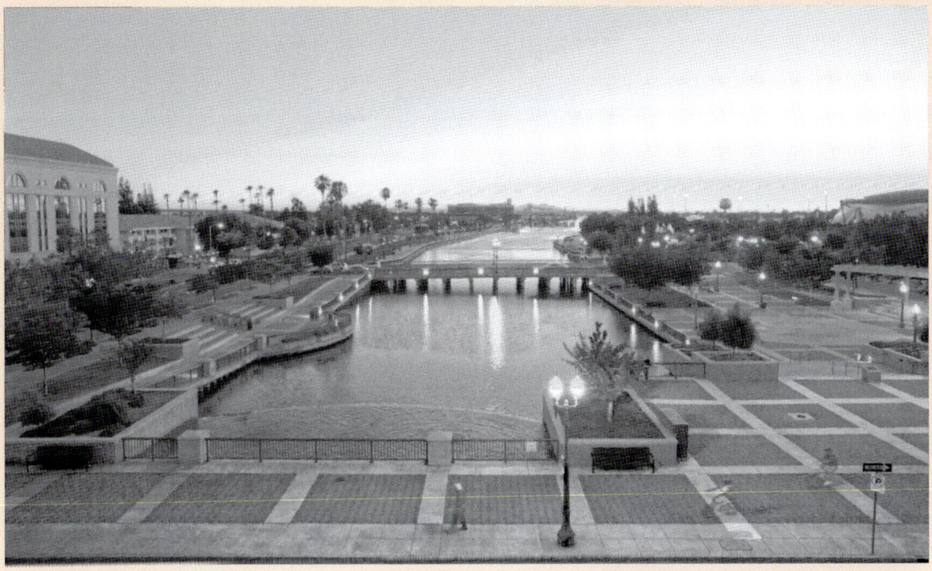

In 1930, the Head of Navigation at El Dorado Street and Bridge Place featured a billboard announcing the progress toward dredging Stockton's Deep Water Channel. The deepwater channel opened to large vessels on February 2, 1933. Today, the DeCarli Plaza bears no reminders of the steamship era. The *Capt. Weber* (left) burned in her berth in 1943; the *Fort Sutter* was commissioned by the federal government to carry troops from Camp Stoneman to San Francisco during World War II. (Courtesy of University of the Pacific Special Collections.)

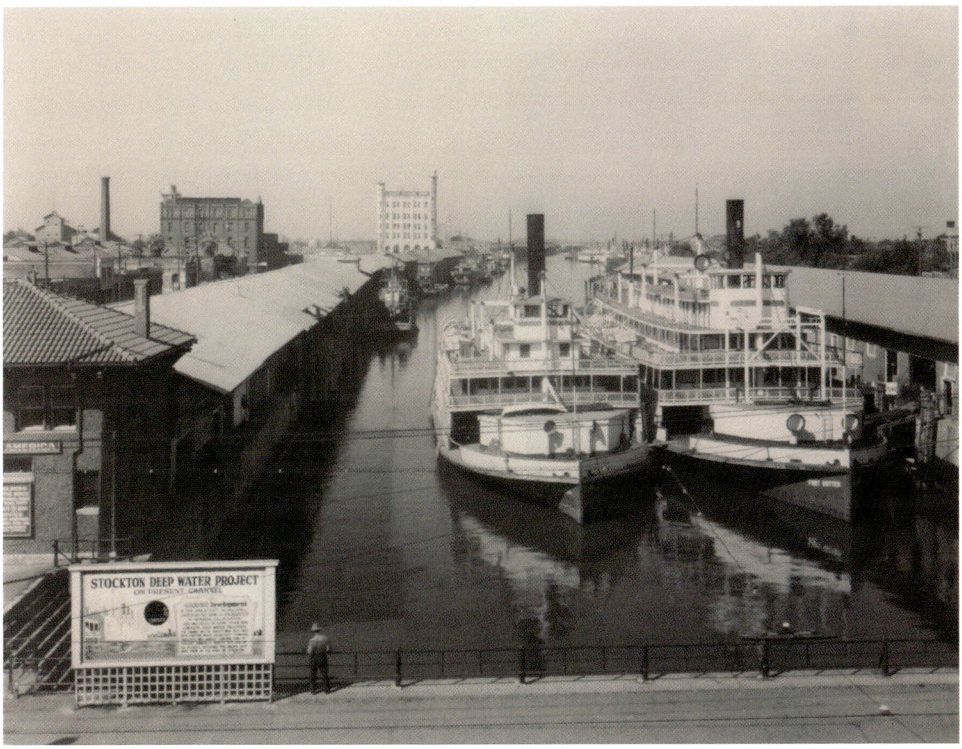

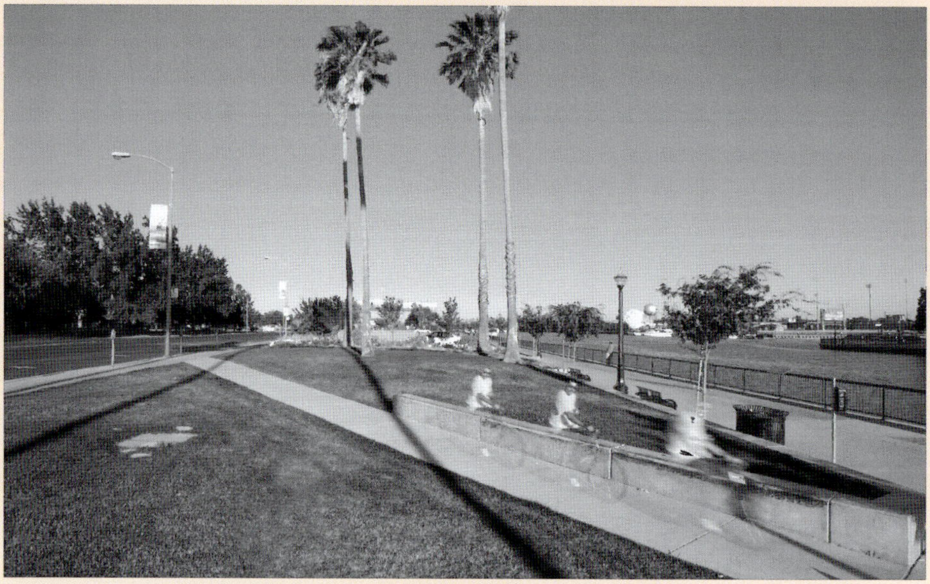

Before the Stockton Channel was dredged, ships with modest draft—such as the USS *Farragut* (TB-11)—visited Stockton's waterfront. The *Farragut* was named after Adm. David Farragut, of Civil War fame, whose order, paraphrased as "Damn the torpedoes, full speed ahead!," is frequently quoted. The boat's commission (1899–1919) was relatively uneventful and included patrolling the West Coast and conducting torpedo-training exercises, along with patrolling the Panama Canal during World War I. Today, the site is a quiet intersection along the Joan Darrah Promenade. (Courtesy of Port of Stockton Archives.)

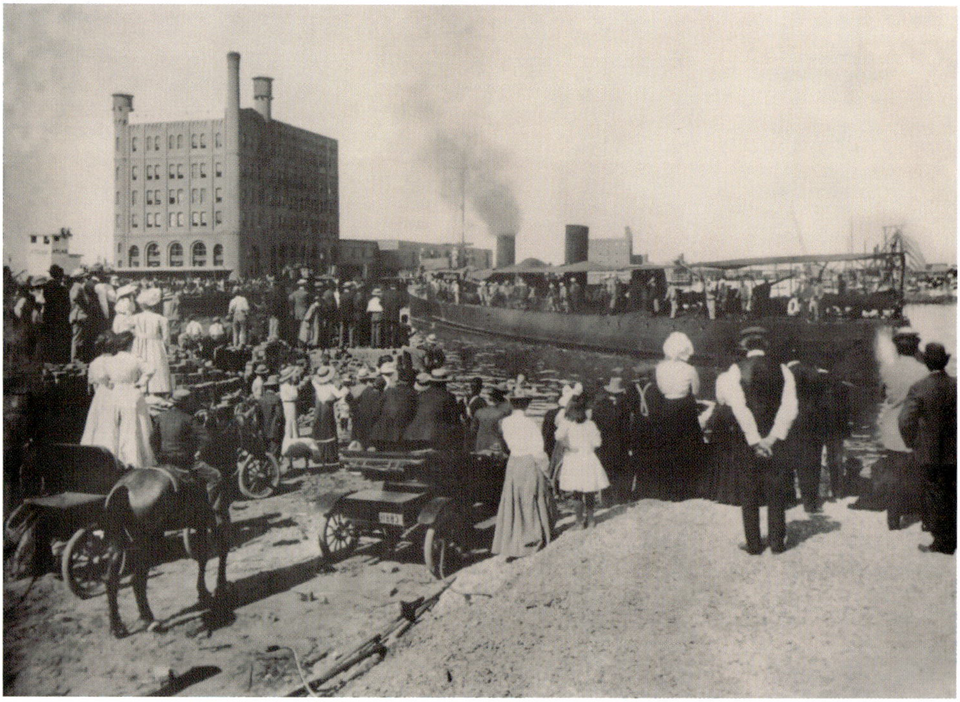

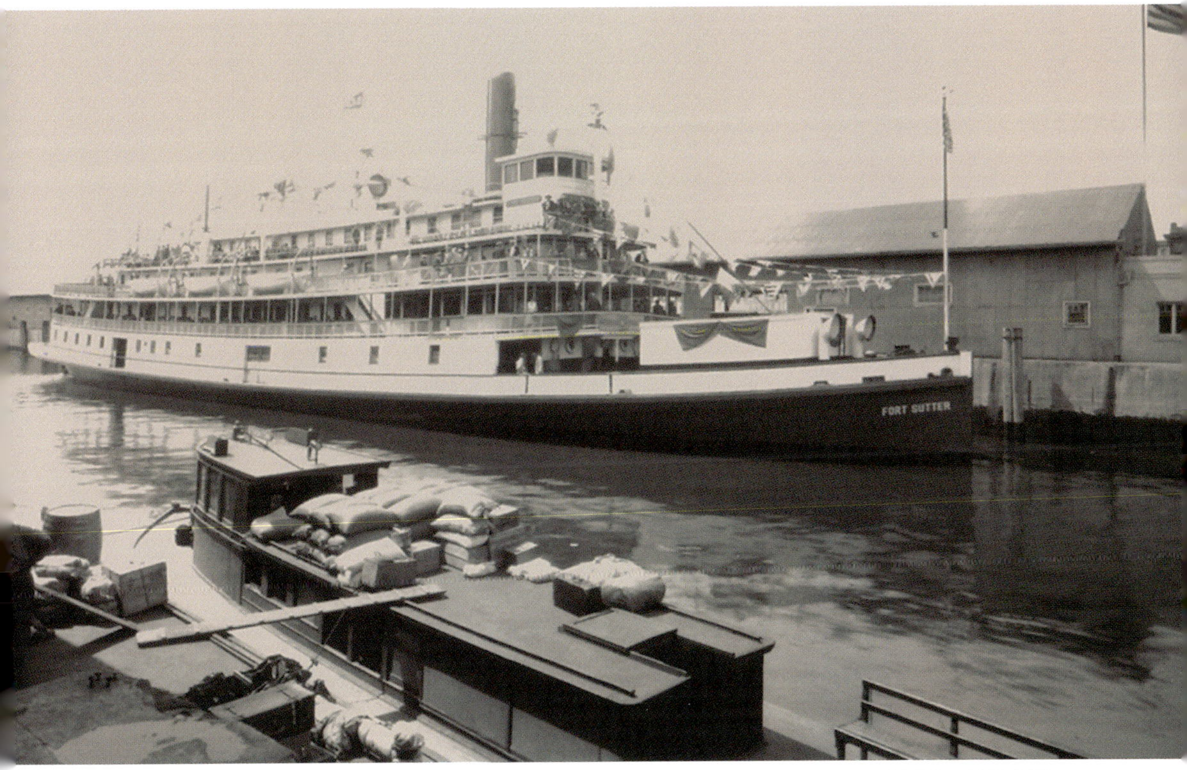

The *Fort Sutter* was among the last steamships to operate on the San Joaquin River by conscription during World War II. It survived the violent fare wars between the California Steam Navigation "Old Line" and the Union Transportation "New Line" companies that provided water transportation service in the delta between 1850 and 1931. Stockton's river-passenger service ended on July 31, 1931. Today, sounds of automobile traffic and a waterfall mingle at DeCarli Plaza. (Courtesy of University of the Pacific Special Collections.)

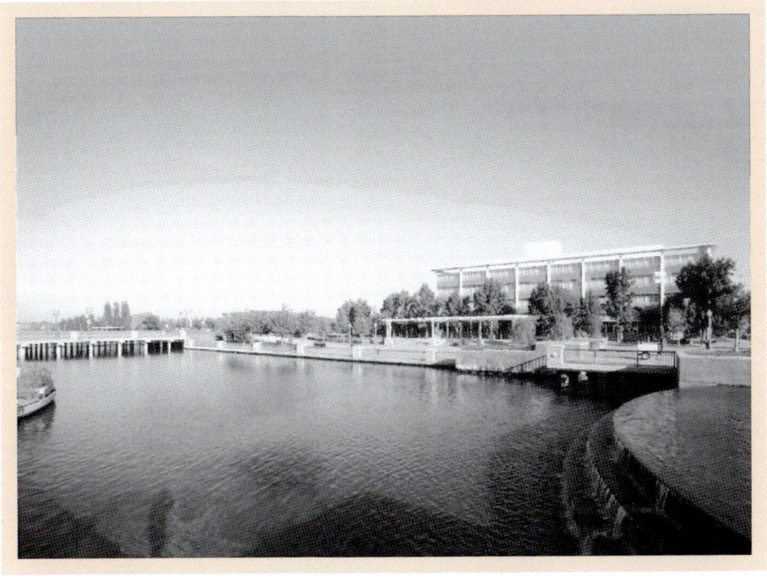

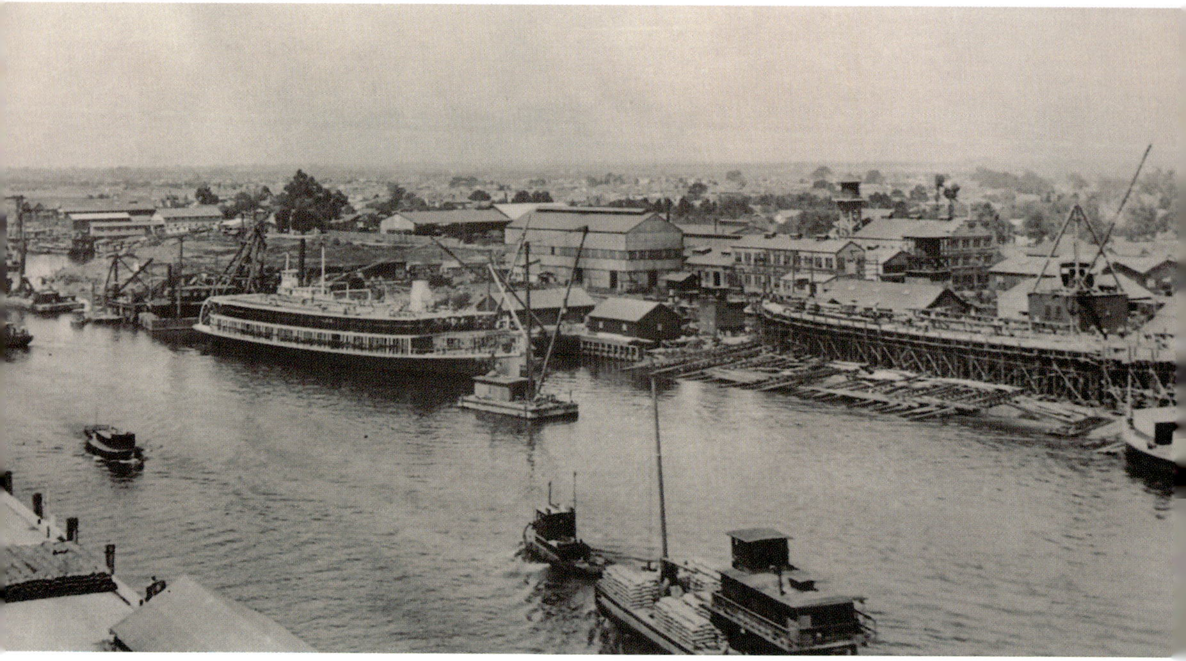

Shipbuilding is a lesser-known chapter of Stockton's history. In 1848, the city's first sailing ship, the *San Joaquin*, was built. During the 1920s, the *Delta King* and *Delta Queen* were constructed along the north shore of the Stockton Channel at Harrison Street and the Stockton Iron Works. Stockton's shipbuilders hammered and sparked through World War II and declined after 1945. Today, the old ironworks provides a rustic reminder of Stockton's maritime past to passing boaters. (Courtesy of Port of Stockton Archives.)

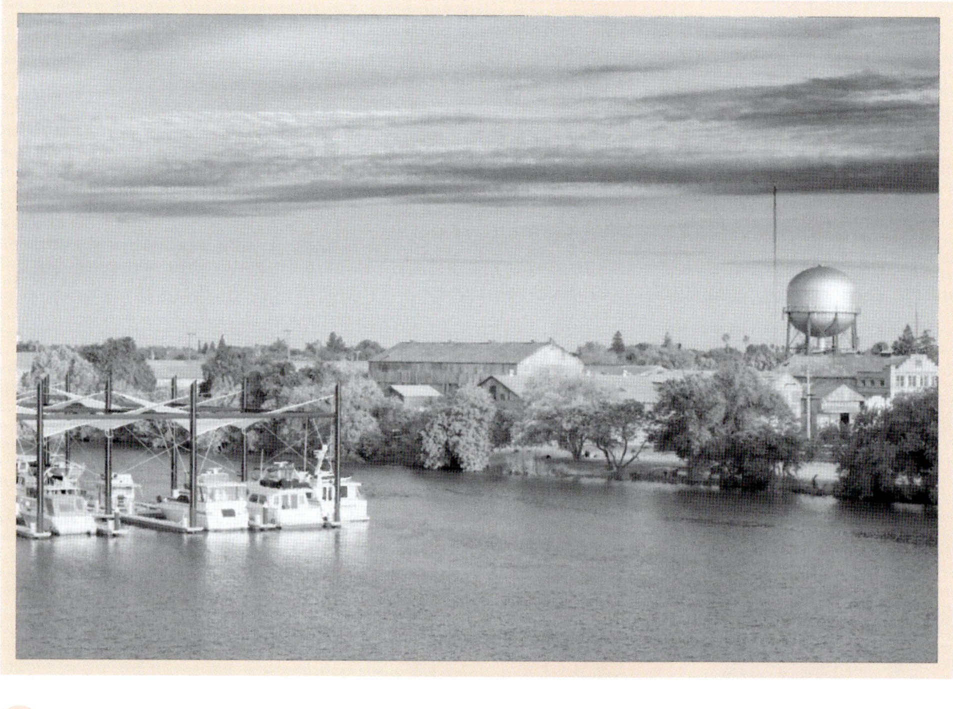

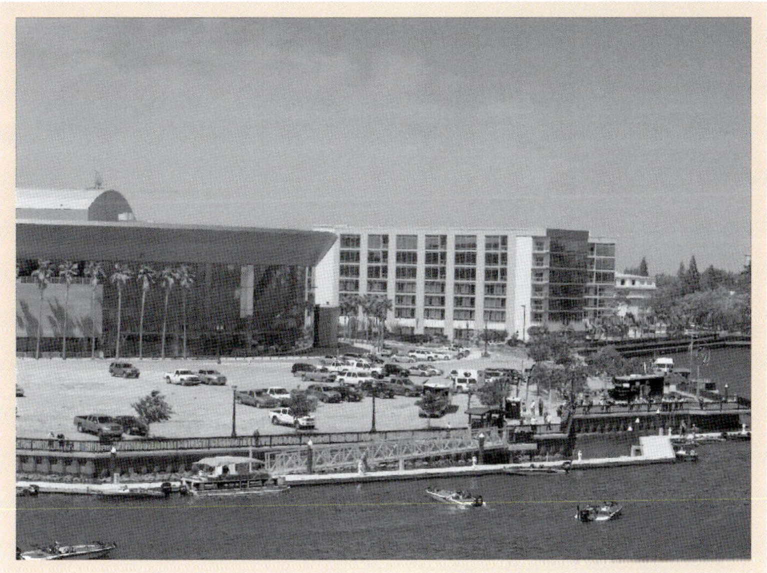

Hickinbotham Brothers was one of several companies that built water vessels for the military during World War II. The company's boat construction facilities fronted Fremont Street, between Commerce and Van Buren Streets. Today, the site has been transformed into the Stockton Arena and a baseball park. This is a success story for Stockton's urban renewal and a classic example of beating swords into plowshares. (Courtesy of University of the Pacific Special Collections.)

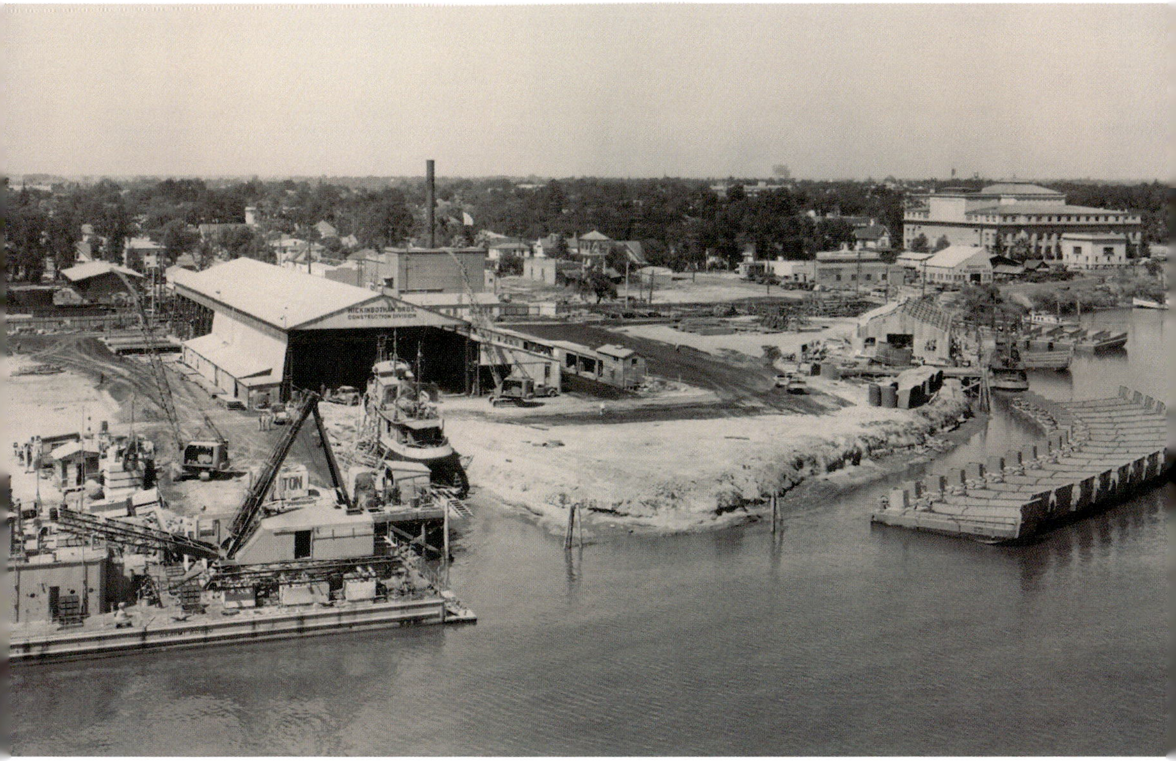

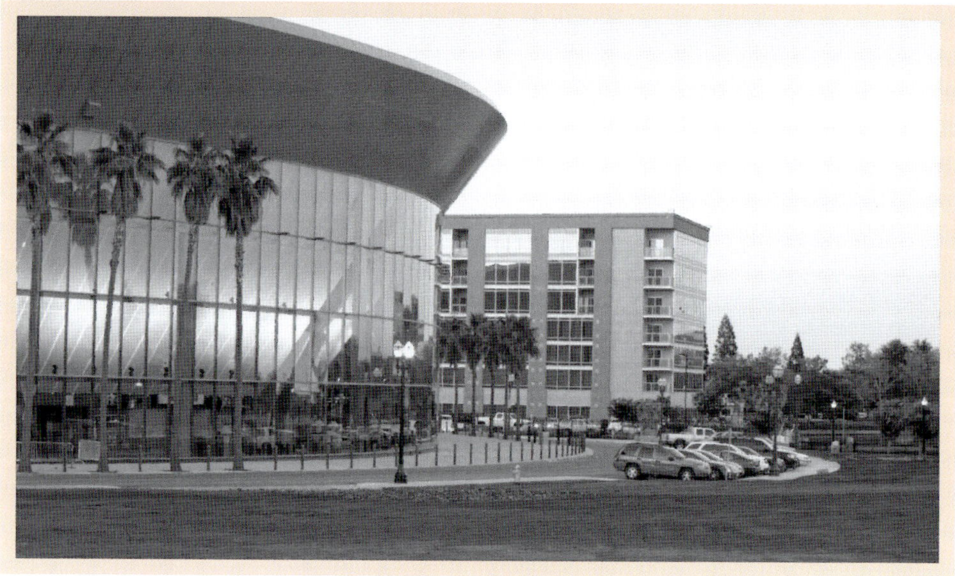

The Hickinbotham Brothers employed a sizeable workforce constructing tugboats for the US Army during World War II. Hickinbotham subcontracted local businesses such as the Carando Machine Shop Associated Welding, pictured in the background. Today, the University Plaza Hotel sits on the corner of Commerce Street and Steamboat Levee, where Carando's once stood. Carando Technologies has become an international company, operating from the old Stockton Iron Works on Harrison Street. (Courtesy of University of the Pacific Special Collections.)

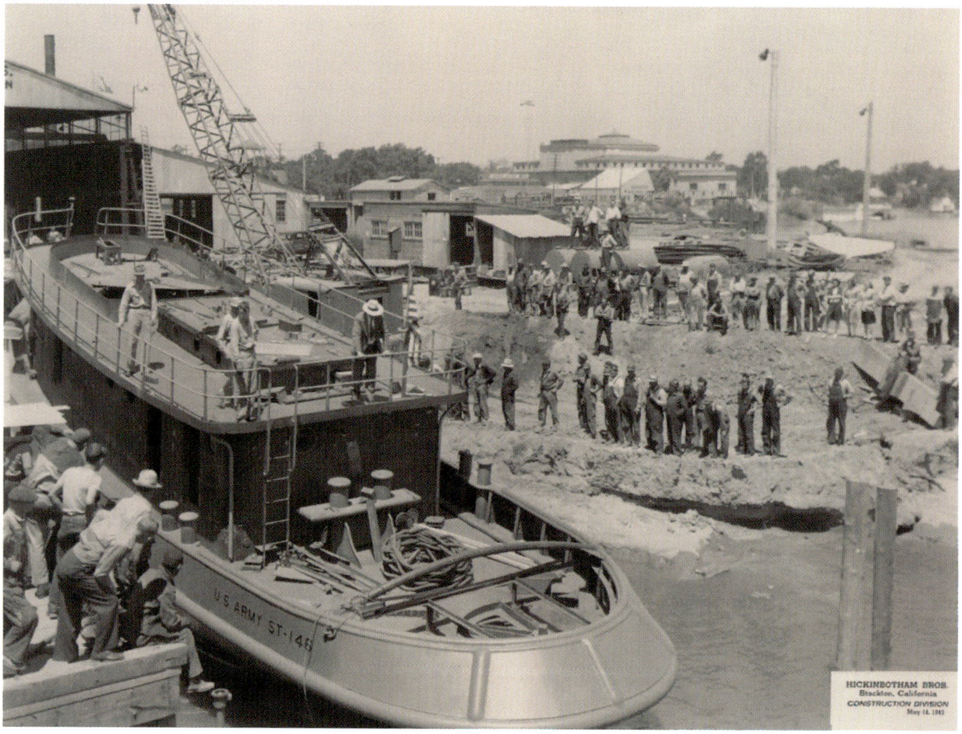

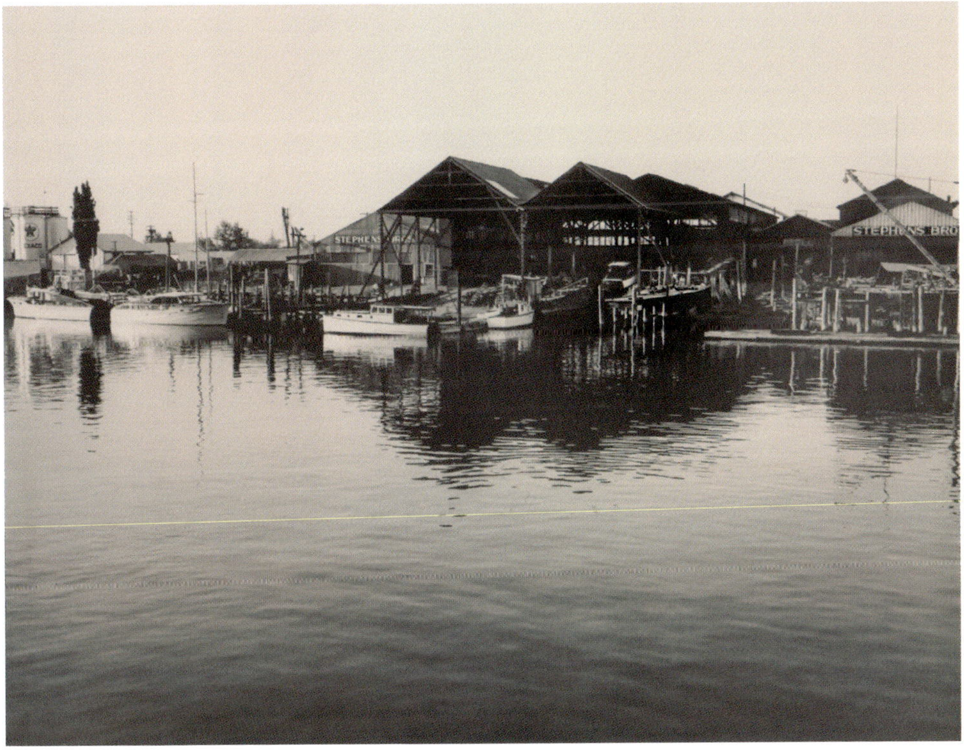

Operating from Stockton's waterfront, the Stephens Brothers Boat Builders were in a class of their own from 1902 to 1987. Working from a modest suburban home, with middle class resources and 1,000 miles of delta waterway surrounding them, Theodore and Robert Stephens built their first sloop, *Dorothy*, in their backyard and launched a new chapter in boating history. The Stephens Brothers history has disappeared from the Stockton waterfront, but an extraordinary display and archive of their achievements can be found at the Haggin Museum in Stockton. (Courtesy of Haggin Museum Archives.)

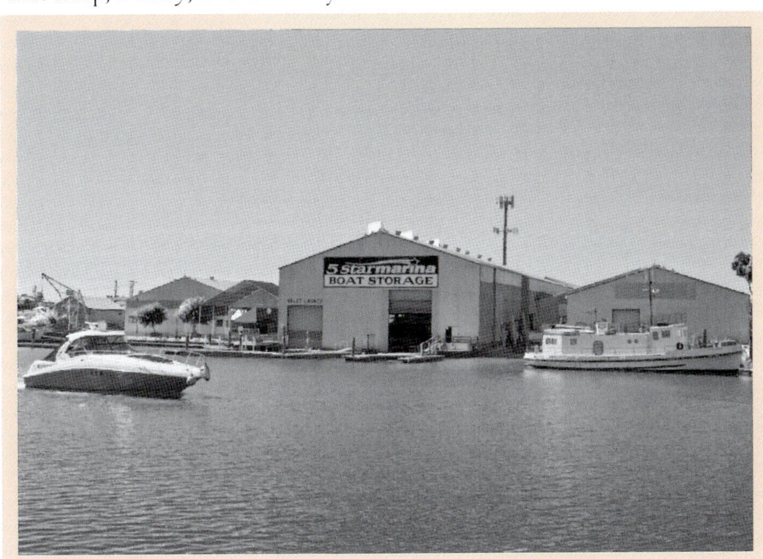

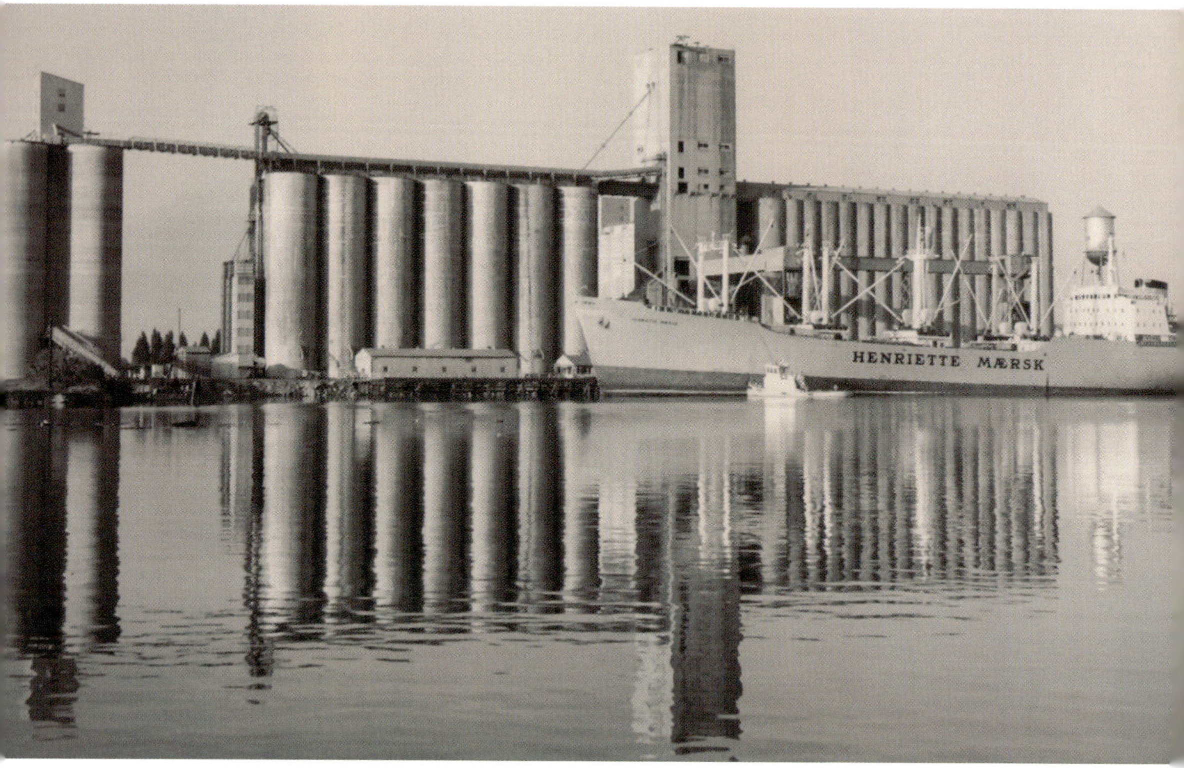

The Penny Newman–owned bulk cargo terminal is an icon for the Port of Stockton. Purchased from the ContiGroup Companies in 2000, the Penny-Newman is one of the largest grain-storage facilities on the West Coast with direct access to international markets. The terminal is located at a transportation nexus—a confluence of truck, rail, and ocean freight lines. From the towering Interstate 5, or the Stockton Channel, the terminal appears much as it did when it was constructed in 1955. (Courtesy of Port of Stockton Archives.)

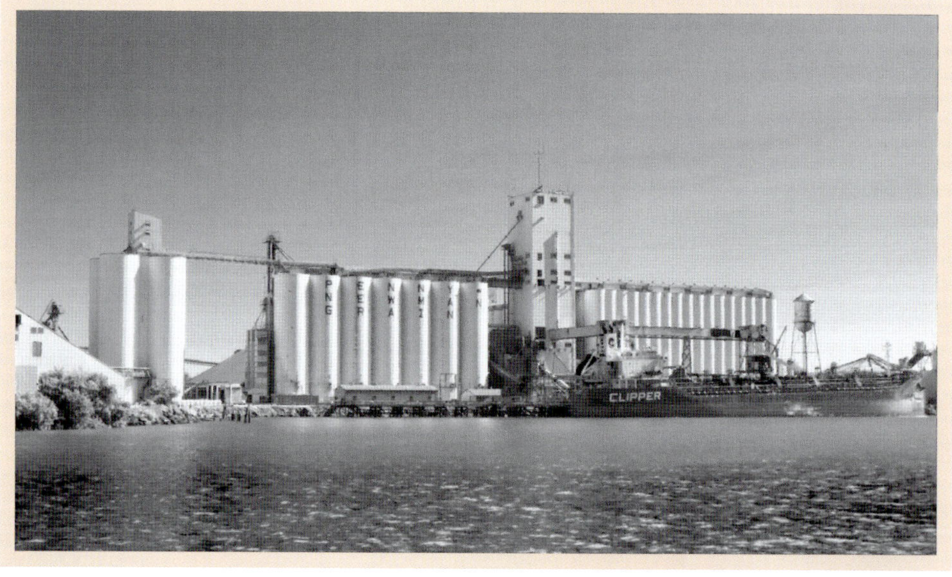

CHAPTER 3

All Roads Lead to Stockton

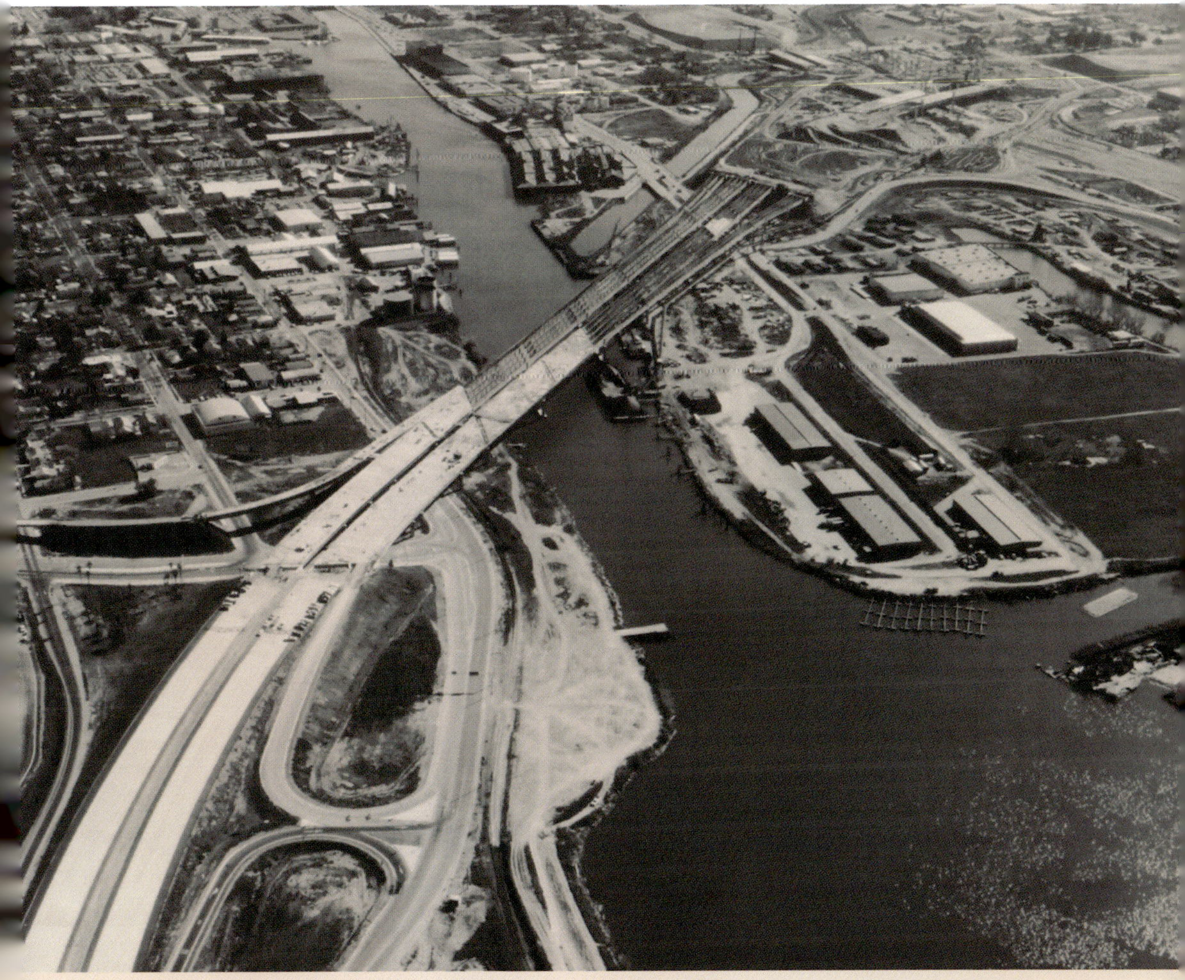

The Interstate 5 freeway along Stockton's west side was completed in 1979 after nearly a decade of stalled development and grassroots action committees lobbying for its completion. The impact to the city while stalled was increased traffic, traffic accidents, and pollution. Completion of I-5 has contribution to Stockton's economy and environment. It has also encouraged suburbanization in northwest Stockton. (Courtesy of University of the Pacific Special Collections.)

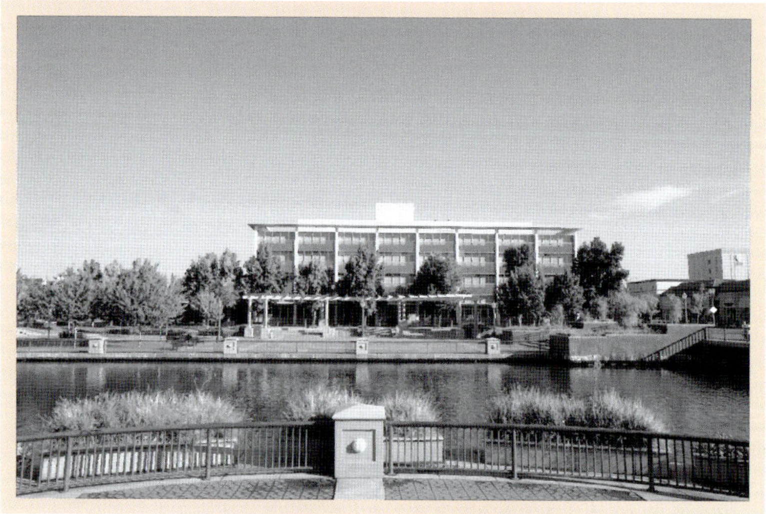

Transportation to and through Stockton coordinated land, water, rail, and air. The first commercial transportation network in Stockton linked water and land by stagecoach. In 1851, the Corinthian Building, located near the waterfront on Channel and El Dorado Streets, contained the first stage depot with passage to Sacramento and the southern mines of the Gold Rush. Today, the State of California Building's International Style architecture blends well with the newly constructed DeCarli Plaza. (Courtesy of the Weber-Murphy Archive.)

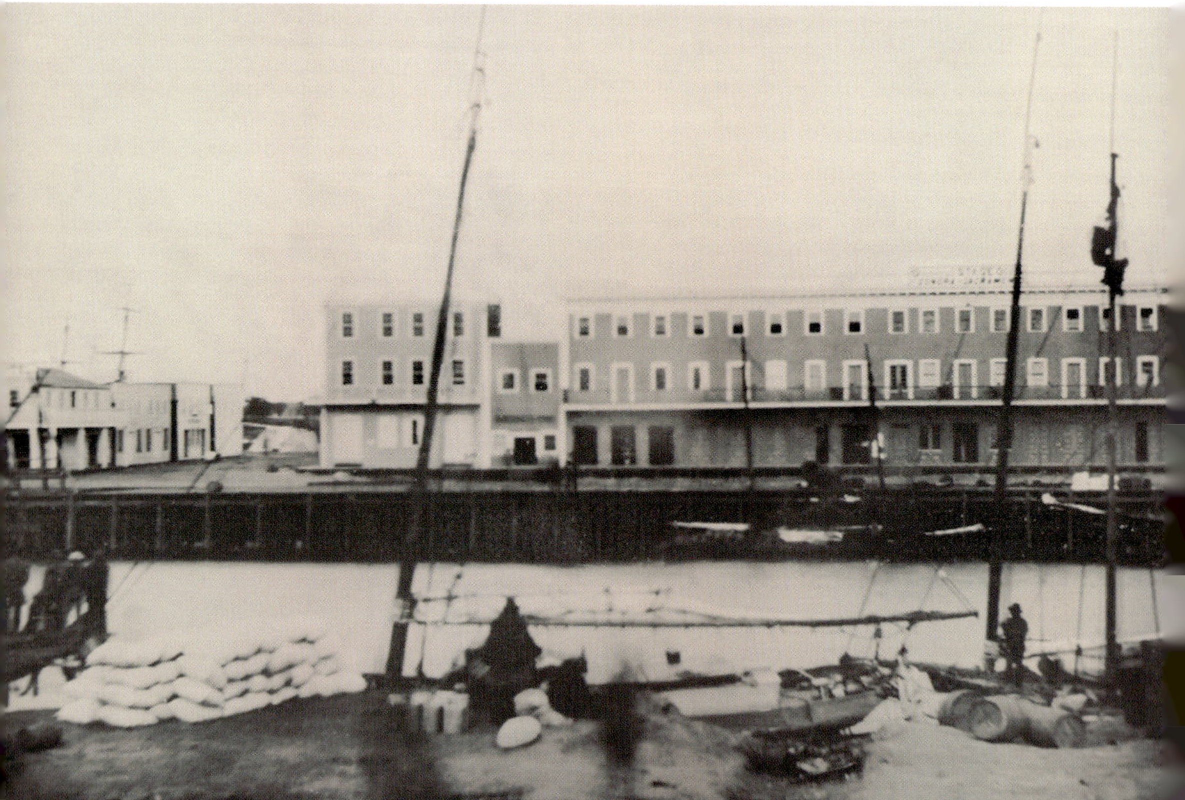

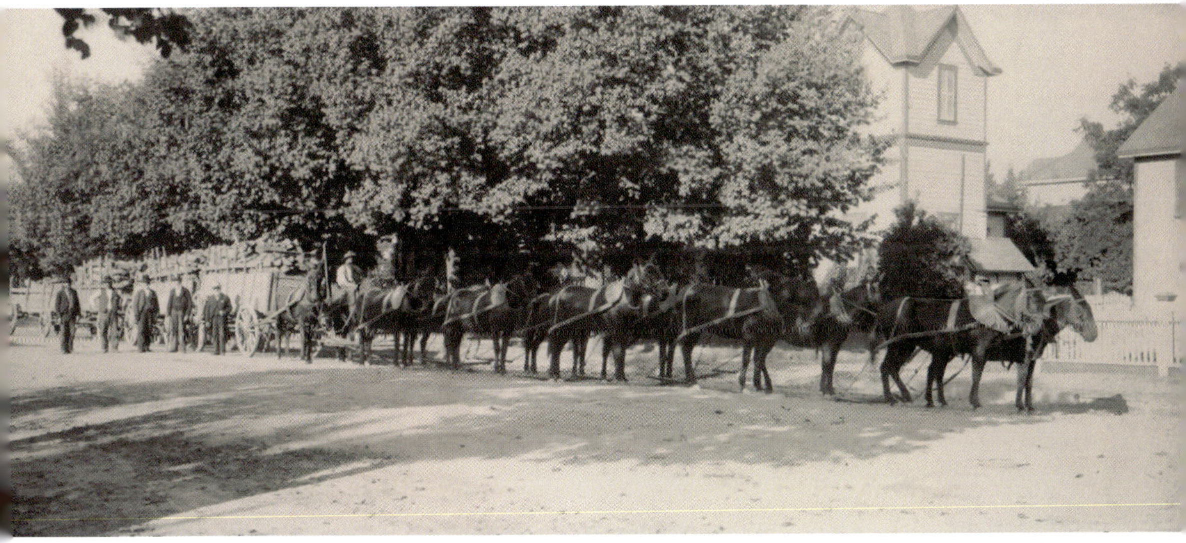

Stockton streets were designed to accommodate commercial activity. Miner Avenue was a wider commercial corridor leading from the embarcadero to roads east and, after 1869, railroad terminals. In the 1870s, 12-mule-team wagons routinely passed through the intersection of Miner Avenue and Stanislaus Street. Today, Miner Avenue is a mixed-use commercial zone with a high rate of vacancies and remembered in as "auto row." The street is scheduled for redevelopment between the Robert J. Cabral Station and Weber Point Events Center. (Courtesy of University of the Pacific Special Collections.)

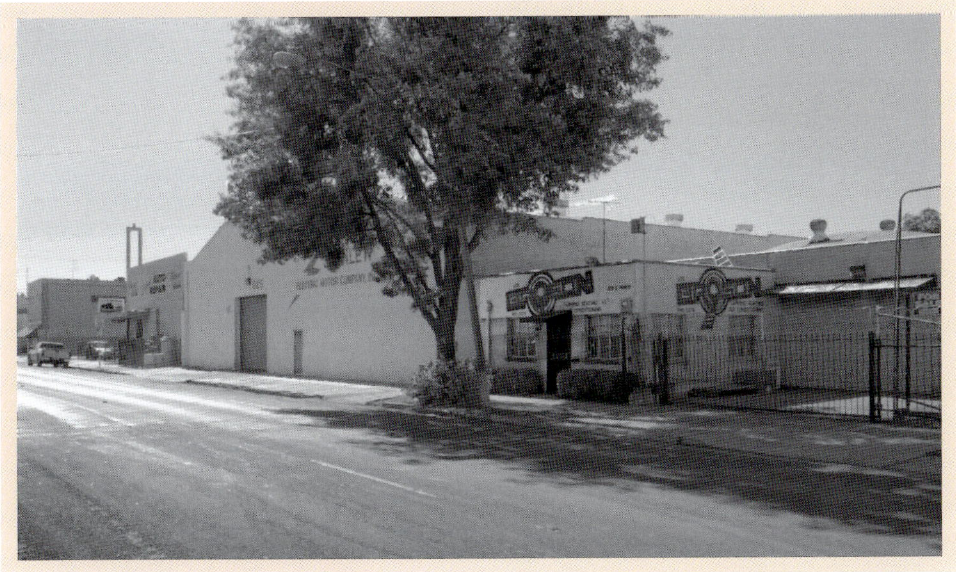

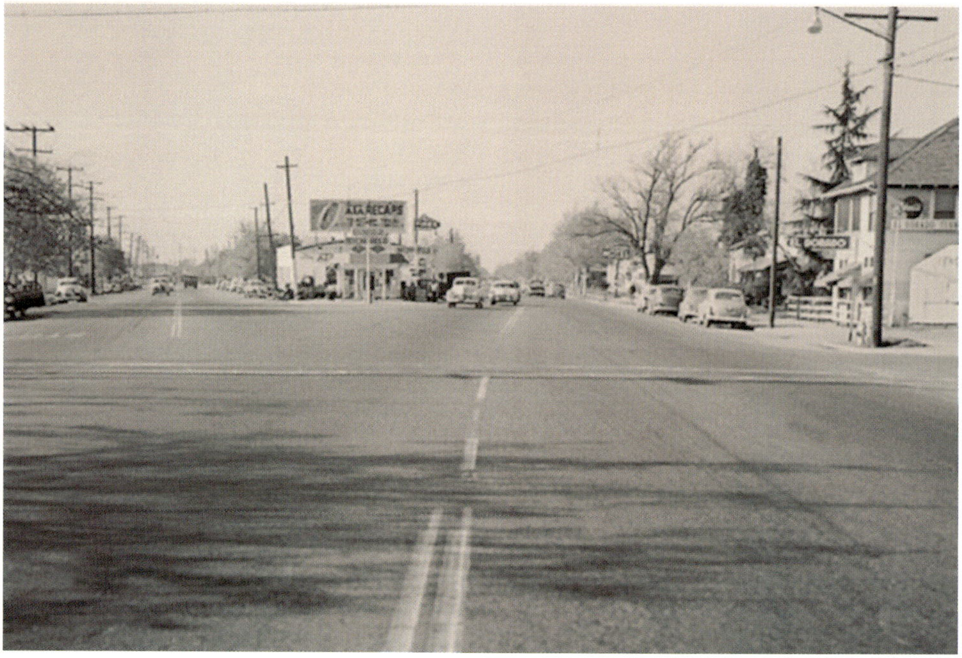

The 19th-century trails to Stockton from the San Francisco Bay region stretched from San Jose to French Camp via Altamont Pass. The French Camp Turnpike was Stockton's southern gateway; as the turnpike entered Stockton, it merged with Jackson, Center, and El Dorado Streets on its way into the central city. Visitors northbound from Manteca and Tracy followed McKinley Avenue, merging with the old turnpike at the Center and El Dorado convergence. The turnpike's distinction and commercial significance declined with the designation of the Lincoln Highway. (Courtesy of Bank of Stockton Archives.)

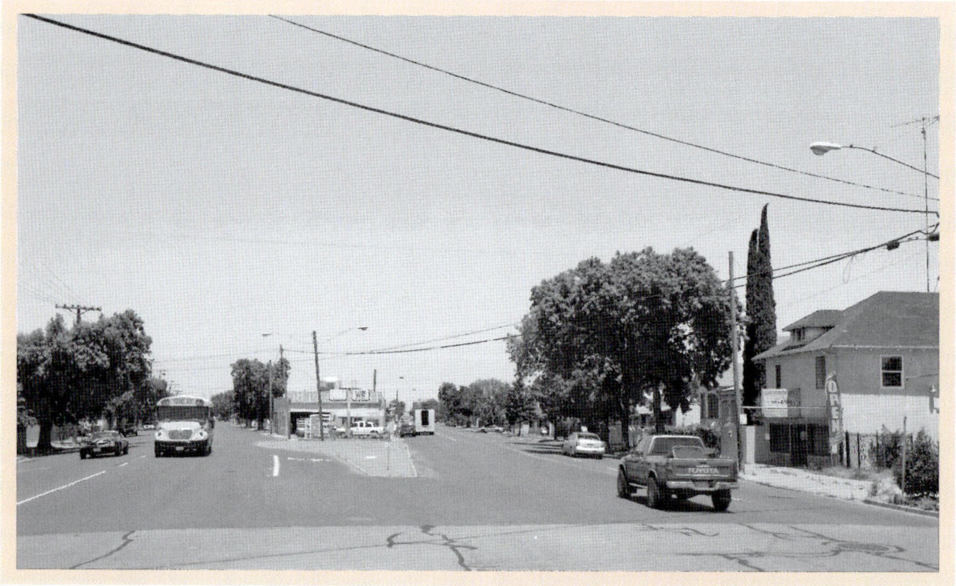

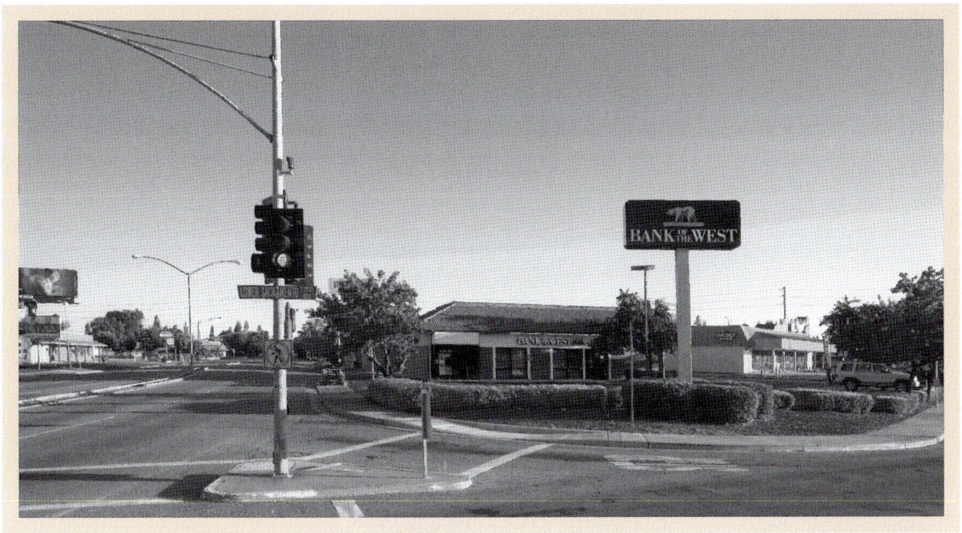

Southbound motorists followed Lower Sacramento Road and the Lincoln Highway to downtown Stockton from 1904 through the 1920s. Otto's Place (aka the Five Mile House) was located at the intersection of Pacific Avenue and Hammer Lane. In 1932, it was a popular diner and recreational park where the highway crossed the historic boundary of Charles Weber's land grant. The roadway has changed very little as the region has undergone steady development since the 1950s. The Bank of the West is the most recent newcomer to this once rural outpost. (Courtesy of University of the Pacific Special Collections.)

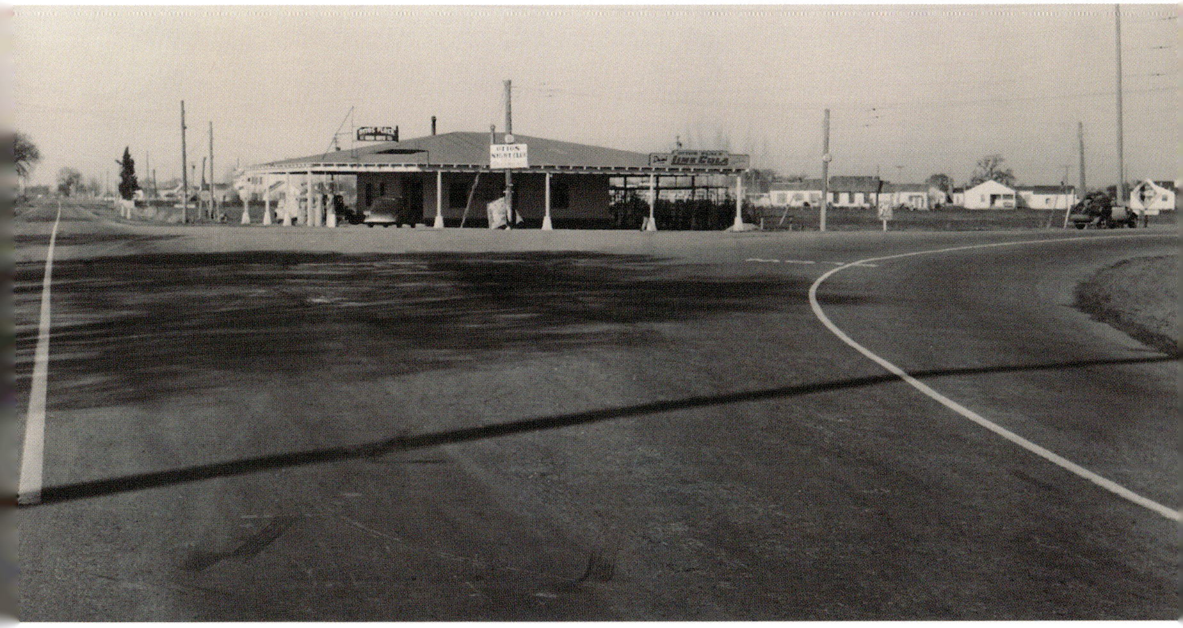

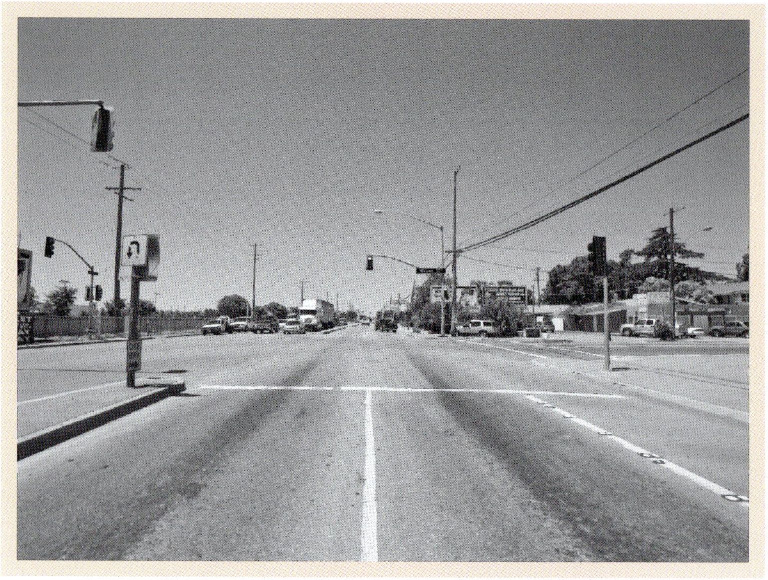

Between 1910 and 1925, the routes through Stockton reflected the country's chaotic roadways. The Bureau of Public Roads was formed in 1915 to unify the system. In 1939, the intersection of Charter and Wilson Ways received northbound traffic arriving in Stockton via the Golden State Highway (99), historic US Highway 50, and State Route 4. This intersection has been progressively enlarged since 1919 to accommodate automobile and truck traffic and the development of the San Joaquin County Fairgrounds directly to the south. (Courtesy of University of the Pacific Special Collections.)

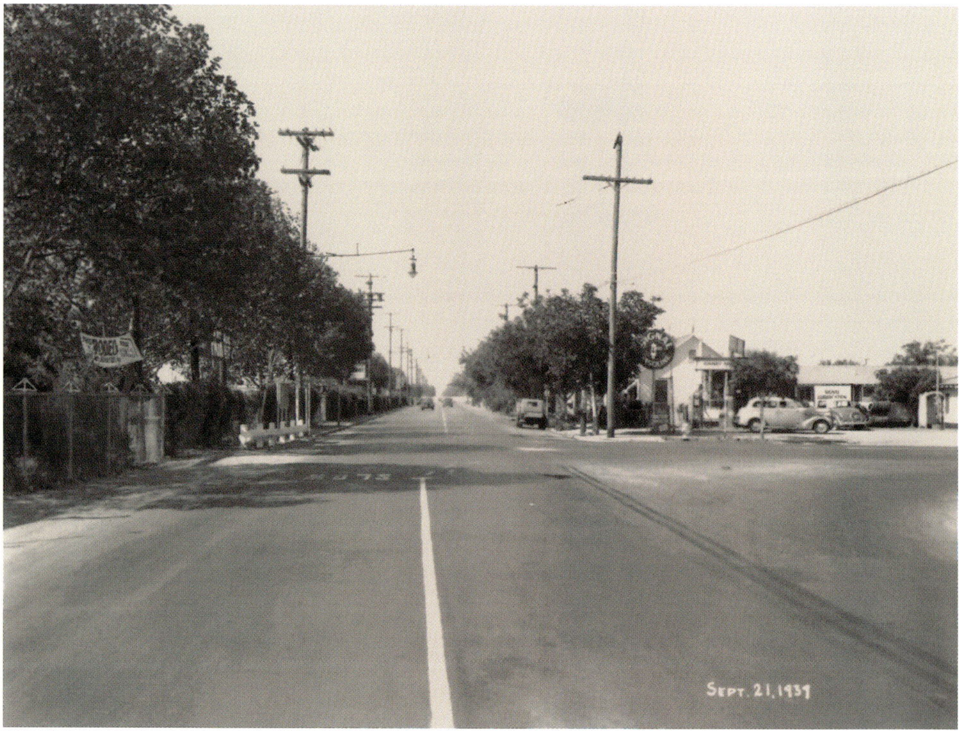

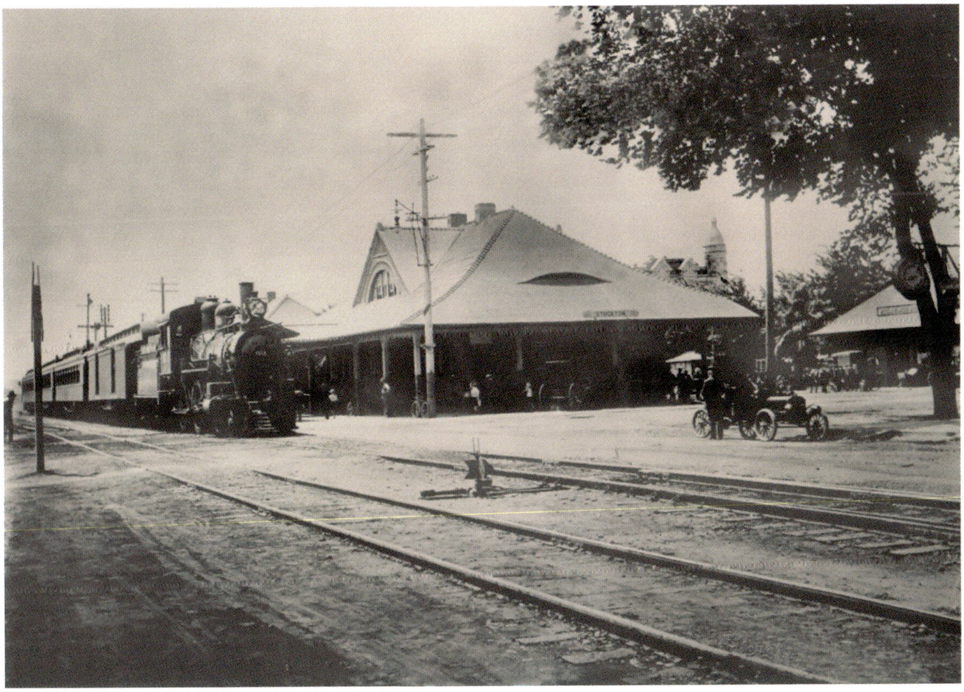

The Western Pacific Railroad arrived in Stockton on August 12, 1869, shortly after the completion of the transcontinental railroad. Leland Stanford insisted on building his railway into central Stockton. The citizens resisted, and the depot was established on the east side at Sacramento and Market Streets. Subsequently, a Southern Pacific Depot was erected near Main and Sacramento Streets in 1892. Today, the old location of the Western Pacific Terminal is a parking lot for commuters to San Jose. A recently revived 1930s depot is now operational. (Courtesy of Port of Stockton Archives.)

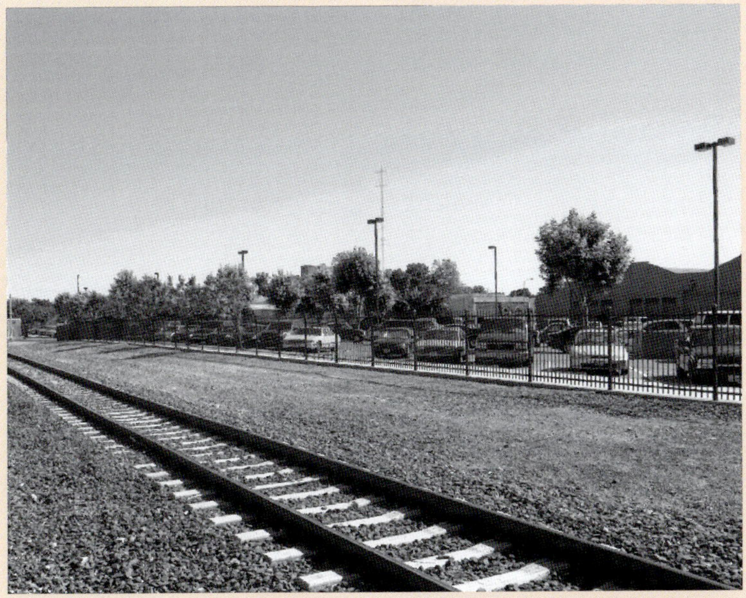

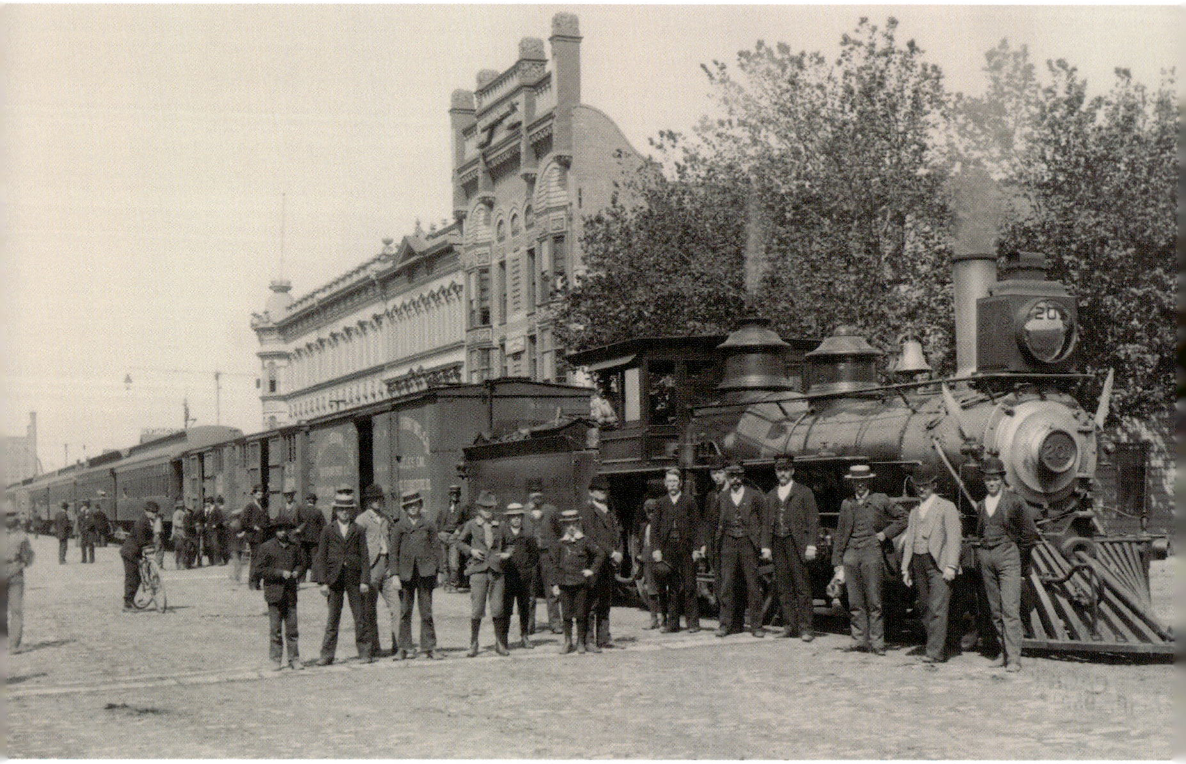

The grand plans for the Stockton and Copperopolis Railroad to the waterfront via Weber Avenue were not completed until 1870, but the enterprise teetered on bankruptcy. The railroad was sold, and after multiple ownerships, absorbed by the Southern Pacific in 1888. These trains were a routine feature of Weber Avenue until 1901, when track was removed and the terminal on Sacramento Street was used. Today, buses from a revived San Joaquin Rapid Transit District are a regular feature on Weber Avenue. (Courtesy of University of the Pacific Special Collections.)

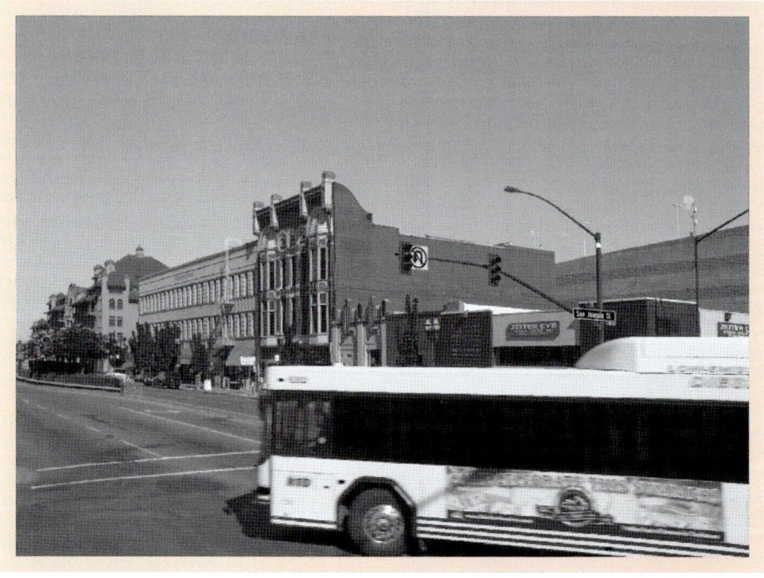

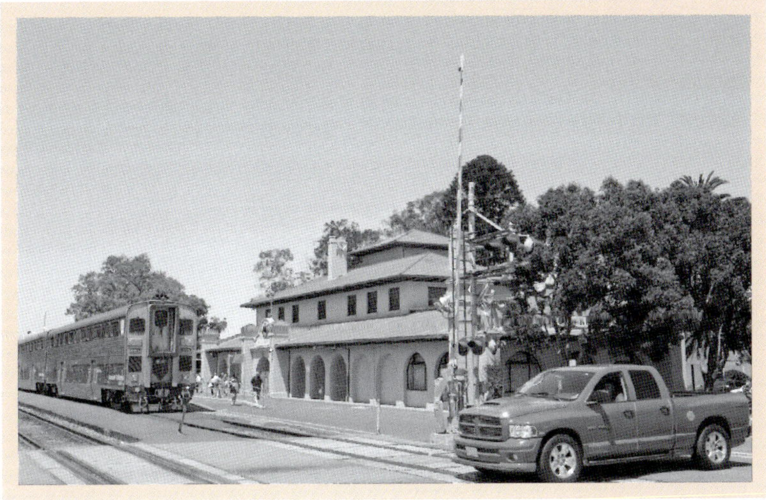

In 1900, the San Francisco & San Joaquin Valley Railway constructed what was known the Old Santa Fe Railroad Depot on South San Joaquin Street. It has been in continuous operation since then. An early innovator in intermodal transportation, the terminal was linked to local transportation systems. Today, it is the San Joaquin Street Station, with regular Amtrak service to Sacramento, Oakland, Bakersfield, and Los Angeles. (Courtesy of University of the Pacific Special Collections.)

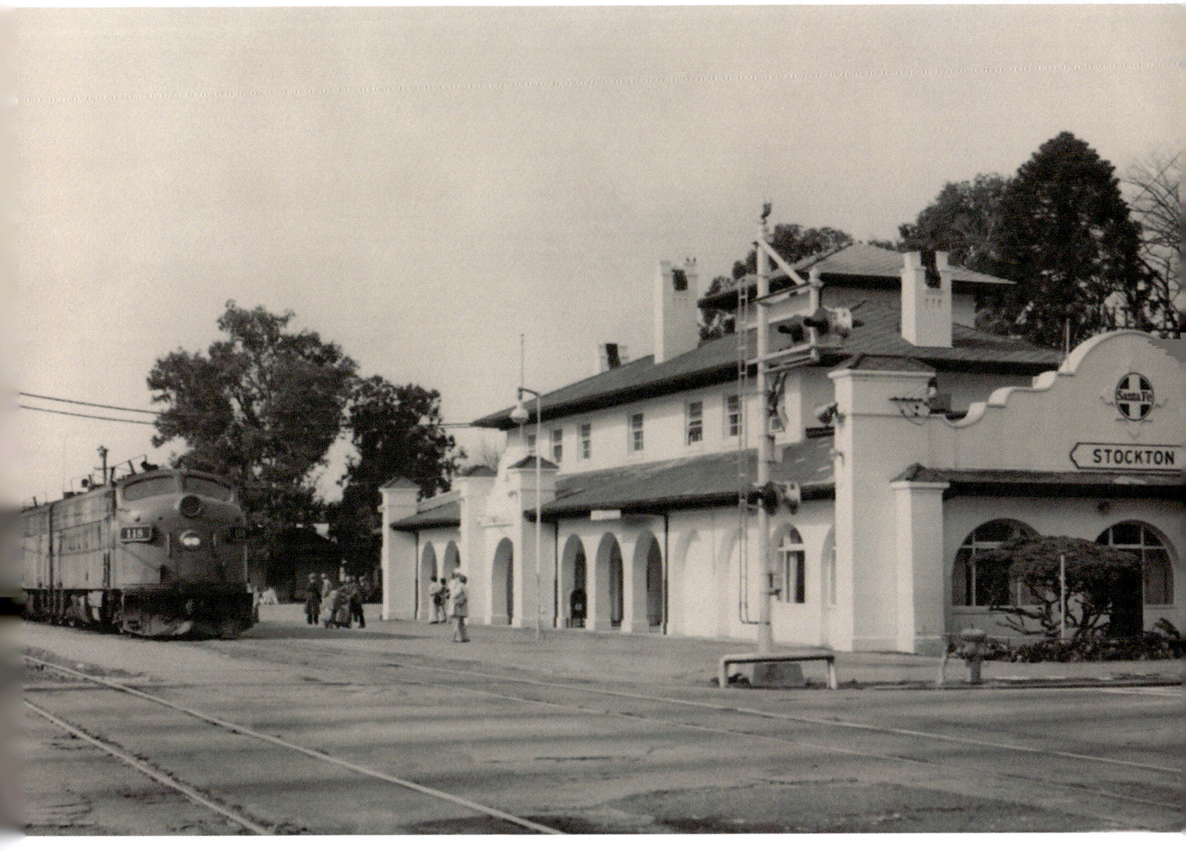

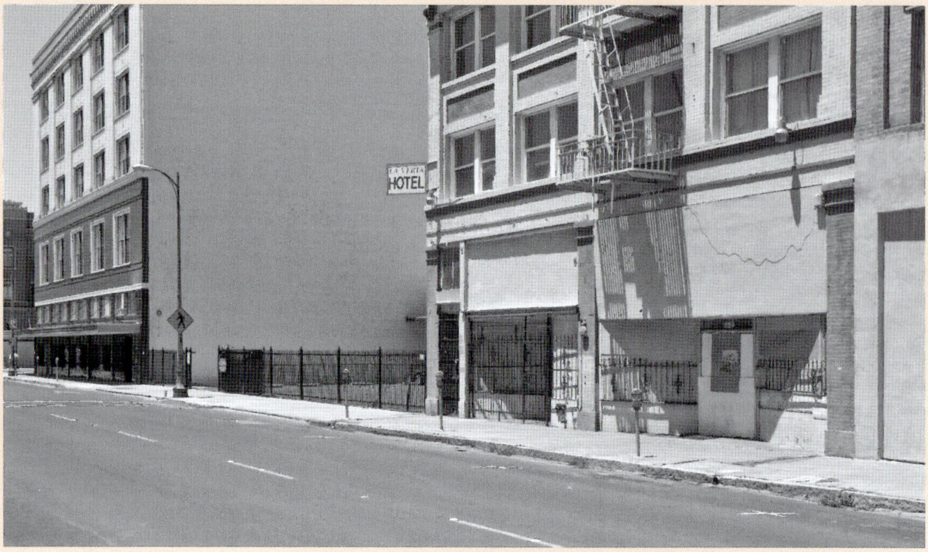

Stockton's public transportation system began in 1875 as the Stockton Street Railroad. The system was horse-drawn until the early 1890s. The main office and maintenance terminal were located on Main Street, east of American Street. Today, the La Verta Hotel sits on the former terminal site, a minor memory of Stockton's golden age, when Main Street was lined with hotels. The old hotel represents another generation entering Stockton's urban history. (Courtesy of University of the Pacific Special Collections.)

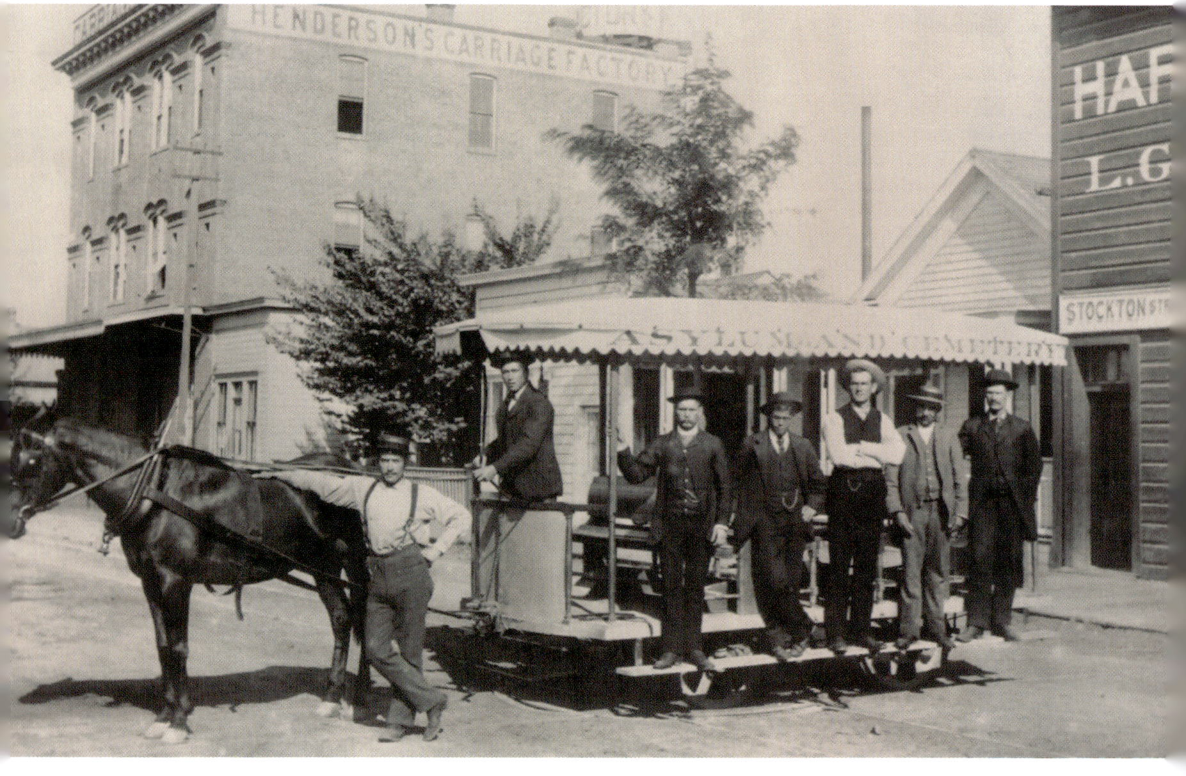

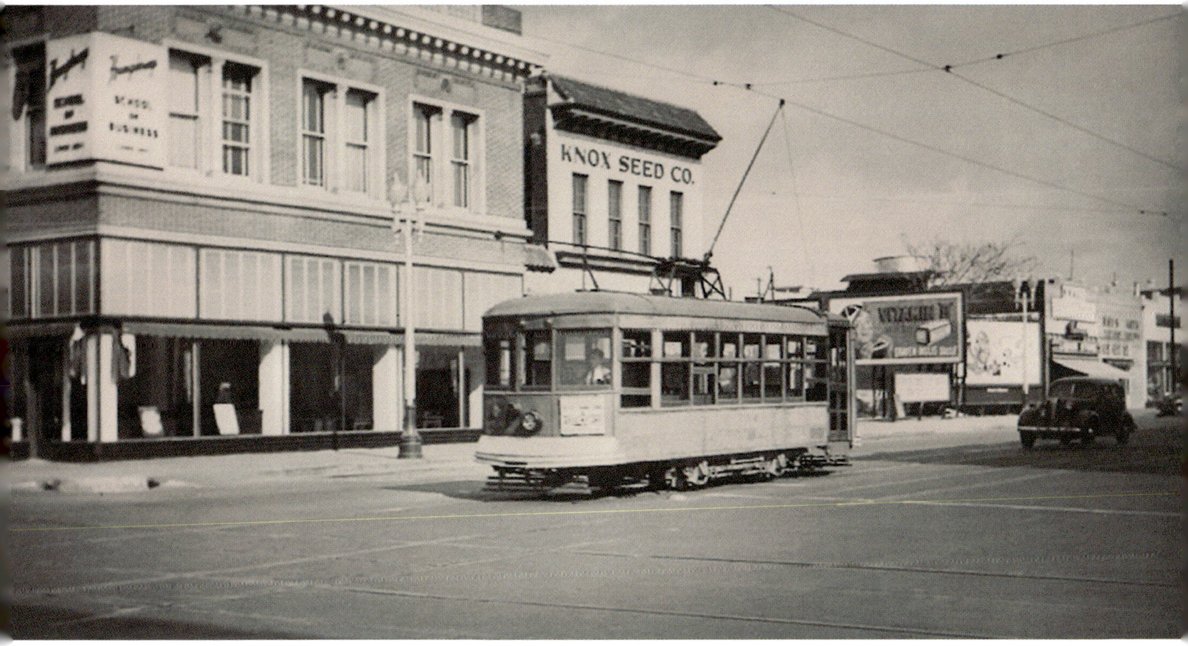

In 1892, the horse-drawn car system was refitted with electric motors and reorganized as the Stockton Electric Railroad Company. In 1924, the line extended as far as the College of the Pacific. Southern Pacific Railroad purchased and operated the Stockton Electric Railroad from 1905 to 1939. Interurban and intraurban electric railroads in Stockton ended in September 1941, replaced by diesel-powered buses. Today, the San Joaquin Rapid Transit District is reemerging with low-emission and hybrid technologies to power public transport. (Courtesy of Bank of Stockton Archives.)

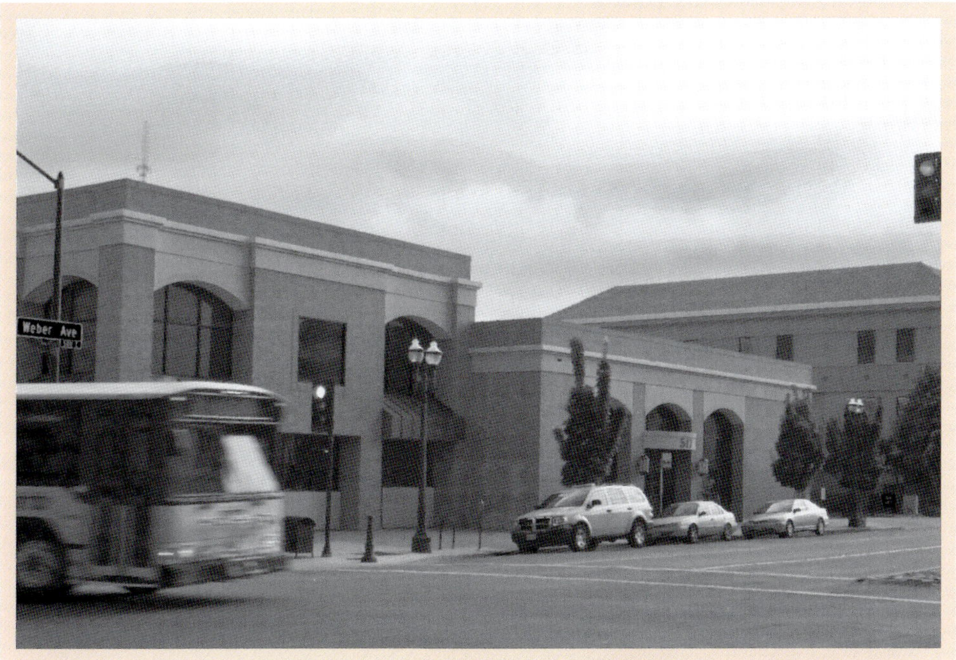

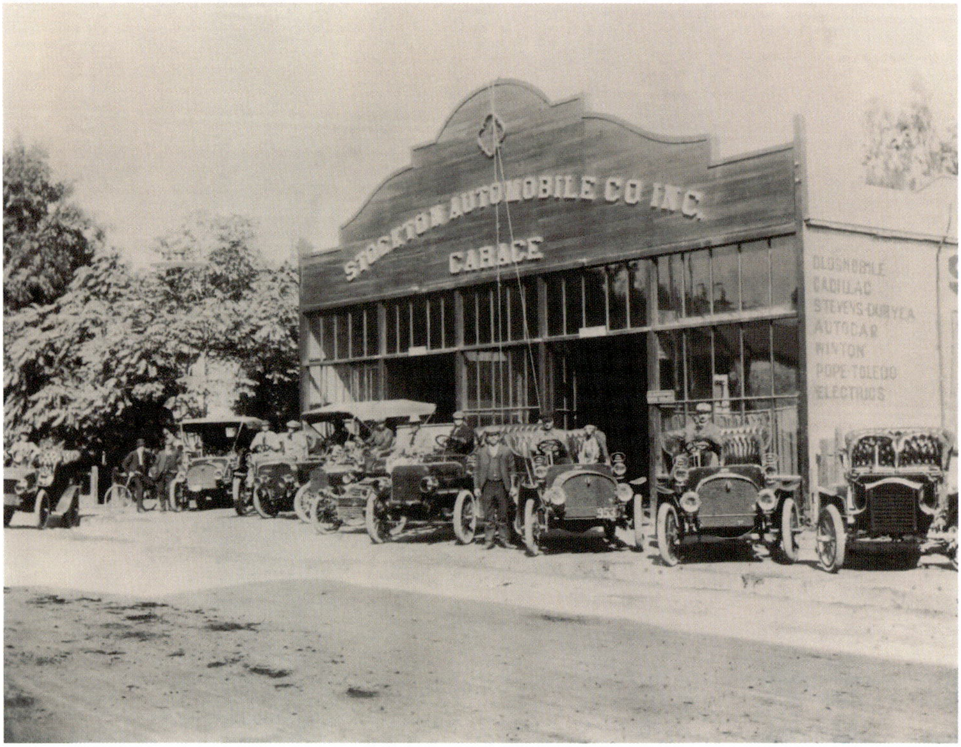

The appearance of the automobile profoundly changed the future of Stockton. Adapting roadways and turnpikes to highways and freeways consumed tremendous amounts of space, time, and capital. Independence from the fixed routes and schedules of public transportation ignited the economy and suburban development. In 1907, the Stockton Automobile Co. was the first of its kind in the city. It was located at 419 East Channel Street. Today, the site is a parking lot, across the street from the new San Joaquin County Transportation Terminal. (Courtesy of University of the Pacific Special Collections.)

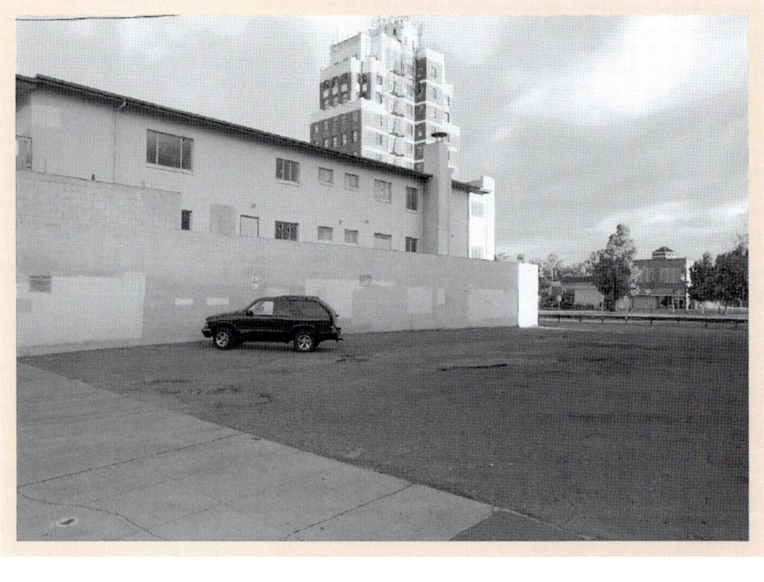

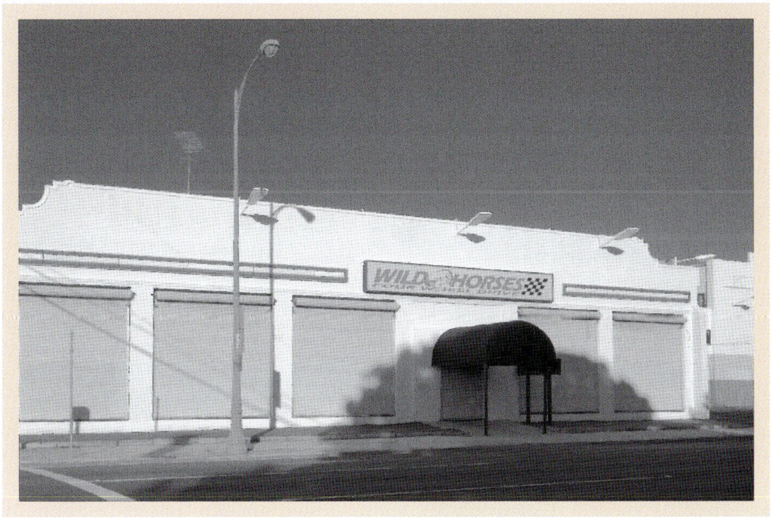

The Test Brothers were successful automobile dealers at the forefront of Stocktonians' embrace of the automobile. In the late 1940s, they franchised the Nash automobile and introduced its streamlined designs to the market. The air-conditioned car was ready-made for Stockton's hot summers. Today, the building reflects the diverse interests and specializations in the automobile business. Wild Horses Four Wheel Drive began in Stockton in 1989 and has developed a national market for its innovative products for the off-road vehicle enthusiast. (Courtesy of Haggin Museum Archives.)

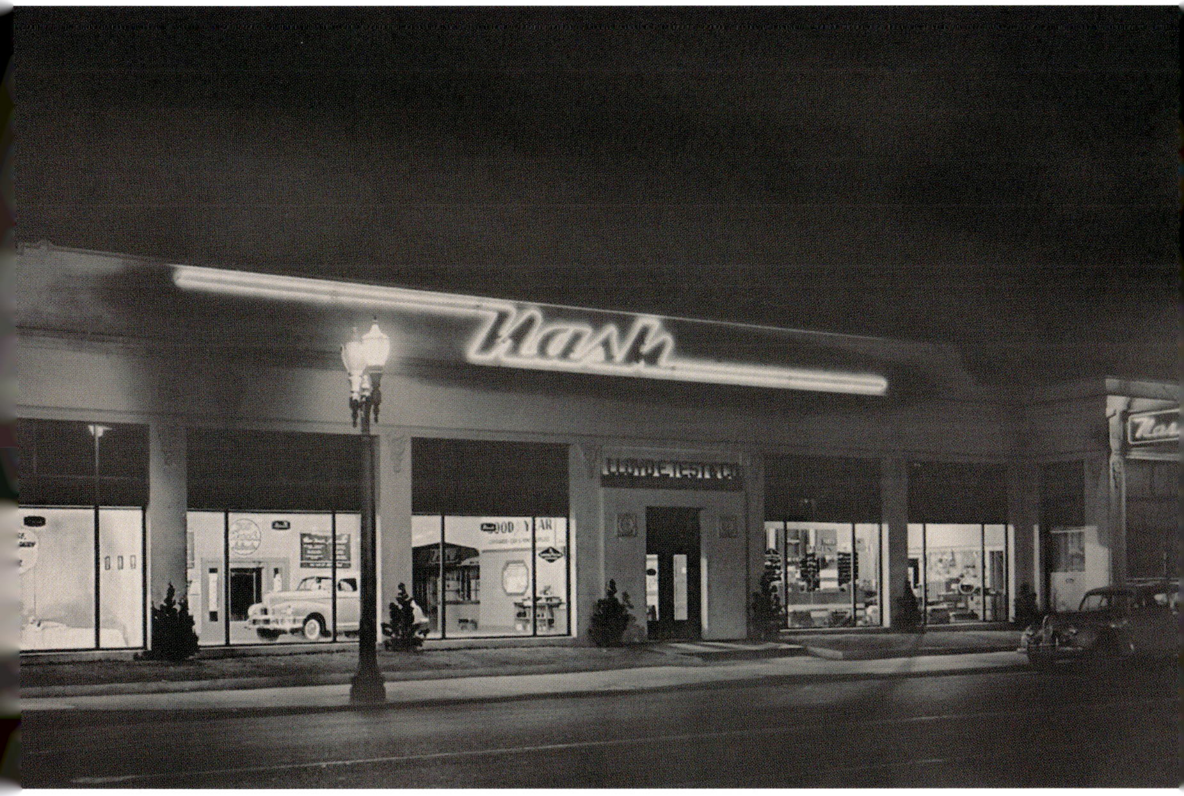

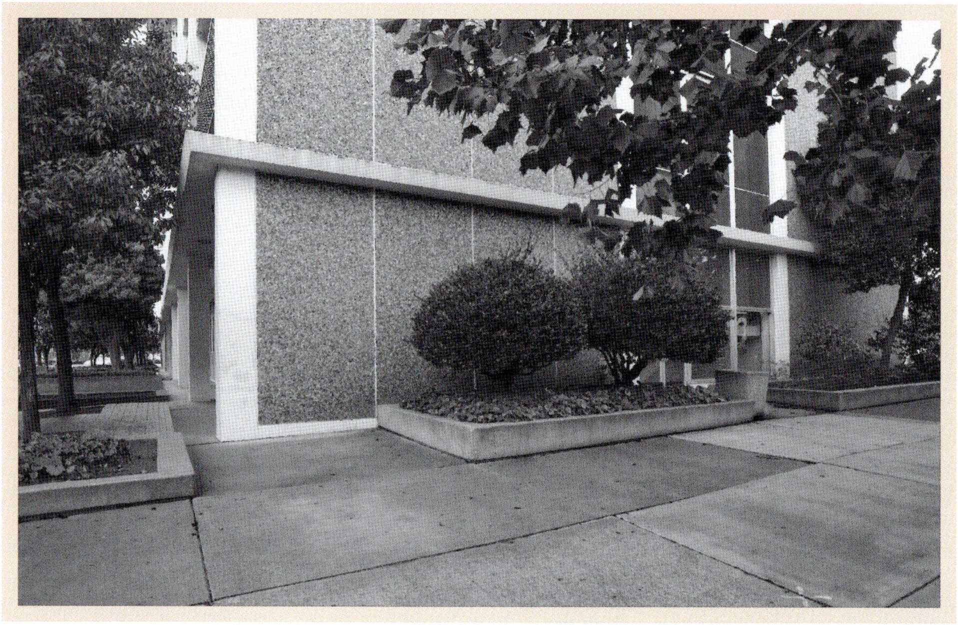

Privately operated jitneys were a common sight in Stockton through the 1920s. Located at 227 North El Dorado Street, the California Transit Company provided Stockton's first commercial bus service throughout the San Joaquin Valley. Today, the State of California Building occupies this site. Its International Style–influenced design was popular in Stockton from 1950 to 1970. Once considered a questionable contribution to local architecture, the building has integrated well into the redevelopment of the new City Center and DeCarli Plaza. (Courtesy of University of the Pacific Special Collections.)

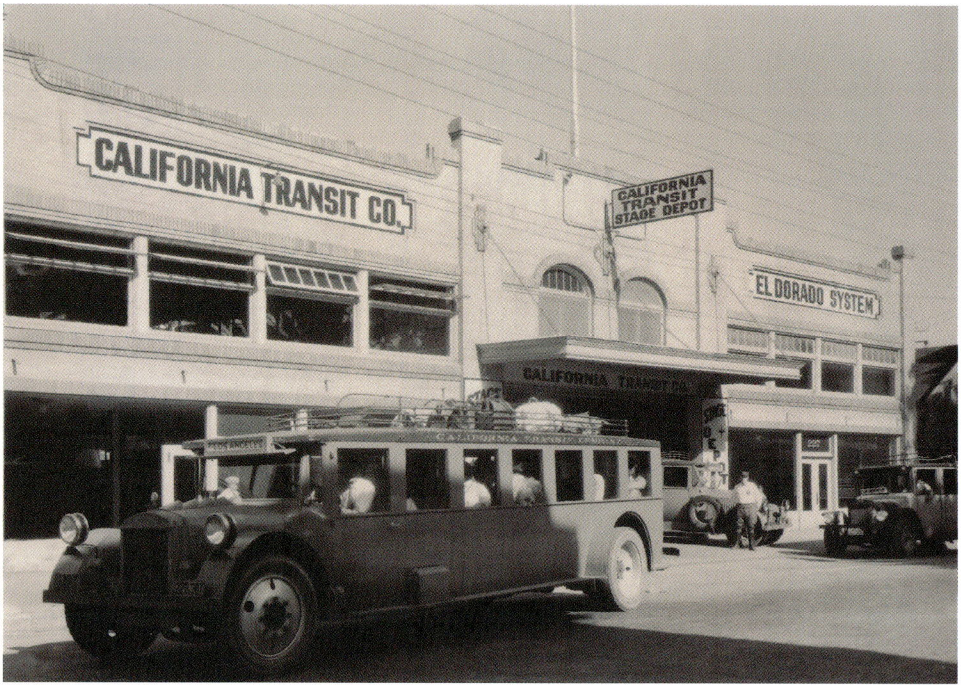

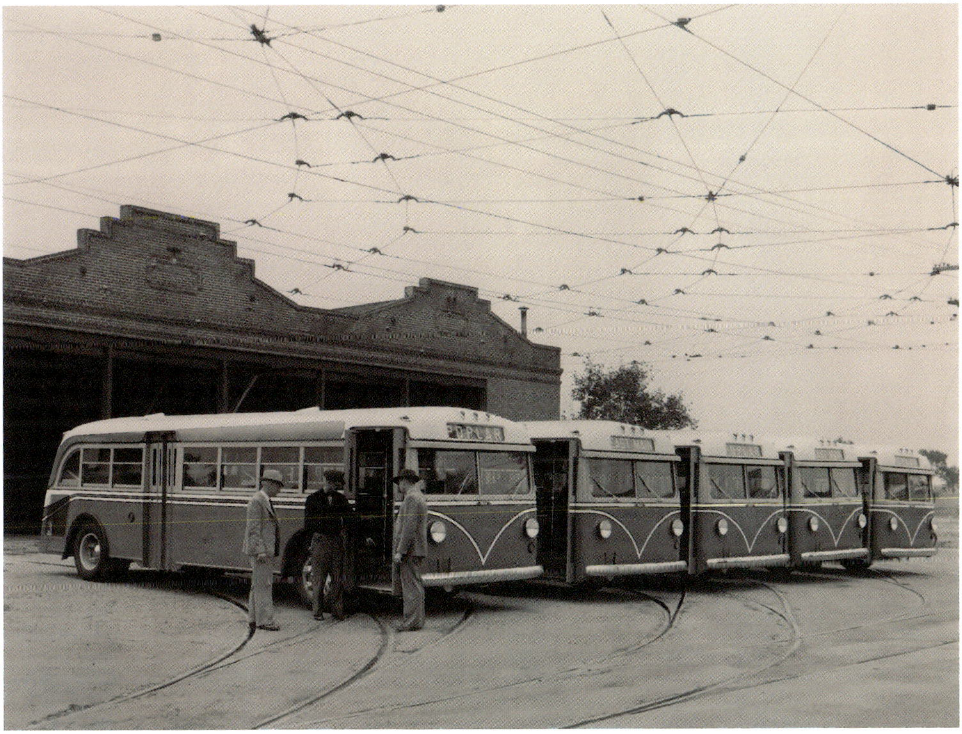

The Stockton Electric Railroad Company maintained a terminal on Northern California Street near Alpine Avenue. In 1939, the company transferred ownership to the Pacific Lines. Stockton Chamber of Commerce proposed a feasibility study for converting the electric railroad system to diesel engines, and five diesel buses began operating in 1941. Today, the old terminal is still a functional building, having once been one of five Gaines Market stores; it is now the Alpine Market. (Courtesy of University of the Pacific Special Collections.)

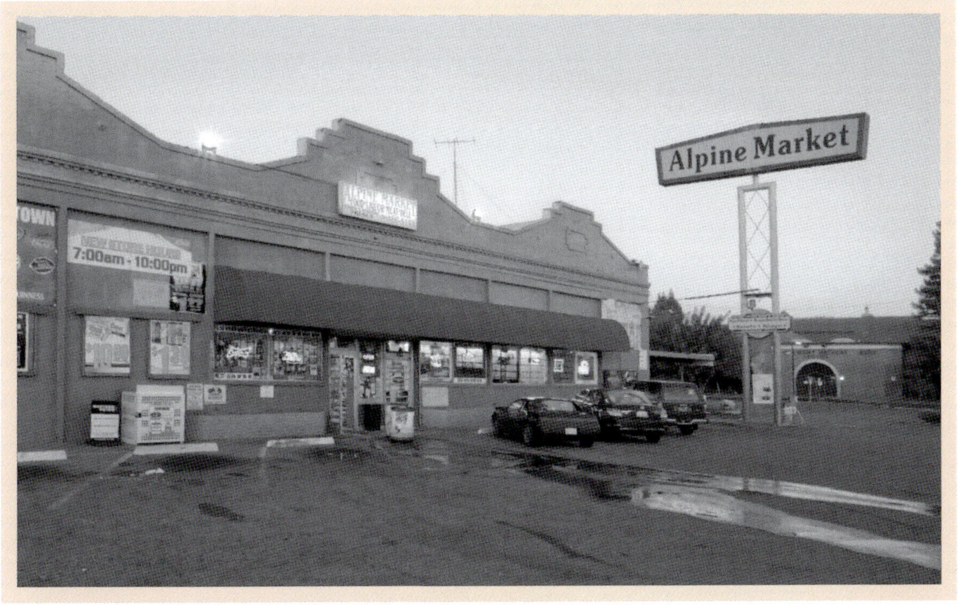

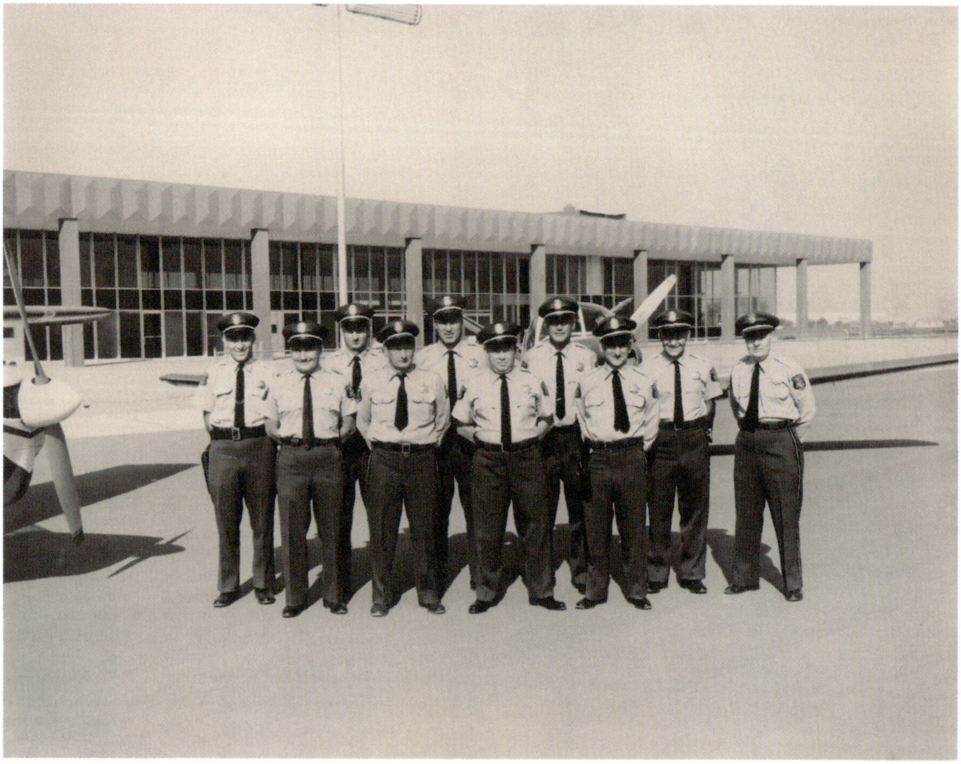

Aviation in San Joaquin County has a long history. Among its many stories is the San Joaquin County Sheriff Air Patrol Organized in the late 1950s to conduct air patrols, reconnaissance, and arrests. Ten members of the 12-man air patrol pose in front of the new International Style San Joaquin Air Terminal in 1965. Today, a new passenger security and staging building has been completed and is ready for service. (Courtesy of Larry Gaines.)

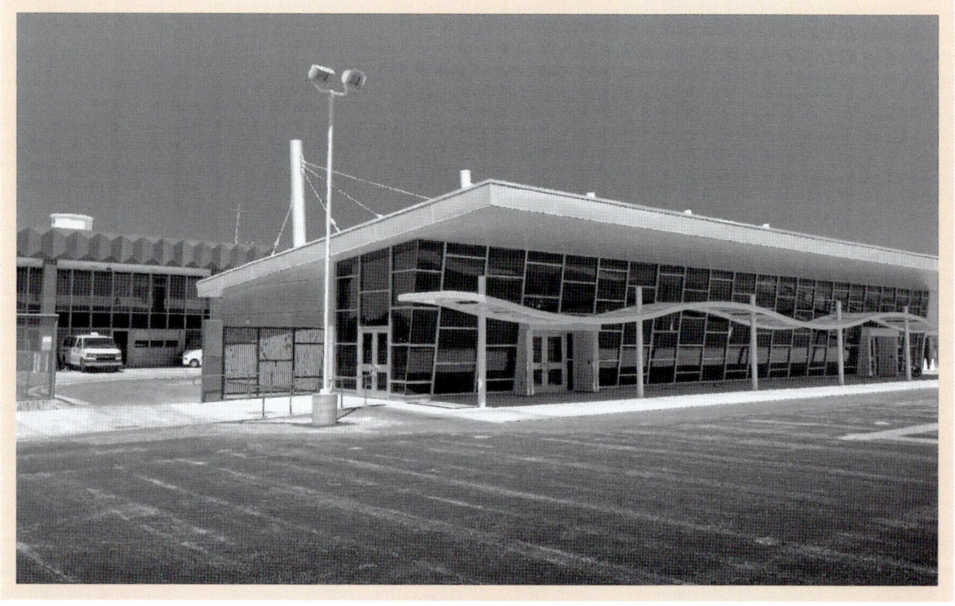

CHAPTER 4

Subdivision and Suburbanization

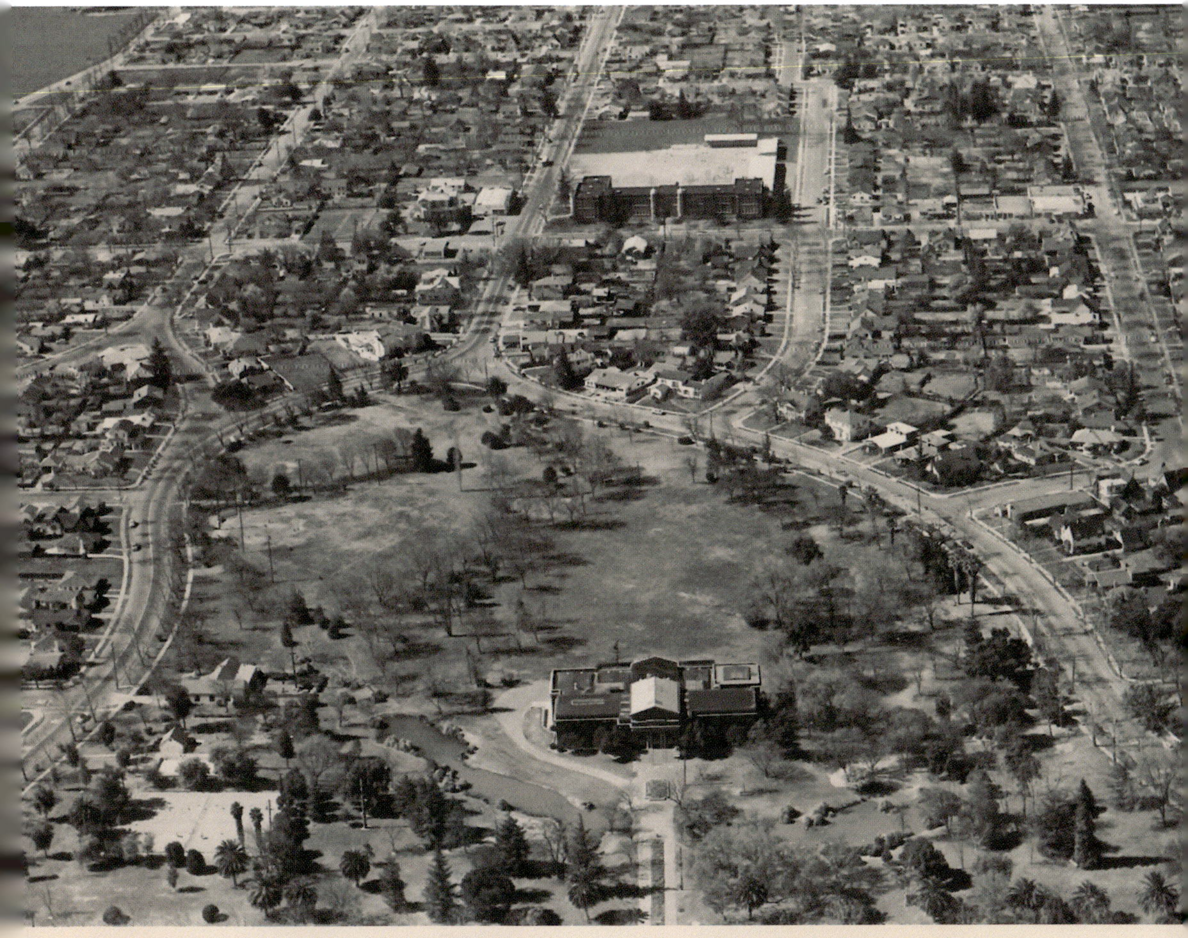

During its first three decades, Stockton achieved a balance of residential, commercial, and industrial life surrounded by an agricultural belt. In 1870, the five-square-mile city boundary was abandoned, and several land speculation booms occurred through 1920 as Stockton ignited with subdivision and suburban growth. Victory Park, west of Pershing Avenue, was the first development of land designated as a buffer from outlying agricultural lands. (Courtesy of Haggin Museum Archives.)

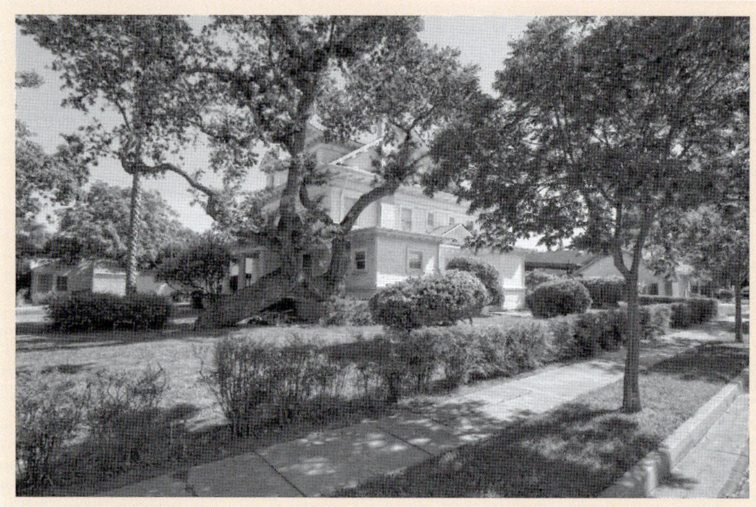

The first waves of suburbanization in Stockton occurred northwest and northeast of the central city between 1880 and 1920. Sperry Park, Bours Park, Victory Park, and Tuxedo Park were well-planned, upscale developments with functional designs and high-quality craftsmanship that remain desirable neighborhoods today. Dr. Daniel Ray's residence, at North El Dorado Street and Walnut Avenue, is an early Sperry Park suburban home. The home elicits smiles from Stocktonians. In 1910, the native oak was already moving east. Today, it literally rests on the porch. (Courtesy of University of the Pacific Special Collections.)

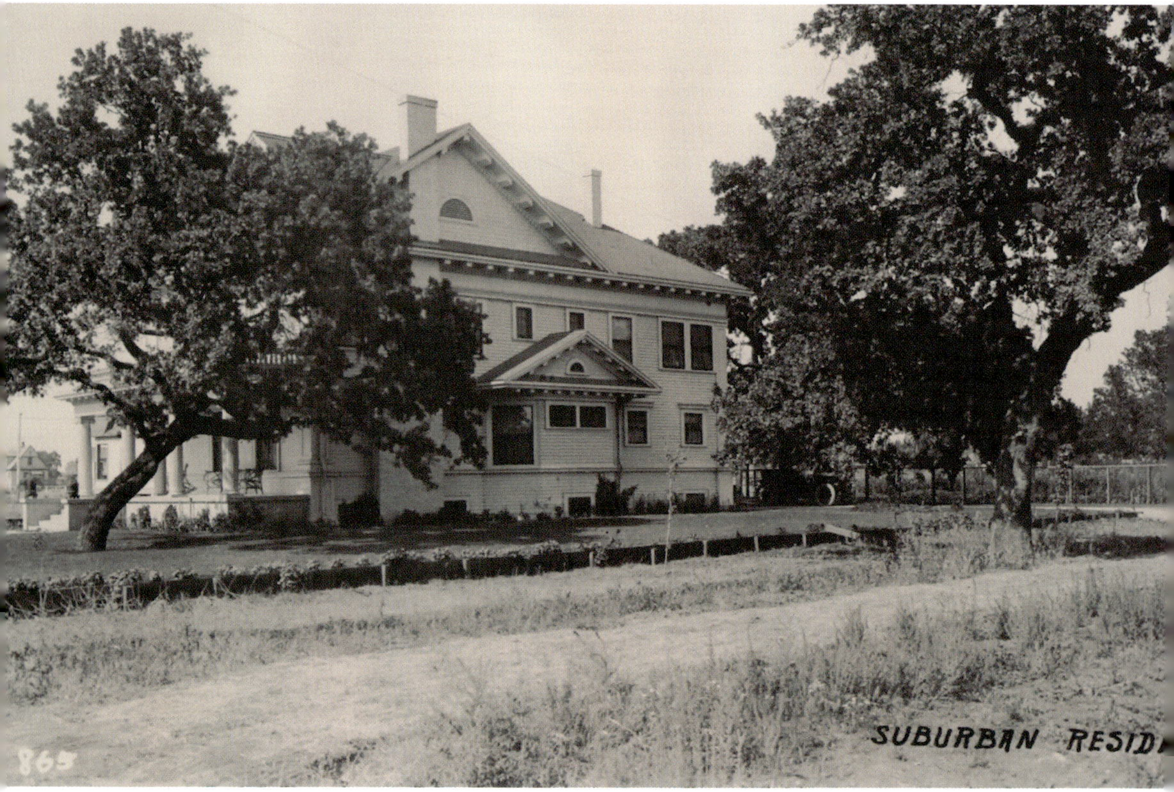

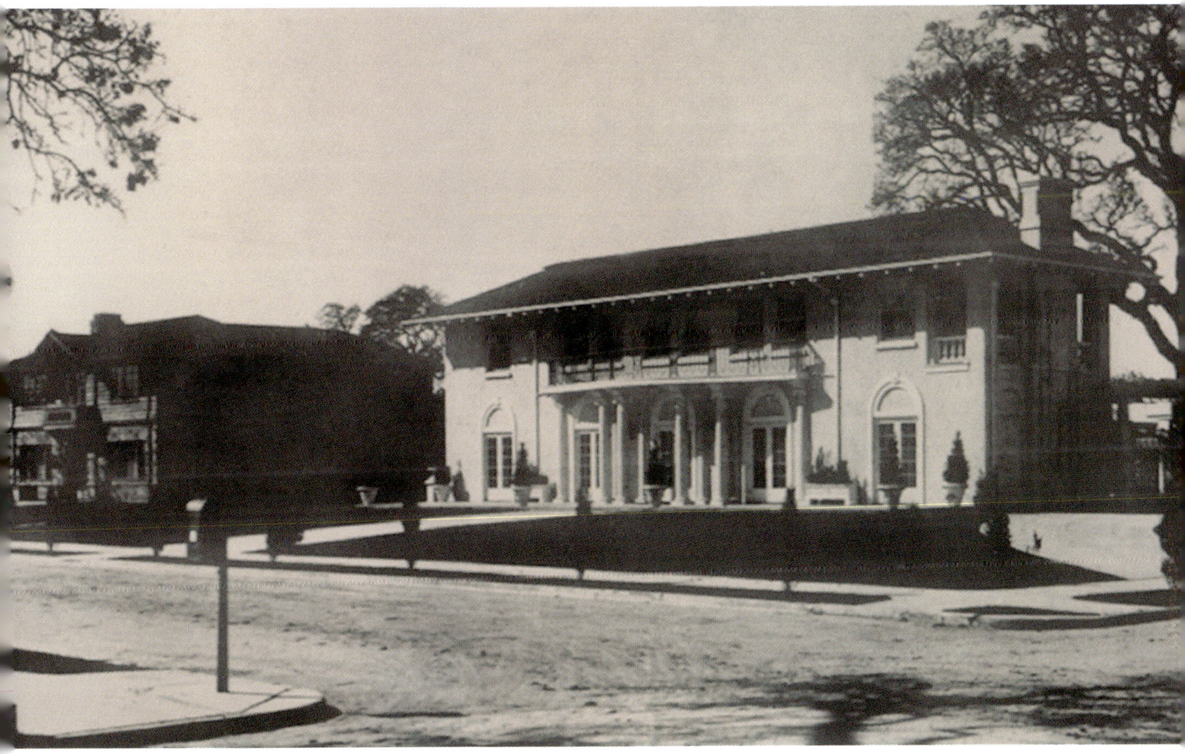

Bours Park is located north of the central city in "The Oaks." The homes in Bours Park represent a mixture of Craftsman and revivalist architecture. Typical of the Spanish Colonial Revival style popular at the time, the Samuel Frankenheimer residence on Walnut Street was constructed in 1916. Today, the house is more elegant than ever. Mature trees shade both street and home, softening and warming its appearance and original design. (Courtesy of Bank of Stockton Archives.)

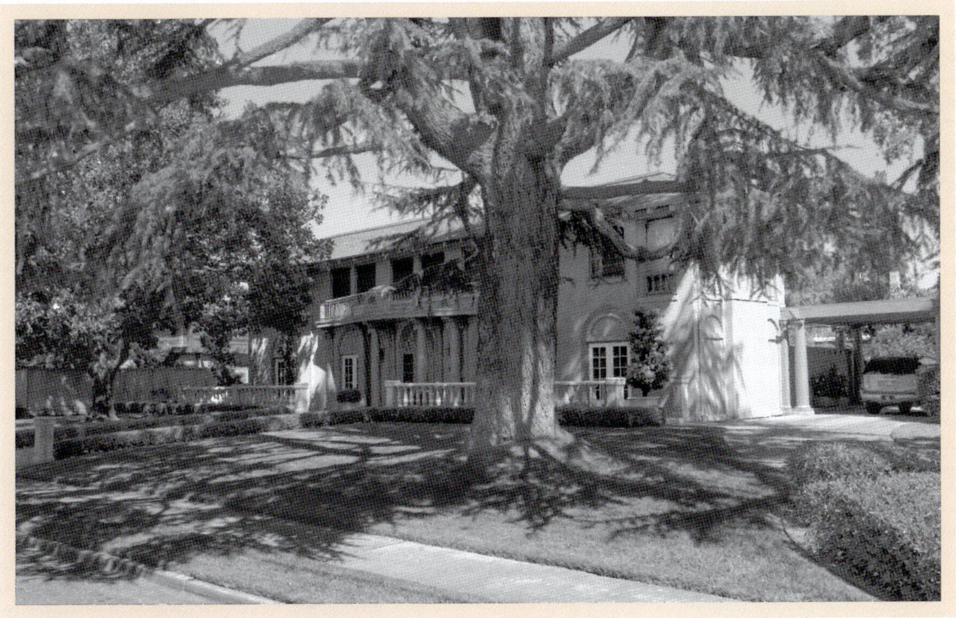

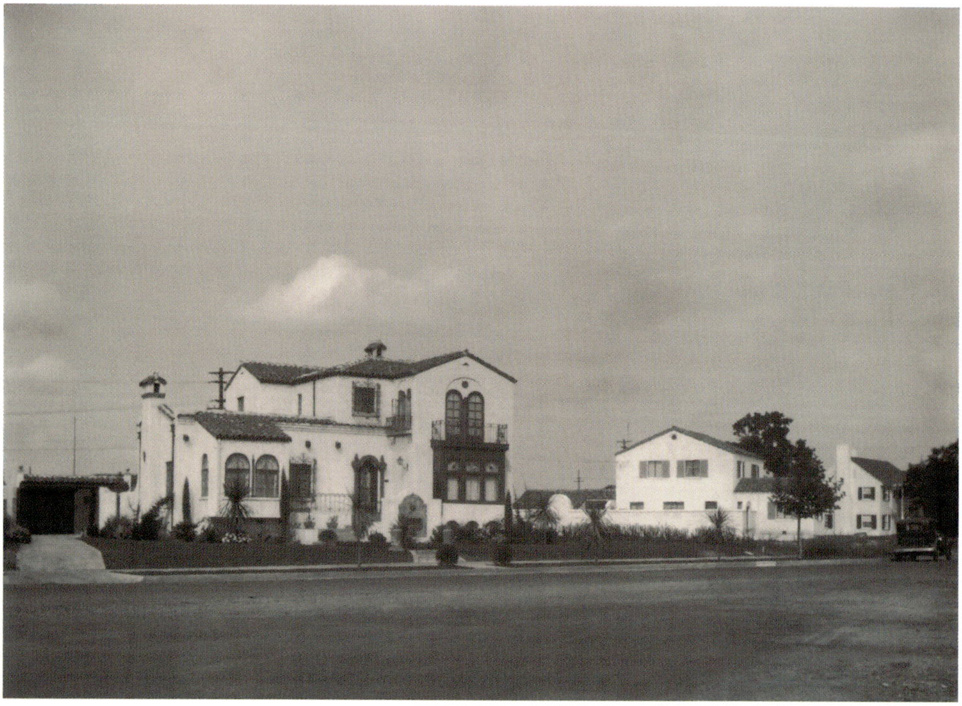

Victory Park was developed as part of the Weber Tract, on the west end of the city, beginning as early as 1890. The development was carefully planned, even as it crossed the line into an agricultural reserve established by Charles Weber to moderate suburban growth. Homes along Argonne Street were built for Stockton's affluent and characterize the prevailing architectural styles of the day. Many Victory Park homes are nearing or have already celebrated 100 years in existence. (Courtesy of University of the Pacific Special Collections)

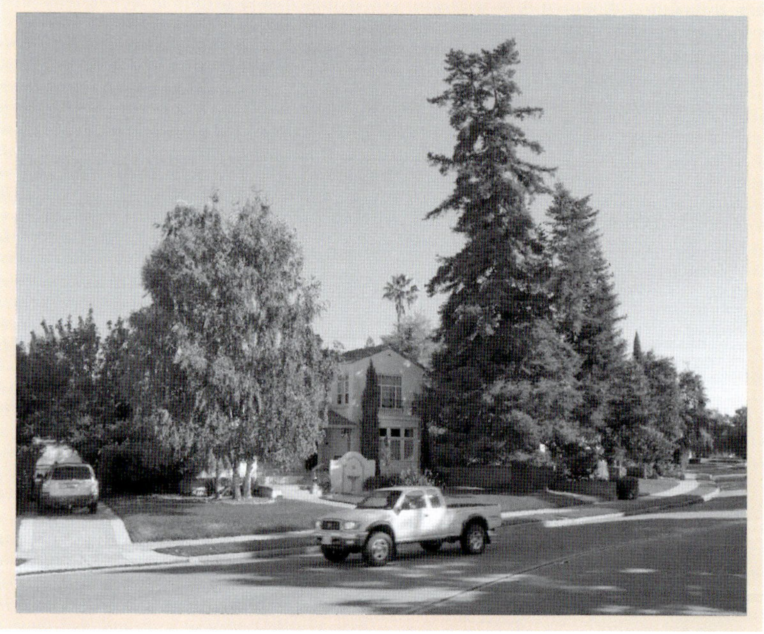

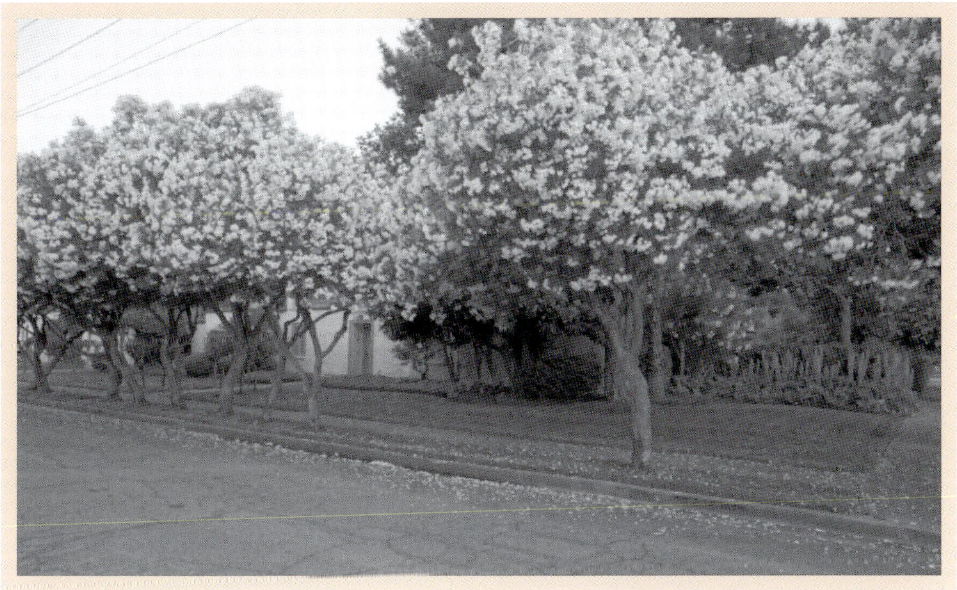

Before 1900, the upscale neighborhoods of Stockton began migrating away from the city center to avoid industrial waterfront pollution. In 1935, Tillie Lewis (later Weisberg), Stockton's "tomato queen" who became internationally famous for her innovations in canning food, purchased a home originally built for the Cleghorn family. The house was famous for its kitchens and entertainment. Today, the home remains in extraordinary condition, even as it is obscured by oleander. (Courtesy of University of the Pacific Special Collections.)

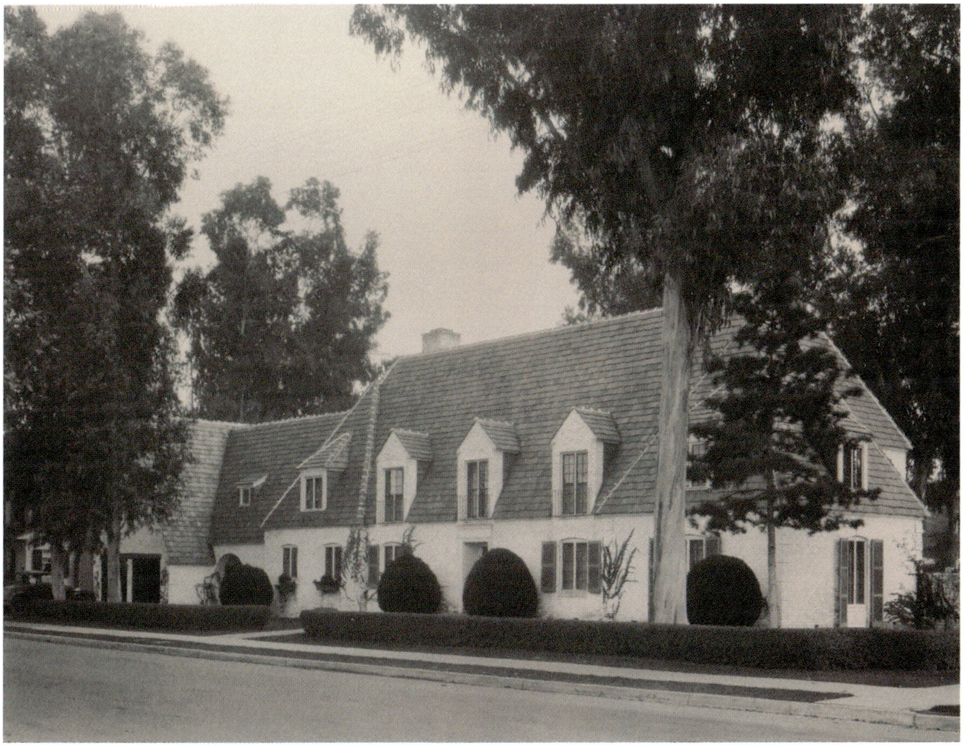

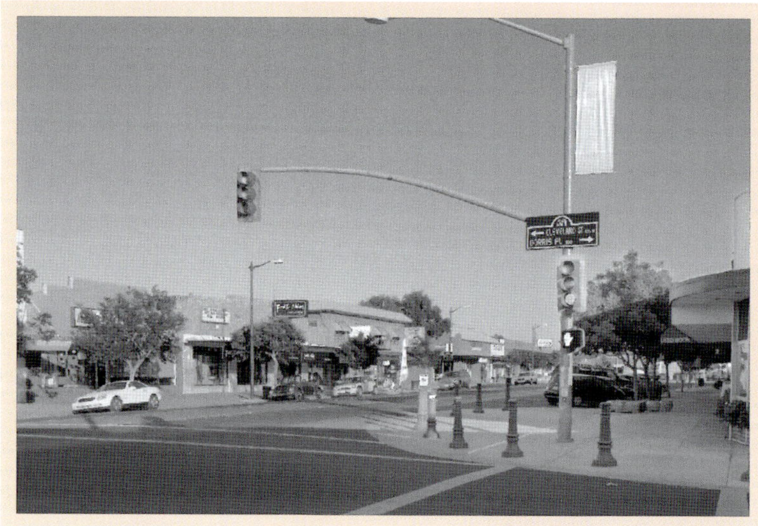

The development of Tuxedo Park commenced in 1913, during Stockton's second wave of suburbanization. It began as a residential/commercial village along Pacific Avenue—the renamed Old Sacramento Road, which once terminated at Harding Way. The earliest development along the eastern side of Pacific Avenue did not display an especially distinctive or progressive architectural style. It has aged well. Today, this is the view from Cocoro, one of Stockton's popular sushi bars. (Courtesy of University of the Pacific Special Collections.)

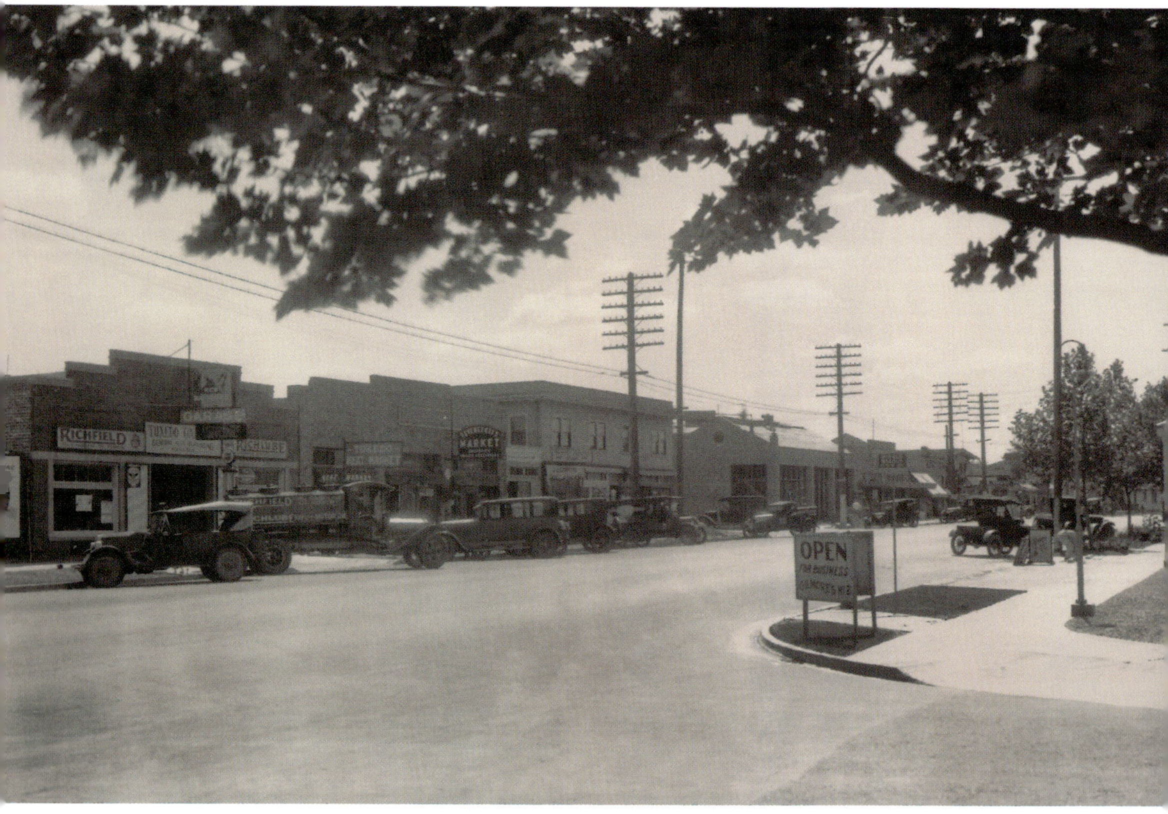

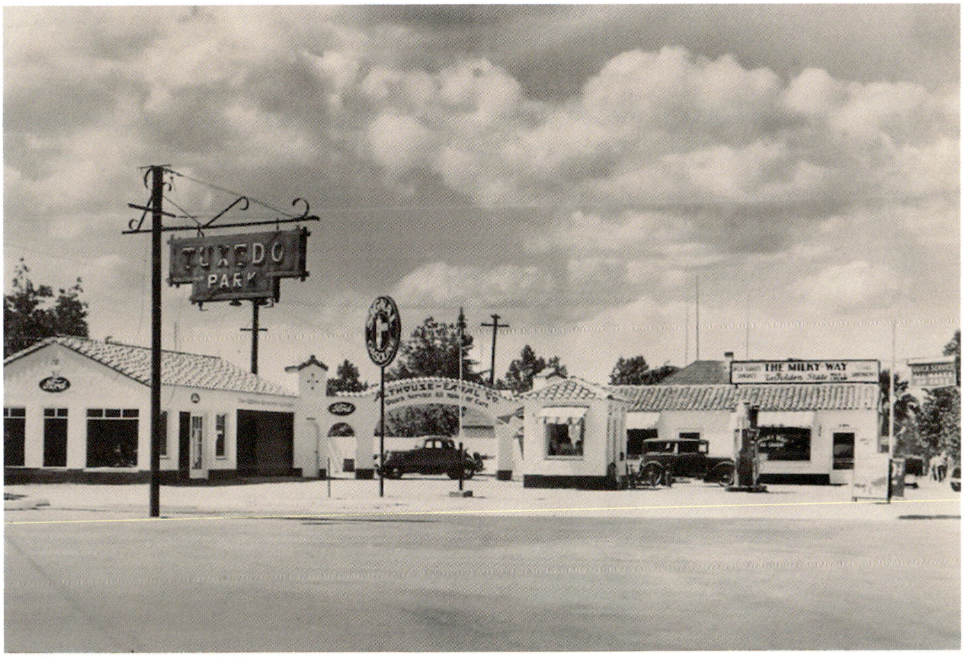

From its inception, Tuxedo Park was a unique community. By the mid-1920s, it became Stockton's first example of an integrated suburban residential-living community, balancing housing, transportation, and recreation. It also featured Stockton's first strip mall. After 1921, Joseph Plecarpo, an inspired Stockton contractor, followed the lead of A.W. Ross's Wilshire Boulevard in Los Angeles and developed the Miracle Mile. Ross's principles shaped commercial modern styles, insisting businesses be easily viewable through the windshield of an automobile going 30 miles per hour. (Courtesy of Bank of Stockton Archives.)

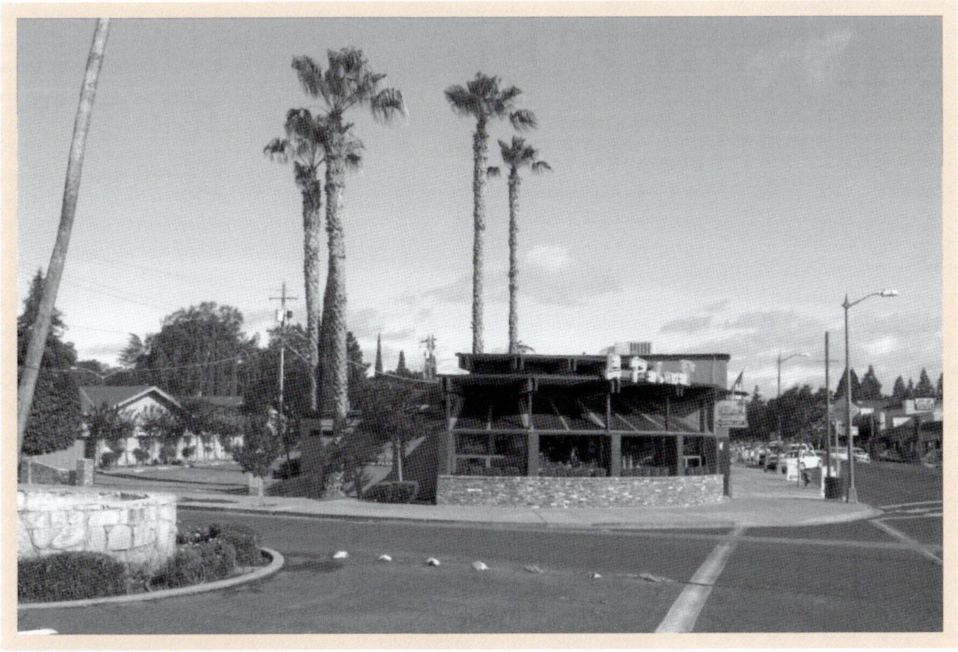

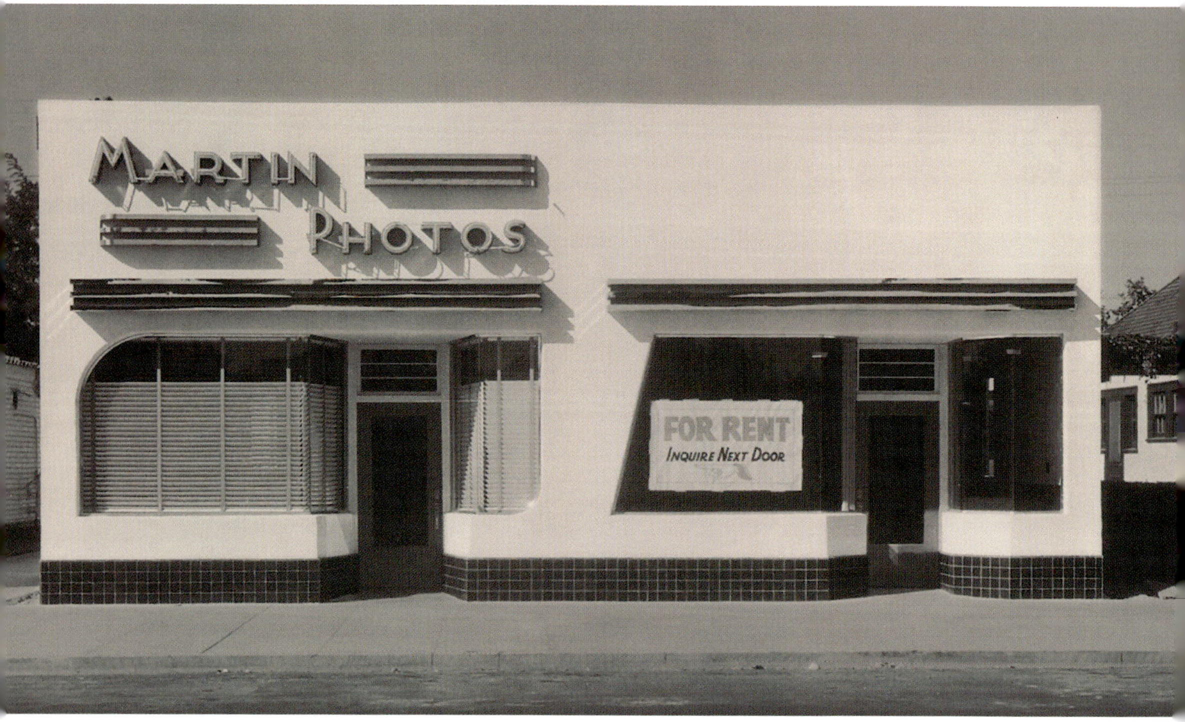

The Stockton photographer Van Covert Martin built his third photography studio on Pacific Avenue. The style of this structure epitomized the principles of Moderne architecture and the rise of the Miracle Mile and strip malls in the United States during the 1920s and 1930s. Broad simple building facades and bold, well-defined typographic signage characterized the Moderne style. Today, all evidence of the original building has disappeared through several generations of tenants and interpretations of commercial trends. (Courtesy of University of the Pacific Special Collections.)

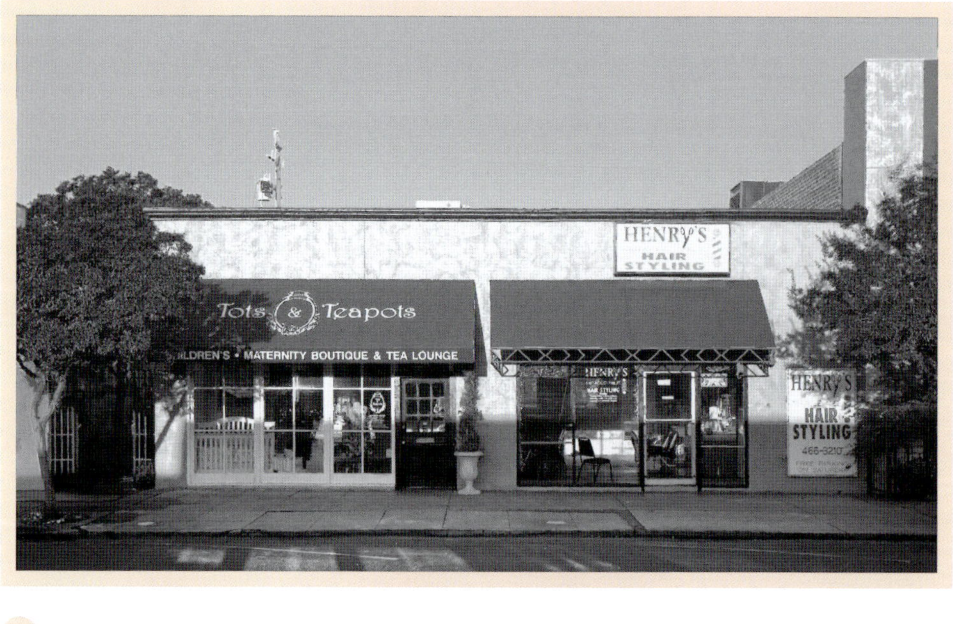

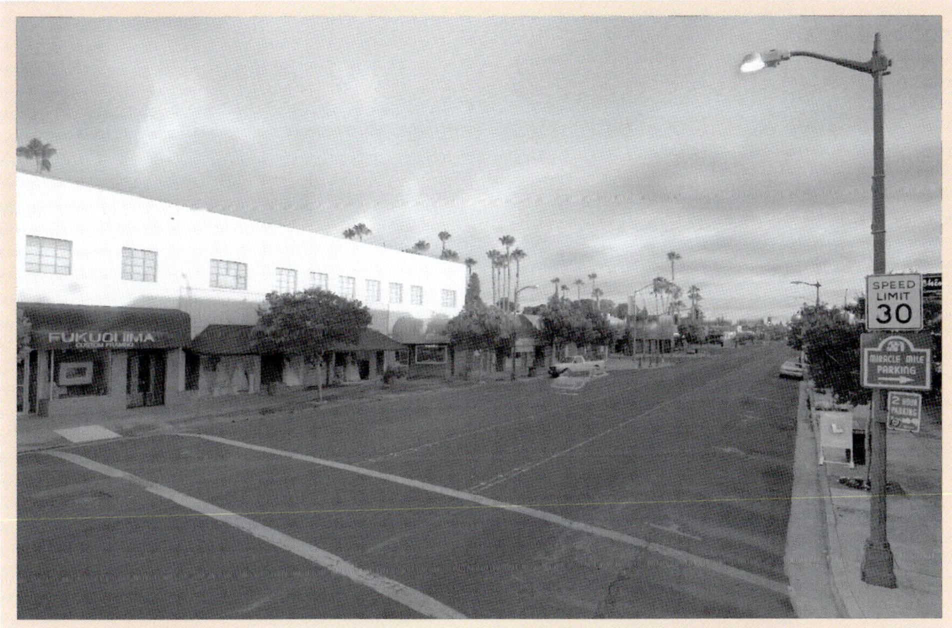

By 1955, the Miracle Mile commercial zone along Pacific Avenue was successfully integrated with the residential life in Tuxedo Park to the west. The Miracle Mile was Stockton's northern commercial zone, and it has remained economically viable since it was established in 1913. Among the Miracle Mile's most enduring qualities is its commitment to locally owned small business. Today, this tradition has defined the neighborhood's popularity as an evening dining and entertainment destination in Stockton. (Courtesy of Bank of Stockton Archives.)

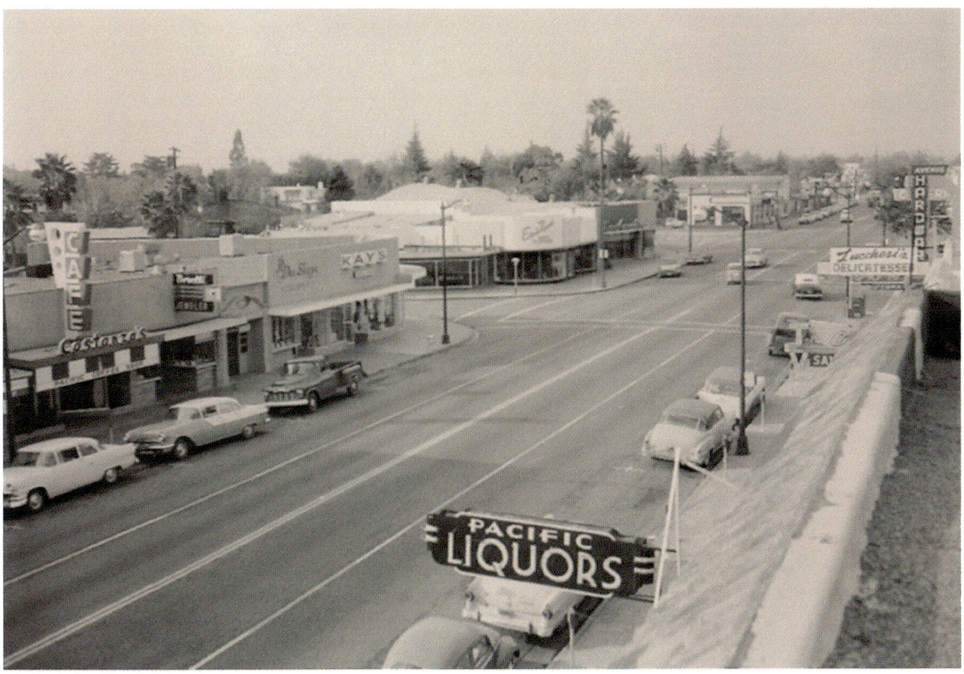

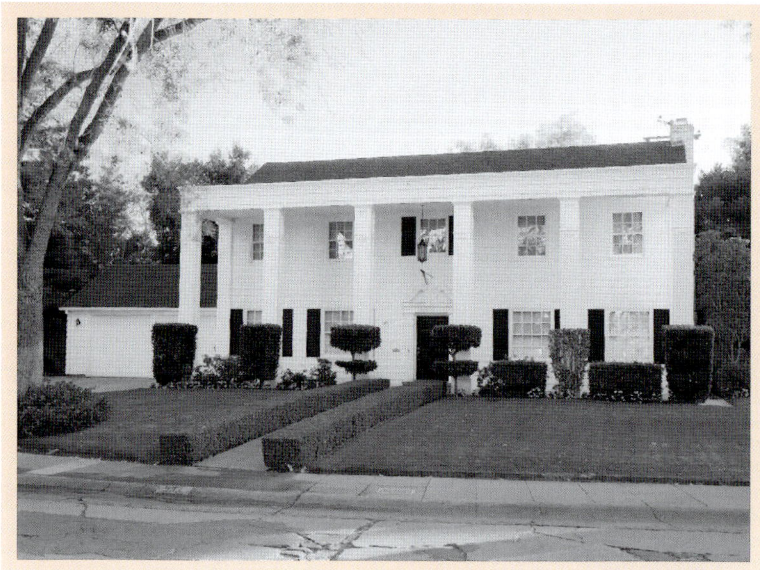

The Oxford Manor Park development commenced in the late 1920s. Part of the subdivision of the Smith Tract platted between 1890 and 1920, it completed the original platting for the contiguous Tuxedo Park and Avondale neighborhoods. The architectural diversity and lot size within Oxford Manor speak to the success of the development, then and now. Many homes in the neighborhood reflect the waning revival styles prevalent in the 1920s. Federal and Colonial Revival styles were popular during the development of Oxford Manor. (Courtesy of Bank of Stockton Archives.)

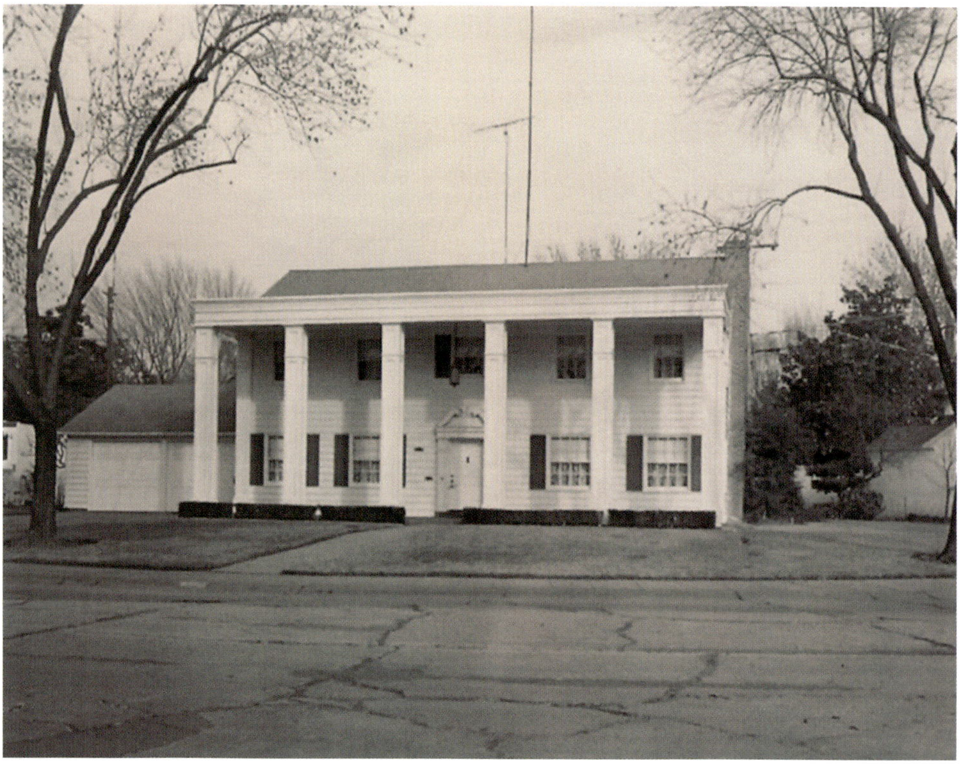

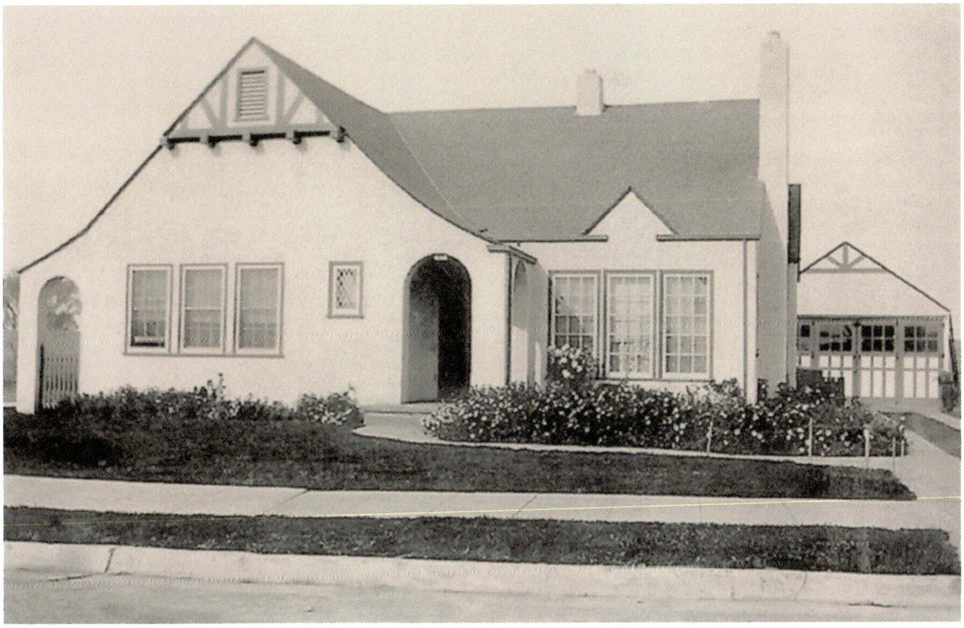

The Victory Park subdivision and adjoining neighborhoods commenced in the early decades of the 20th century. This region was originally set aside as a land reserve separating residential communities and reclaimed agricultural lands banding Stockton on the west. Victory Park experienced controversy in its early years. Aggressive speculators subdividing and redividing lots strained right-of-way and civil services. Today, shady streets, architectural variety, and the aura of cultural programs presented by the nearby Haggin Museum characterize the neighborhood. (Courtesy of Bank of Stockton Archives.)

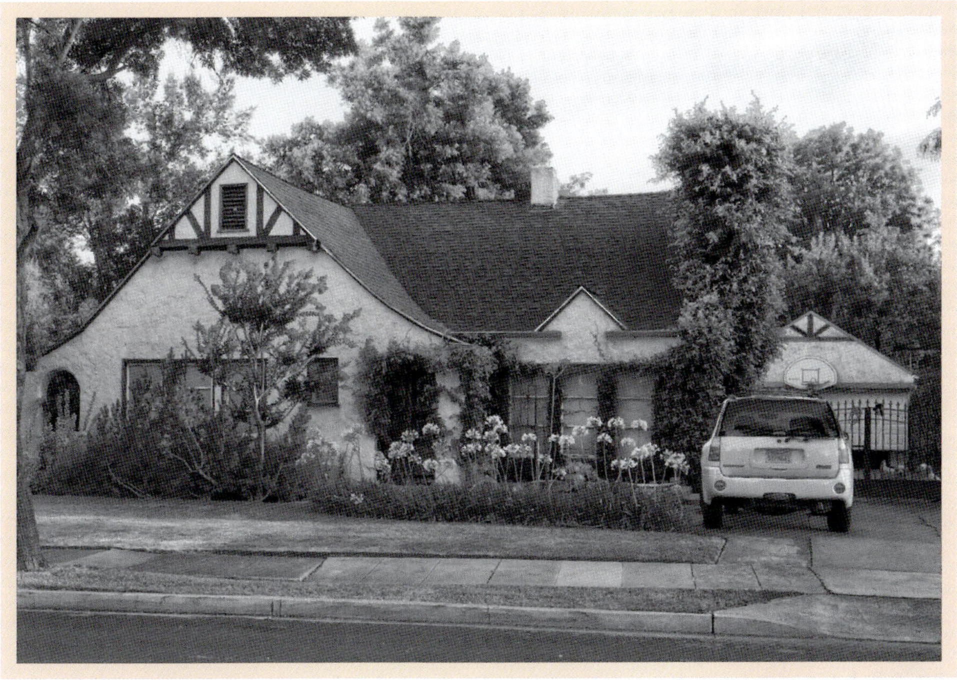

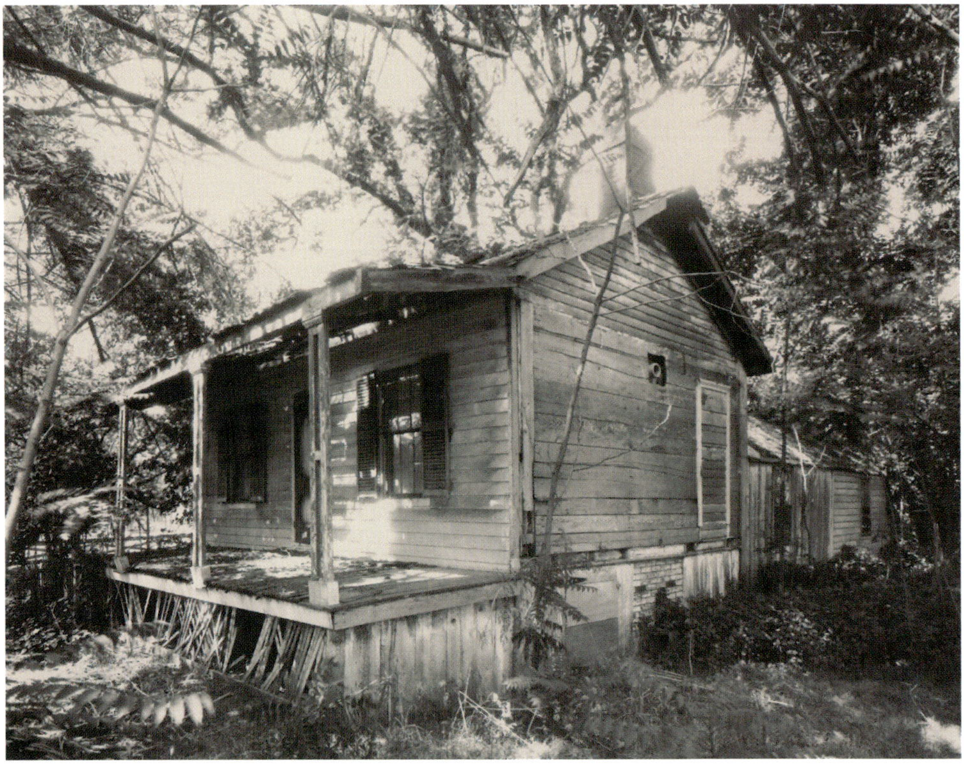

The Pacific Avenue corridor defines the suburbanization of Historic Stockton from 1913 to the present. Pacific Avenue has been at one time or another also known as Lower Sacramento Road, Telegraph Road, and the Lincoln Highway. William McCarson first graded the road from the north to the vicinity of Harding Way in 1856. The original home was located near present-day Lincoln Village. Today, a branch office for the Bank of Stockton sits in the shade of the original McCarson property. (Courtesy of University of the Pacific Special Collections.)

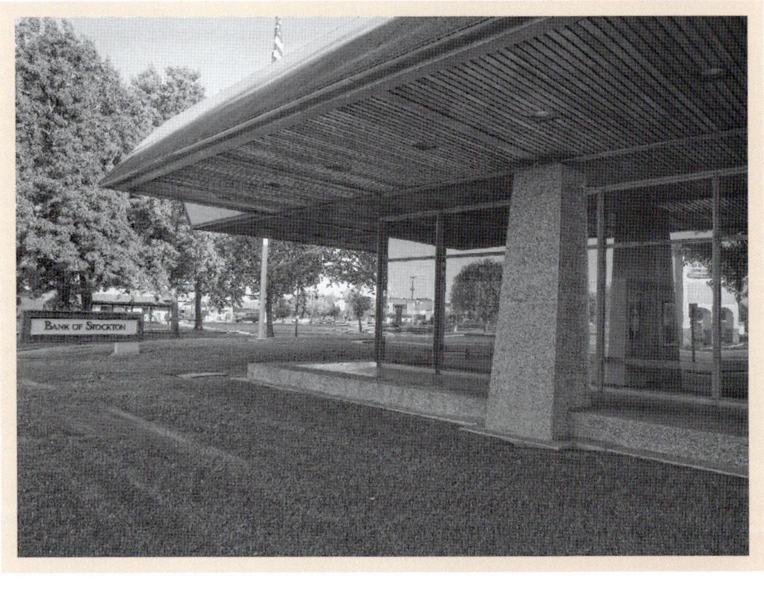

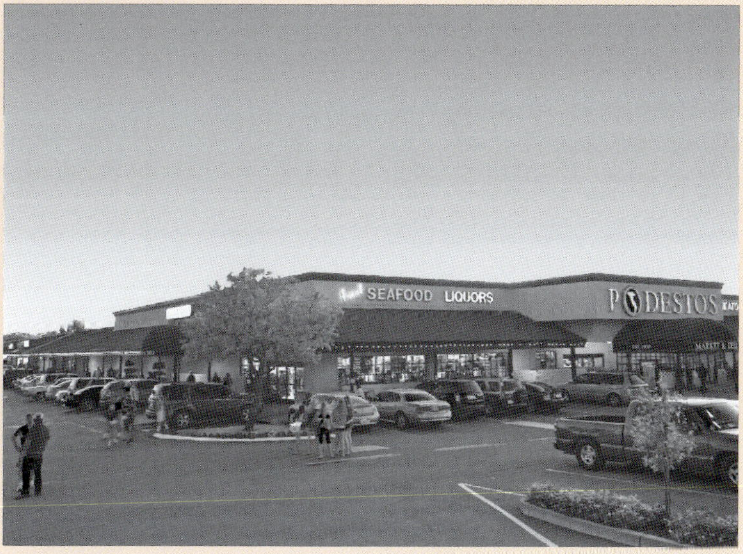

Lincoln Center opened in 1951 in conjunction with Lincoln Village, Stockton's first post–World War II suburban residential and commercial development. Lincoln Center initiated expansion along Pacific Avenue that continued into the 1960s. Development patterns initiated by Lincoln Center and the construction of arterial branches to Pacific Avenue from Interstate 5 in the late 1970s had concomitant effects on Stockton's Historic Downtown. Northern development offered a spacious and modernized alternative and drew attention away from Stockton's blighted core that developed after the war. (Courtesy of Lincoln Center Archives.)

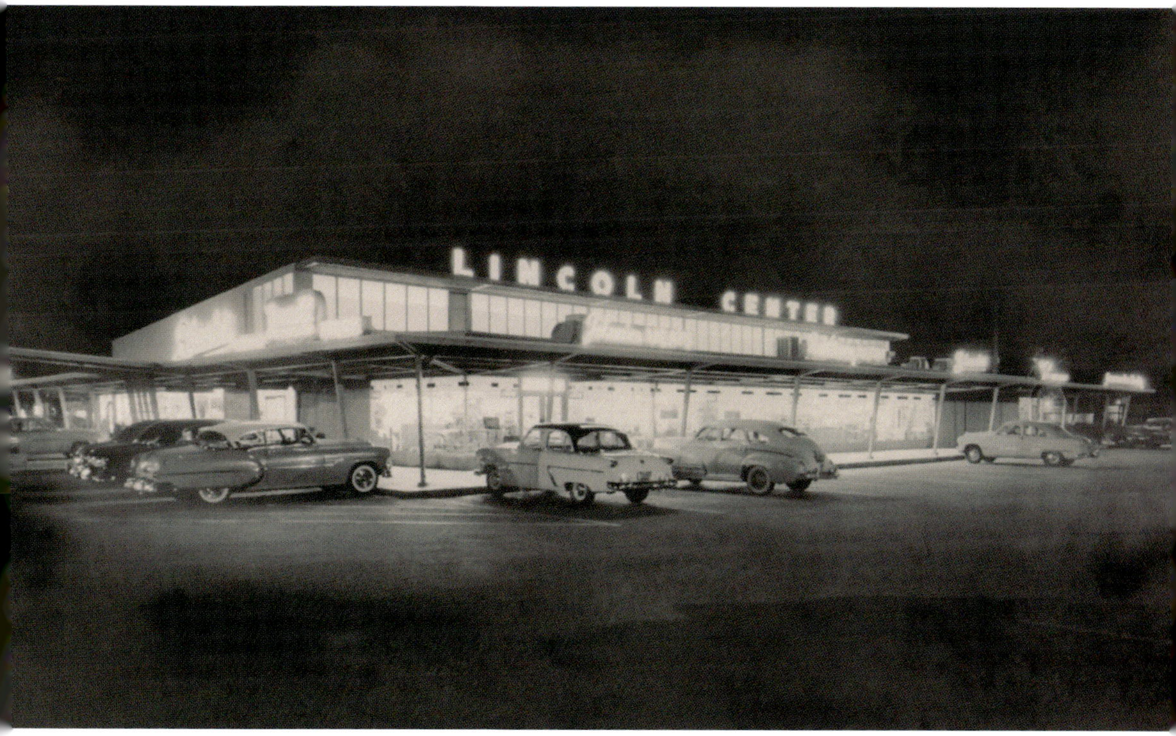

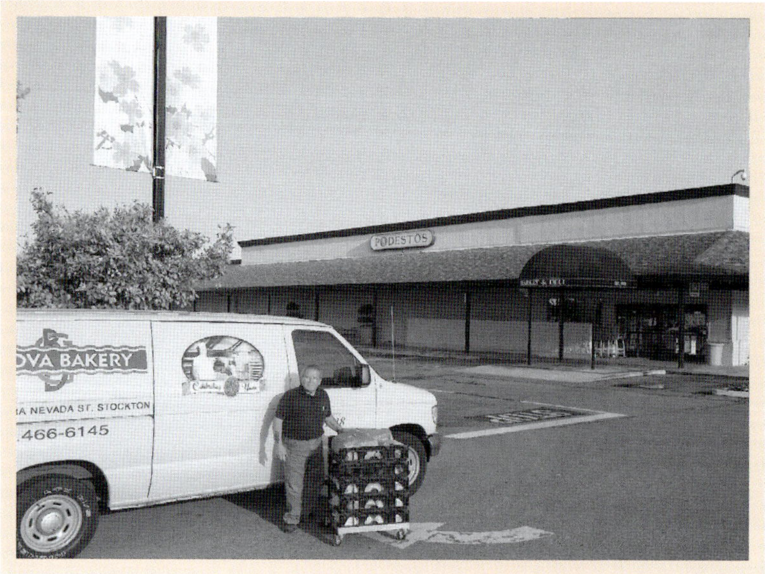

There have been four full-service grocery stores in Lincoln Center in its 60-year history. Black's Market was the first grocer to locate in Lincoln Center, followed by Don Quick's, and then Gaines Market. All three of these businesses were devastated by fire. Today, Podesto's Market is a widely popular shopping destination. With over 90 vendors, Lincoln Center epitomizes a suburban Stockton community. In the "now" photograph, Jay Pilkington delivers fresh bread from the Genova Bakery to Payter's Grill—two traditional Stockton companies still working together. (Courtesy of Lincoln Center Archives.)

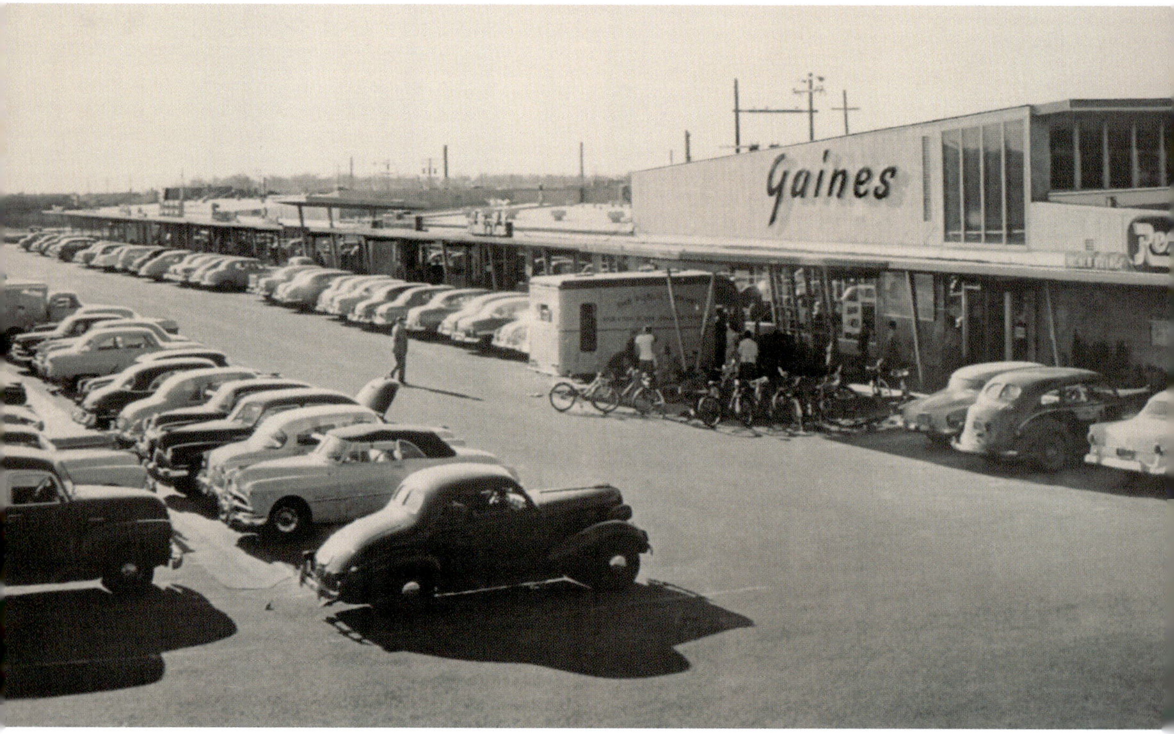

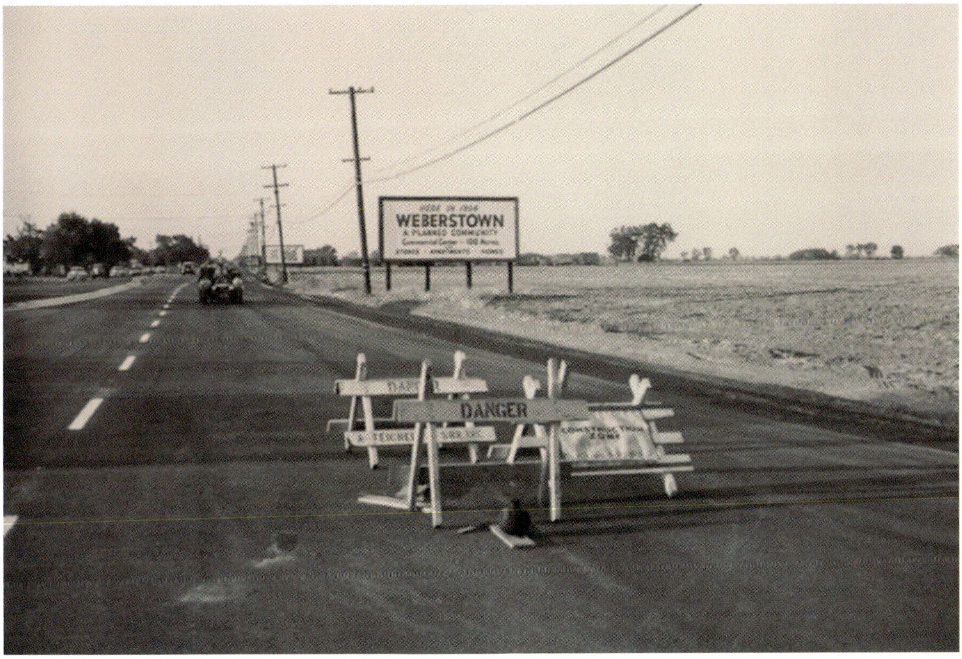

The Weberstown residential community, along Pacific Avenue north of the Calaveras River, was developed in the late 1950s. Consistent with suburbanization trends, Stockton's first enclosed, climate-controlled shopping mall followed in 1962. Local lore says that Charles Weber II proposed the shopping center for downtown Stockton but was refused. The automobile-friendly Weberstown Mall, featuring national department stores, became an attractive alternative to navigating Stockton's foggy winters, hot summers, and the failing prospects downtown—by then mired in urban blight. (Courtesy of Bank of Stockton Archives.)

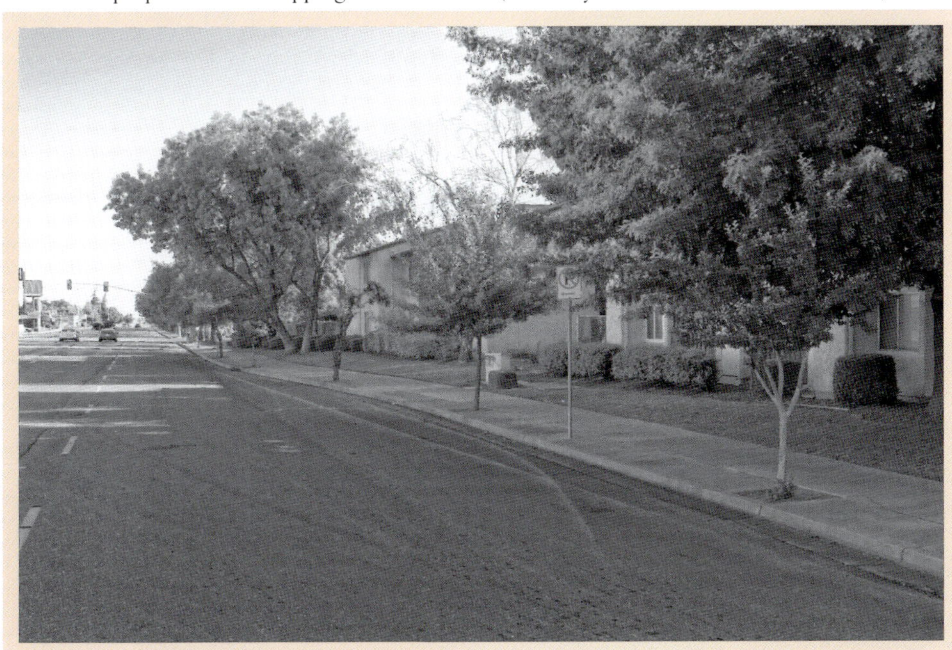

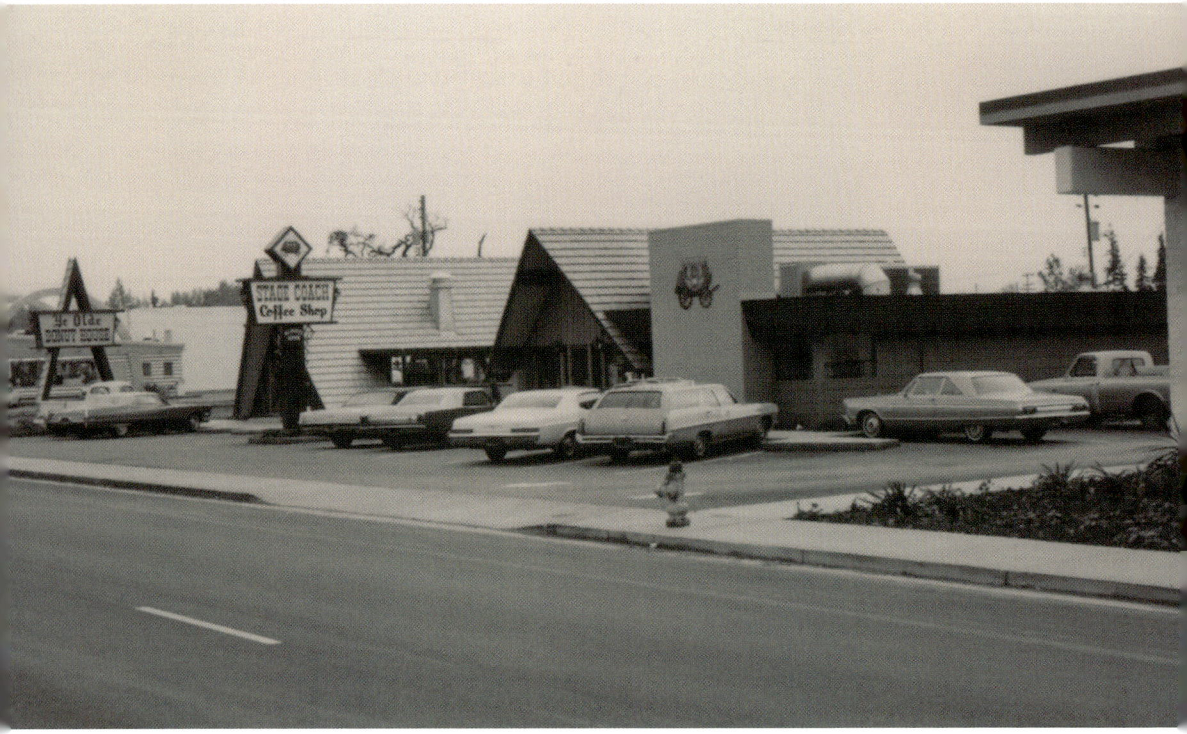

While arcade-style malls grew in popularity, the principles of strip development influenced Stockton's northern suburbanization during the 1950s and 1960s. Several are still present along the Pacific Avenue corridor, north of the Calaveras River. The A-frame building trend, excited in 1951 by San Francisco architect John Carden Campbell, led to the mass production of A-frame kits that were highly adaptive, cheap, and quickly assembled. These buildings were also simpatico with social trends of the period. (Courtesy of San Joaquin County Museum Archives.)

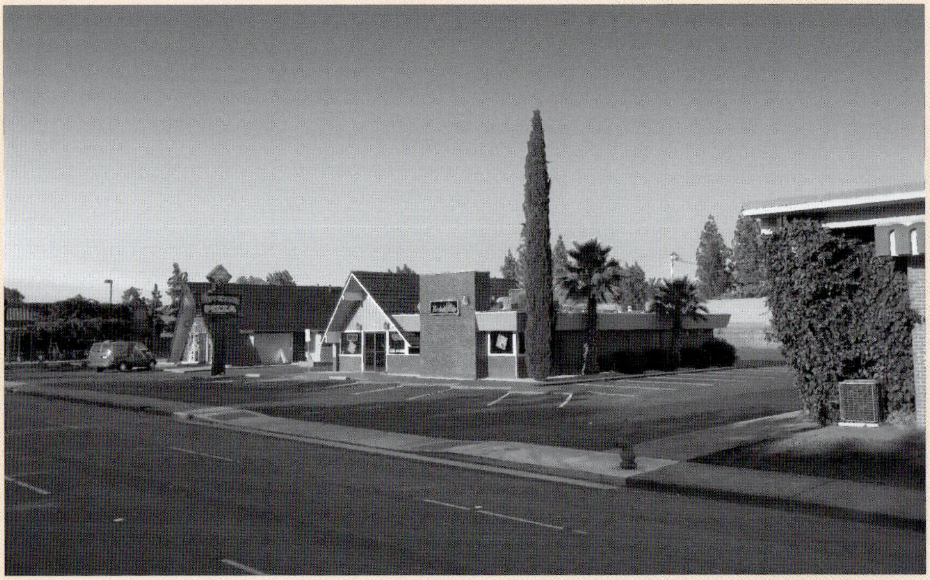

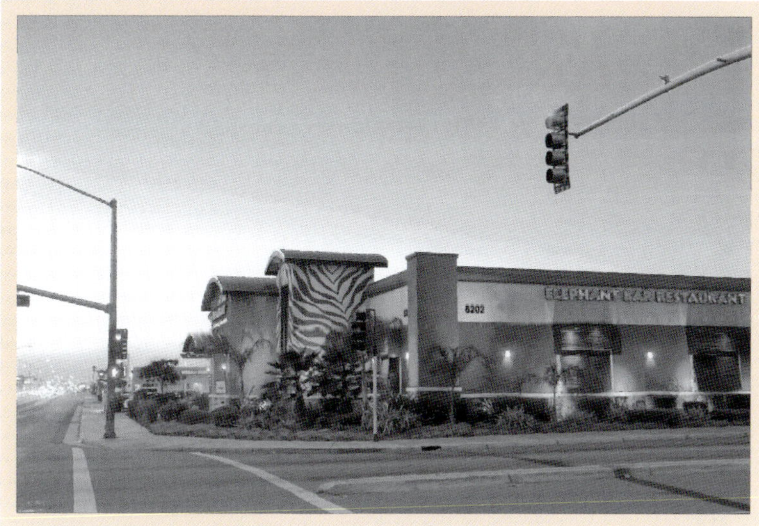

The Lyon's Restaurant chain once had over 70 locations throughout California but went bankrupt in 1998 and continued struggling well into the 2000s. The Stockton store, located near Macy's, survived through 2008 and made an architecturally distinct statement on Pacific Avenue. The Elephant Bar restaurant, following similar market trends to those that once produced the popularity of Lyon's, now occupies the site. (Courtesy of Haggin Museum Archives.)

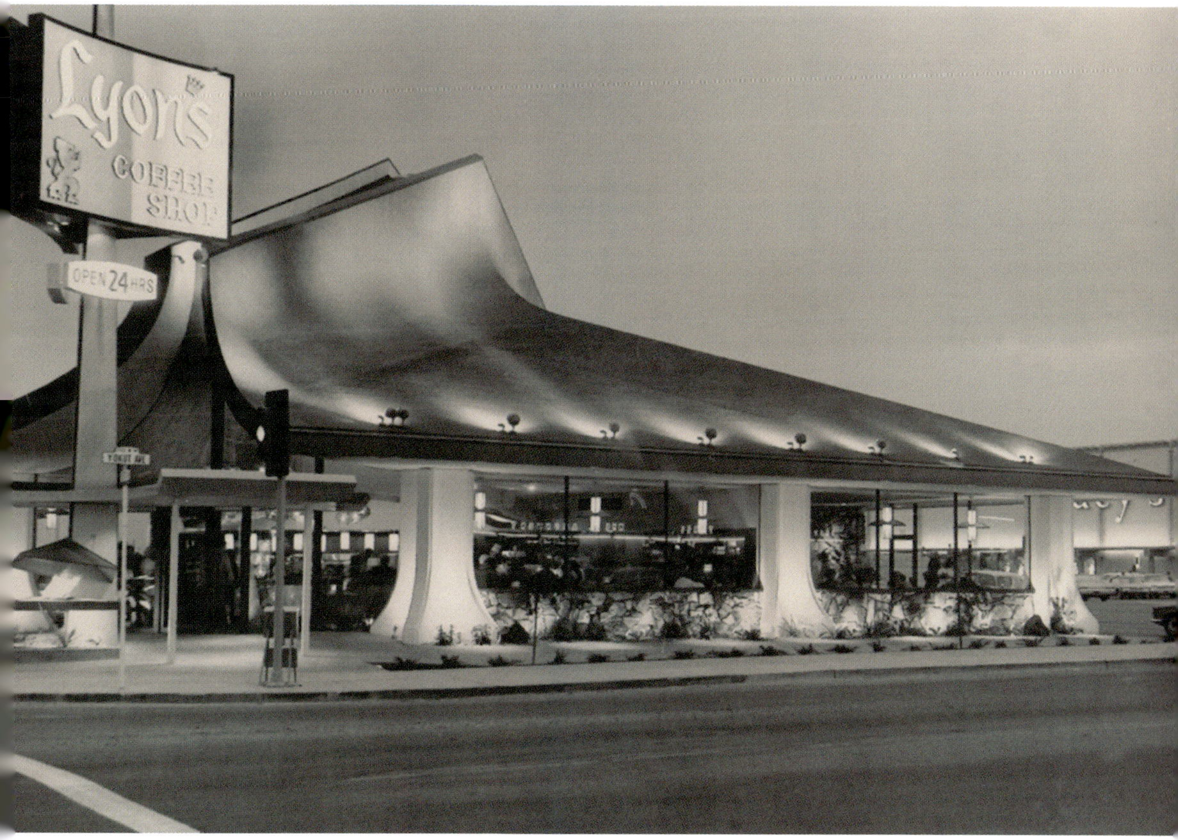

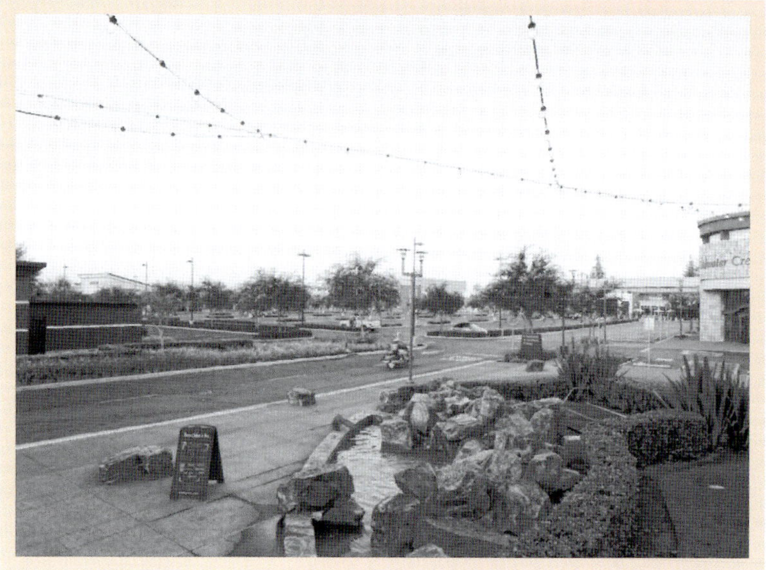

Max and Merrill Stone developed the Sherwood Plaza in 1969. Waning profitability and market opportunity ended a life cycle for Kmart and incentivized redevelopment. In 2007 and 2008, a new generation of the Stone family created the Stone Creek Village, "a life style center," breathing new life into the old strip-mall concept. In the 1950s, the Stone family had envisioned the future of suburban development in Stockton north of the Calaveras River. (Courtesy of Stone Brothers Archives.)

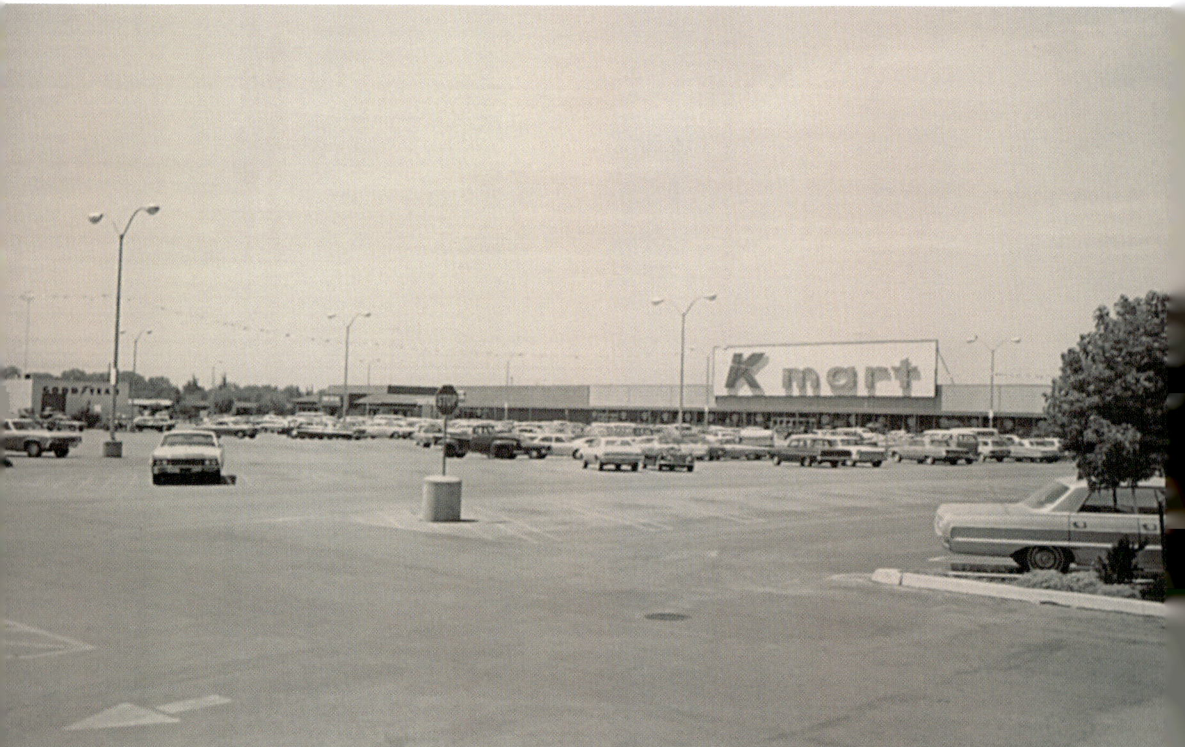

CHAPTER 5

The Urban Life Cycle

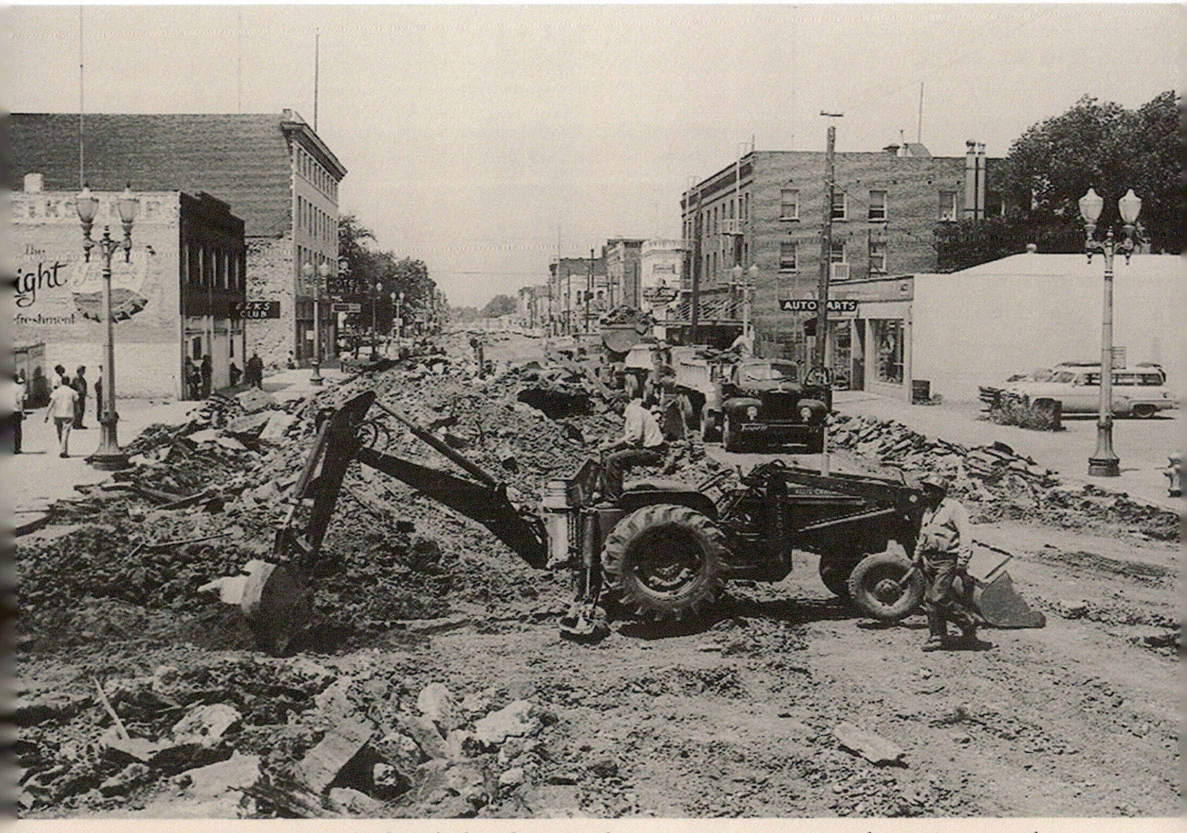

Numerous American cities launched urban redevelopment projects in the 1960s. Stockton's was defined as the West End Redevelopment District. This region encompassed a nine-block area southwest of the courthouse. Characterized as a skid row, this district experienced profound and conspicuous unemployment, social degradation, and a collapsing infrastructure. The demolition of streets and buildings accelerated the urban life cycle of Stockton. (Courtesy of Bank of Stockton Archives.)

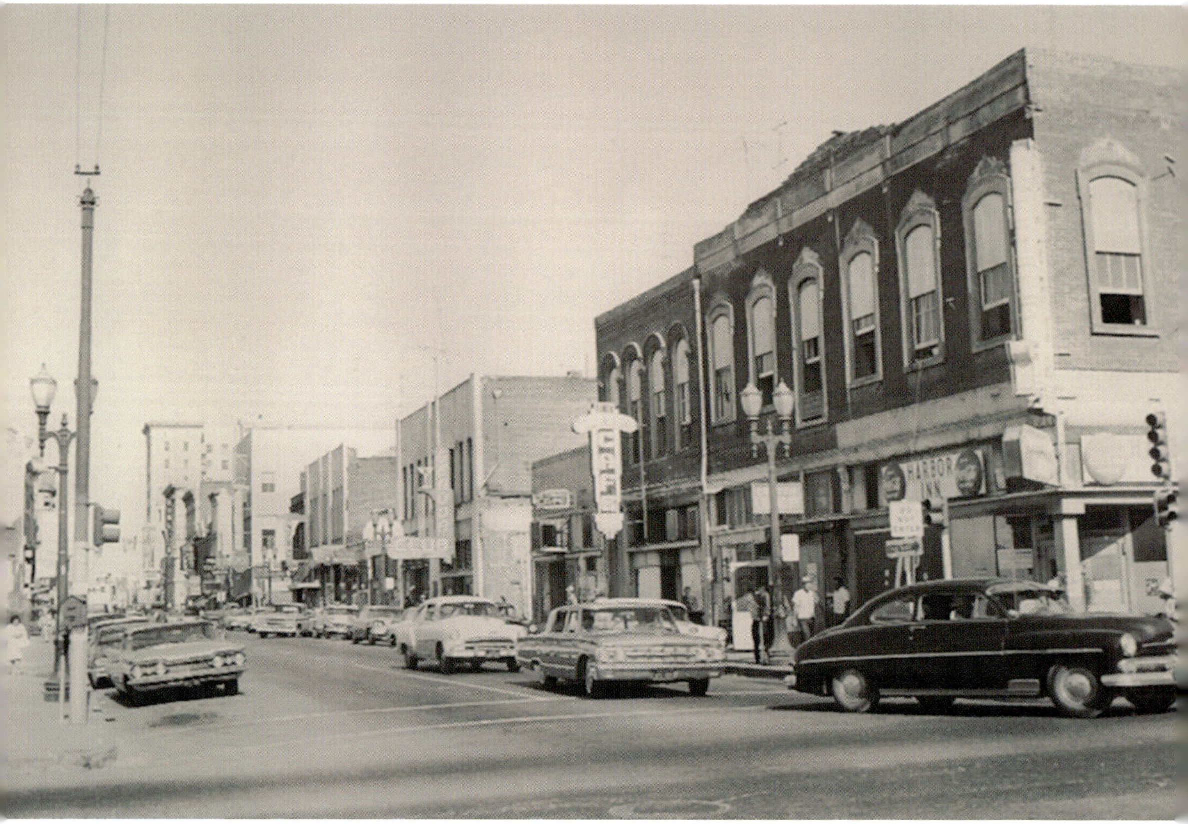

The intersection of Main and Center Streets became a symbolic epicenter for Stockton early in its history as a manufacturing city. From 1860 to 1945, Main Street accommodated and connected the civic, cultural, commercial, and manufacturing sectors of the city. In the 1960s, this intersection became the crossroads of the city's urban redevelopment initiative. In 1965, Main Street was permanently closed to automobile traffic. Today, it is has become a tree-lined pedestrian corridor. (Courtesy of Bank of Stockton Archives.)

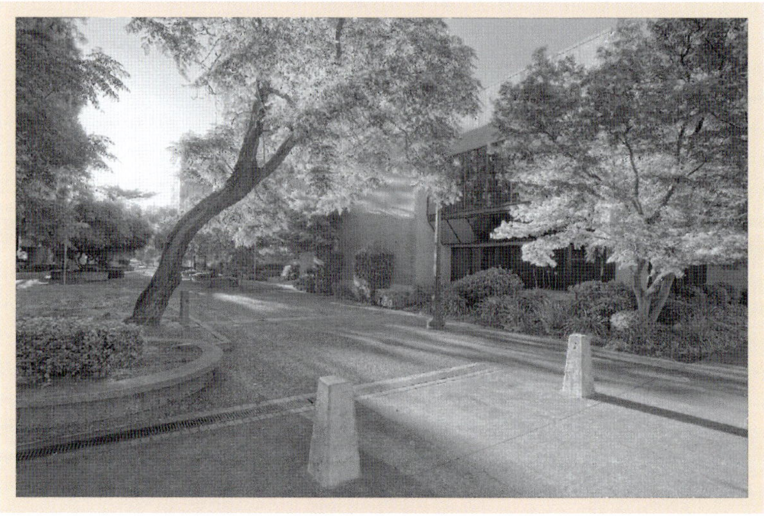

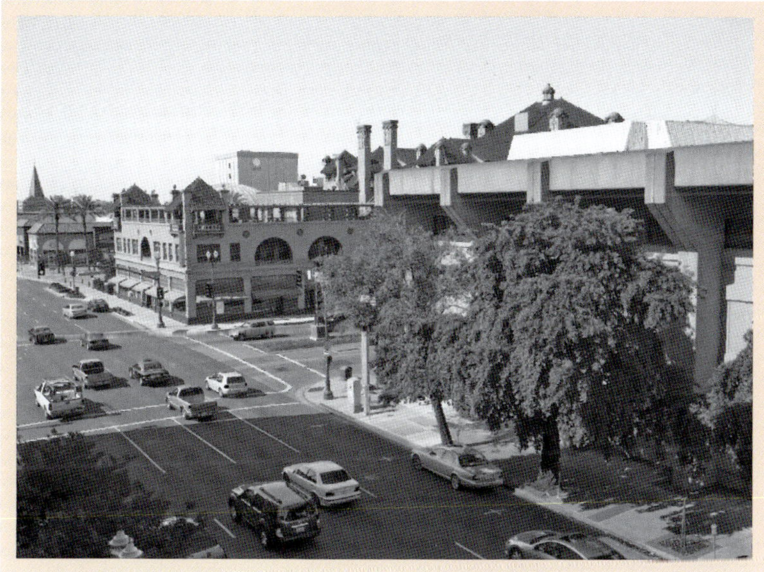

In 1965, multiple buildings surrounding the El Dorado Street/Weber Avenue intersection were razed. Considered "a vast monument to Mission Revival architecture," the Hotel Stockton (1910) was spared. It has been repurposed several times since its heyday before 1940. In 2005, it became a cornerstone of Stockton's downtown renaissance. The Sass Bar and Grill is the newest addition to the venerable landmark's history. The Sass offers fine dining and a remarkable westward view of the Stockton Channel from Stockton's City Center. (Courtesy of Bank of Stockton Archives.)

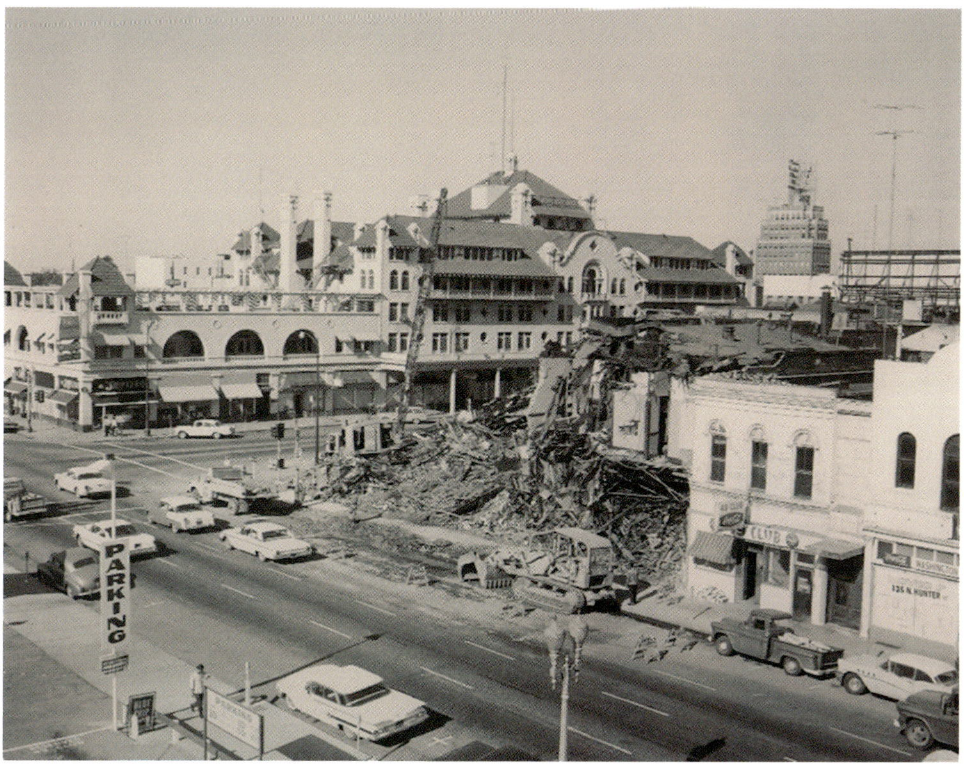

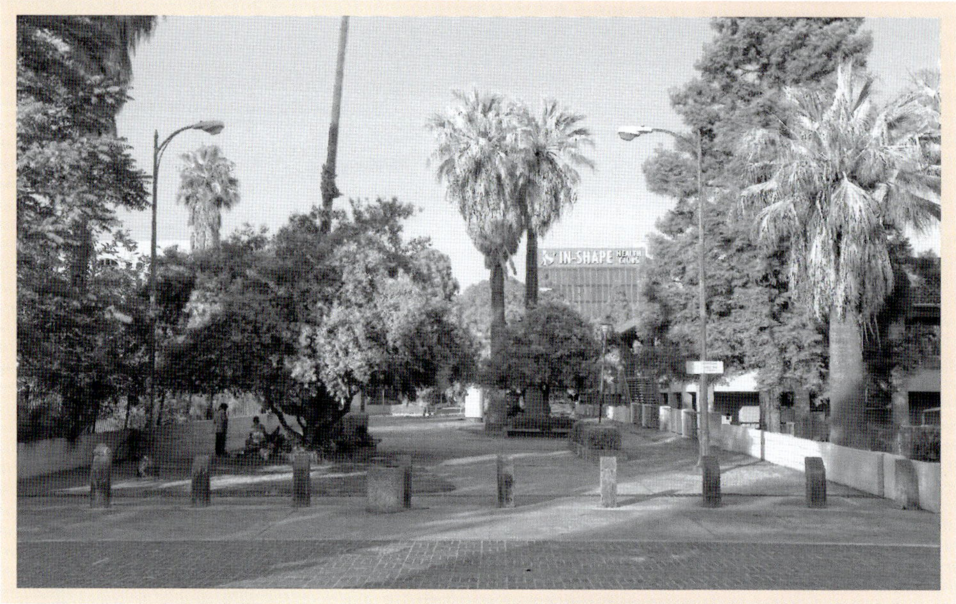

Urban renewal stirred Stockton's early struggles and achievements toward prosperity to the surface. Flooded and impassable streets characterized the early decades of Stockton. Graveling and paving the roadways became an essential ingredient in Stockton's economic success by the 1860s. In 1965, Jack Werner poses on a pile of cobblestones at the intersection of Main and Commerce Streets for a Stockton *Record* photojournalist. Today, the cobbles are being recycled throughout the downtown area as decorative finish. (Courtesy of Stockton Record/Haggin Museum Archives.)

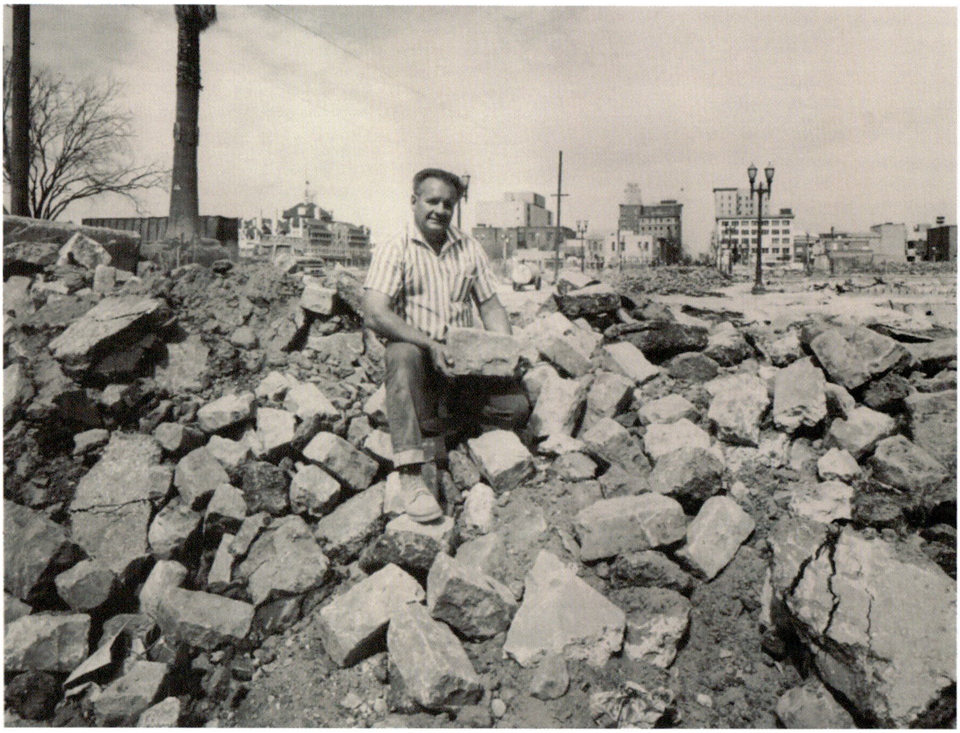

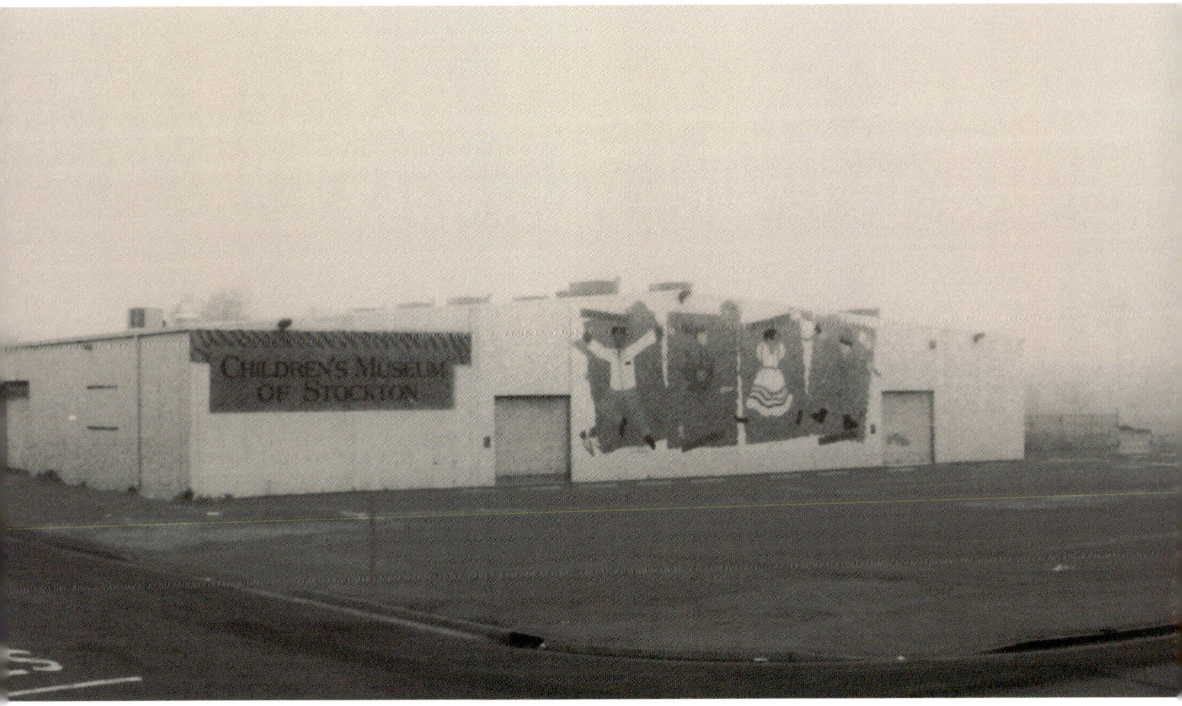

Hope slowly transformed a tragedy in Stockton. Through inspired community collaboration, the Children's Museum of Stockton opened in January 1994. The museum was the vision of Janet Geng, its first director and a teacher who was wounded during the deadly school shooting at Cleveland Elementary School on January 17, 1989, which ended the lives of five children and wounded 31 people. The Children's Museum was an ember of light from its inception, and today it is a beacon on the west end of Weber Avenue. (Courtesy of Stockton Re-Photographic Survey.)

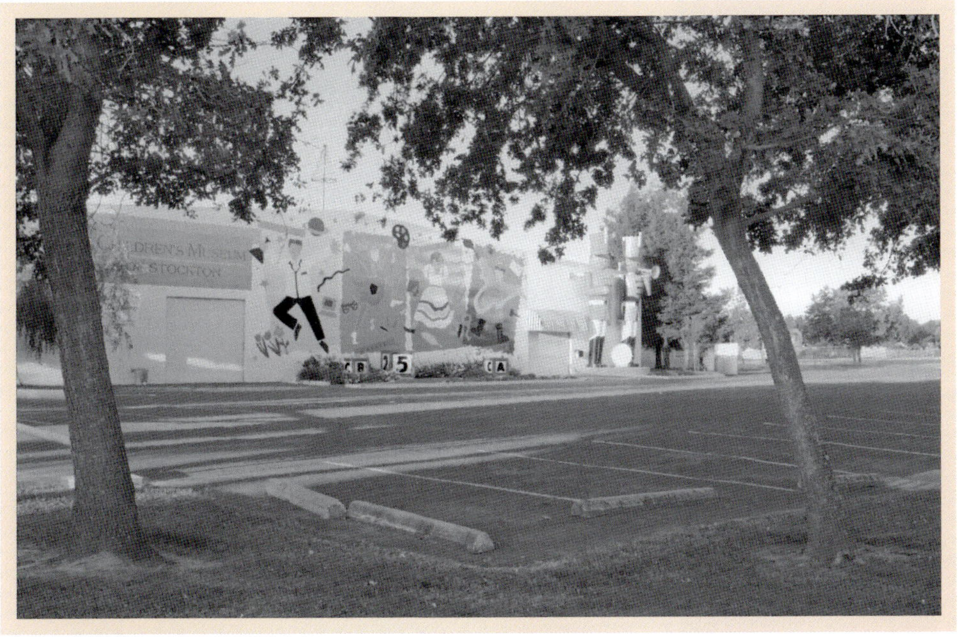

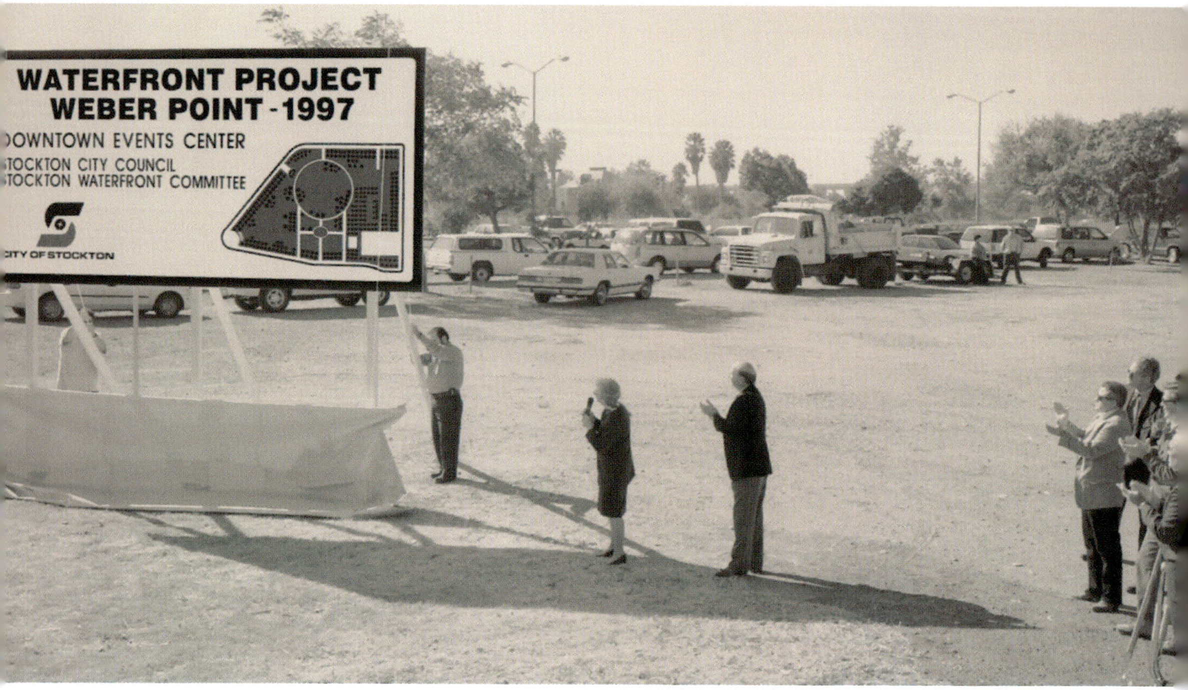

Weber Point is Stockton's historic epicenter. During Stockton's first decade, the Weber family's home and gardens defined the city. The point declined after the 1862 flood and the longer-term consequences of industrialization. Subsequent revitalization attempts through commercial development were short-lived. Committed civic groups lobbied for redevelopment, and in 1997 Mayor Joan Darrah and Duane Isetti unveil the announcement to rebuild. Today, the point is home to the Asparagus Festival. In 2011, the California Repercussions, a St. Helena–based band, opens the festival. (Courtesy of Stockton Re-Photographic Survey.)

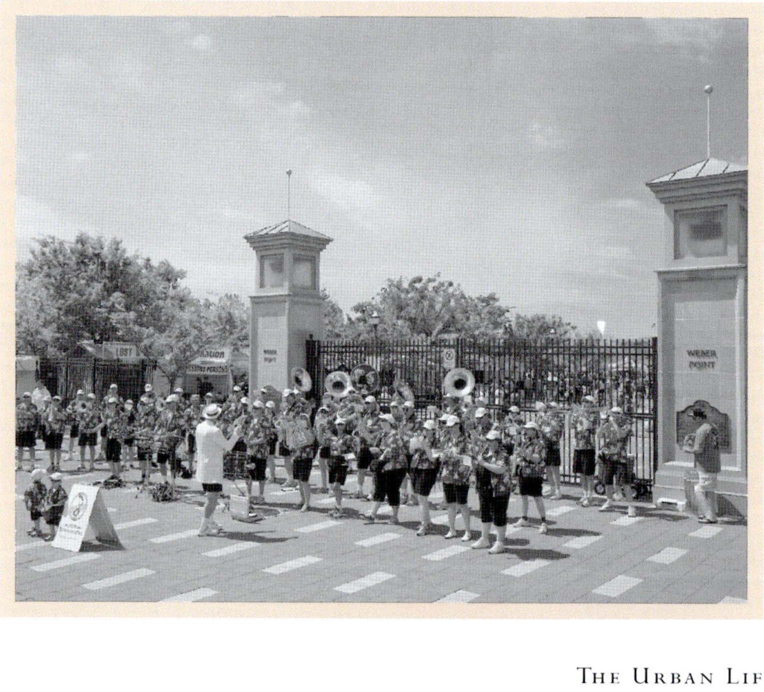

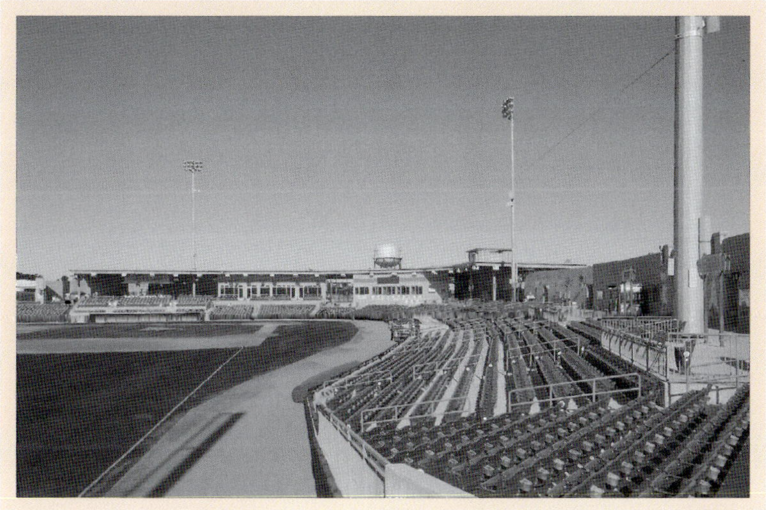

The north shore of the Stockton Channel has an understated maritime history. Commercial boat building in Stockton dates from 1850 to 1987. During World War II, 10 builders operated along the Stockton Channel. The majority of these companies fulfilled large government contracts for a variety of military vessels. Today, the former sites of the Hickinbotham and Guntert companies' shipbuilding divisions are home to the Stockton Ports baseball stadium. (Courtesy of University of the Pacific Special Collections.)

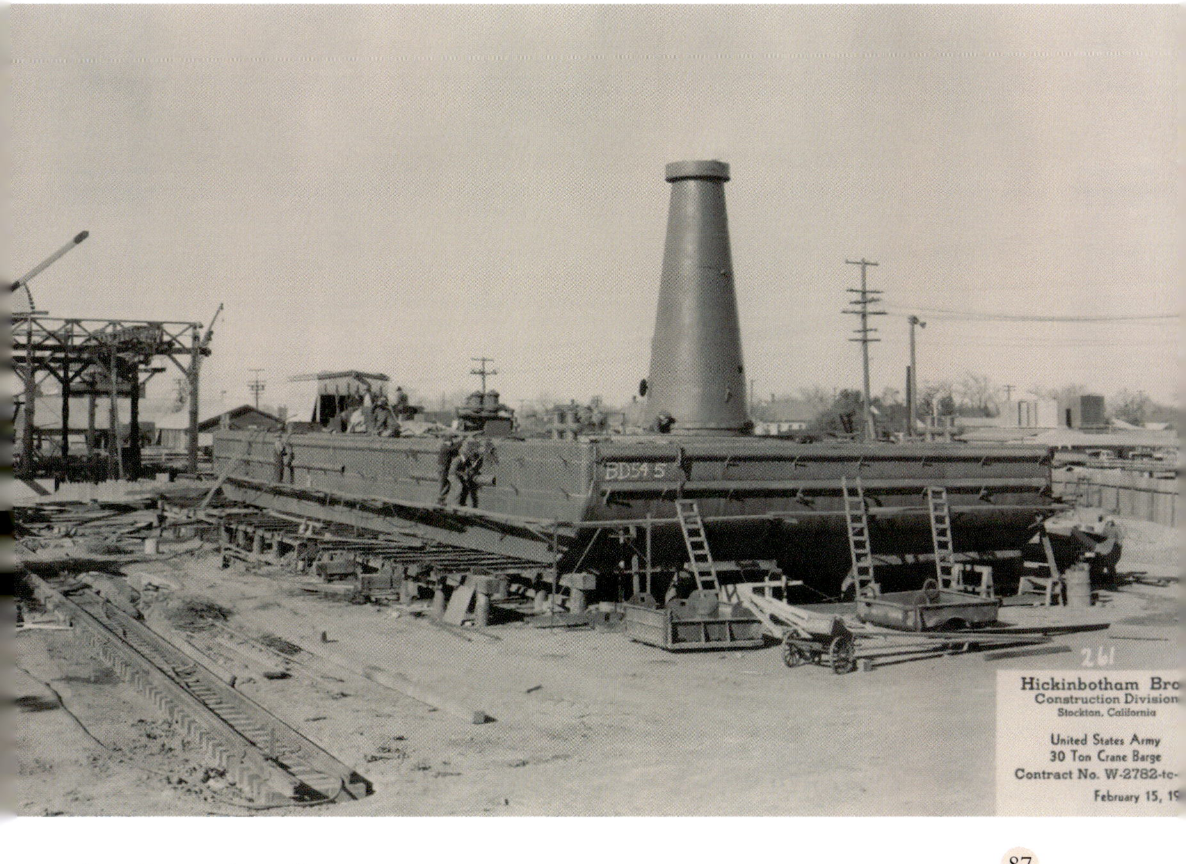

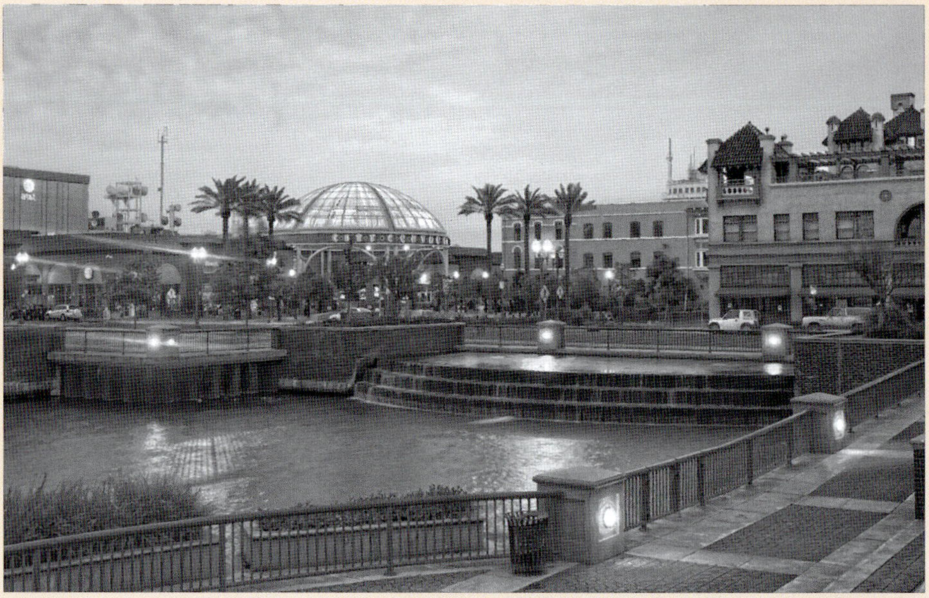

The Head of Navigation provides a wonderful frame of reference for understanding Stockton's urban renewal. It has undergone three relocations since 1948, moving a city block westward each time. By the mid-1990s, the old waterfront that once served the steamship transportation companies was obscured by a parking lot. In the spring of 2001, this reminder of urban blight disappeared. Today, the terraces of DeCarli Plaza create one of the most pleasant urban spaces in downtown Stockton. (Courtesy of Stockton Re-Photographic Survey.)

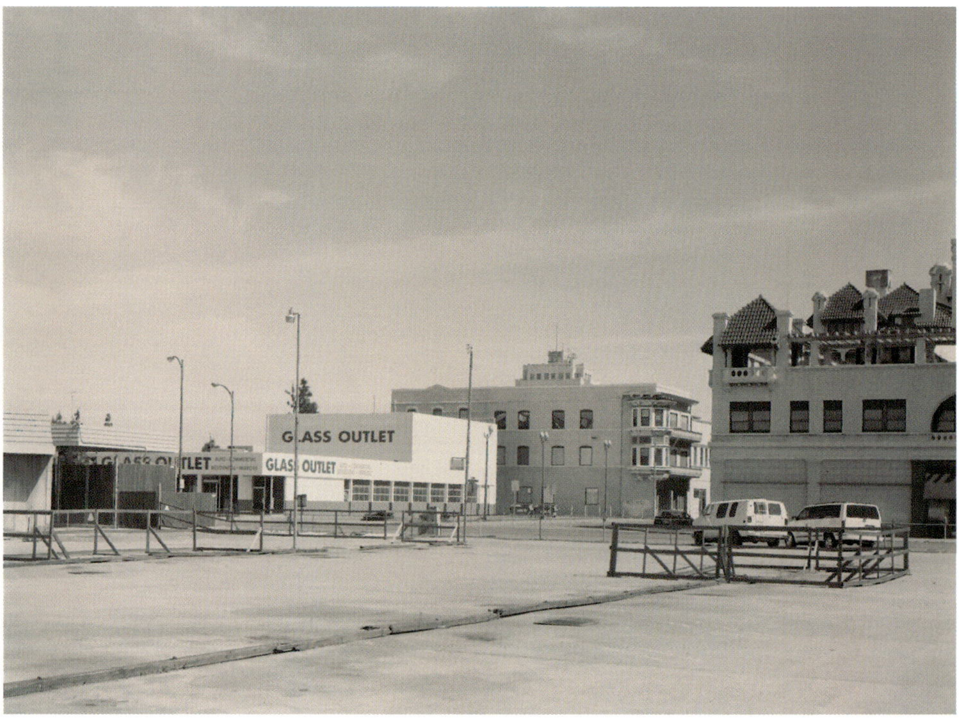

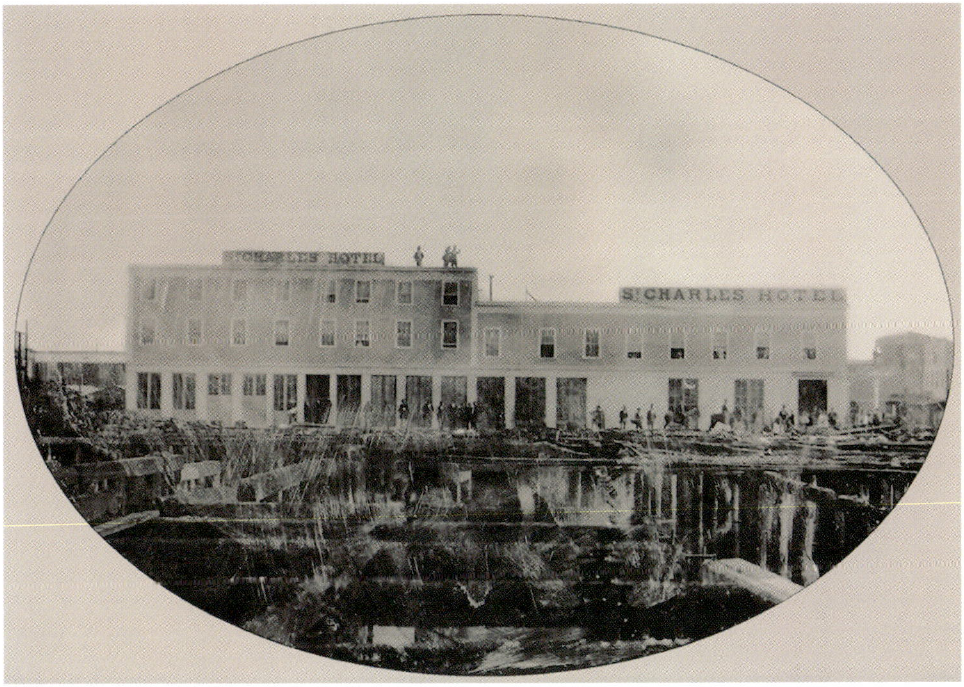

The history of Stockton's Head of Navigation is rich with interesting stories and cycles of development. It has been the location for several significant Stockton institutions and prominent buildings. The St. Charles Hotel, originally opened in 1850 as the Stockton House, featured some of the city's earliest theater and musical performances for a distinguished list of travelers. Today, with the redevelopment of the City Center, the Janet Leigh Square is highlighted by contemporary cinematic features playing daily. (Courtesy of Stockton Re-Photographic Survey.)

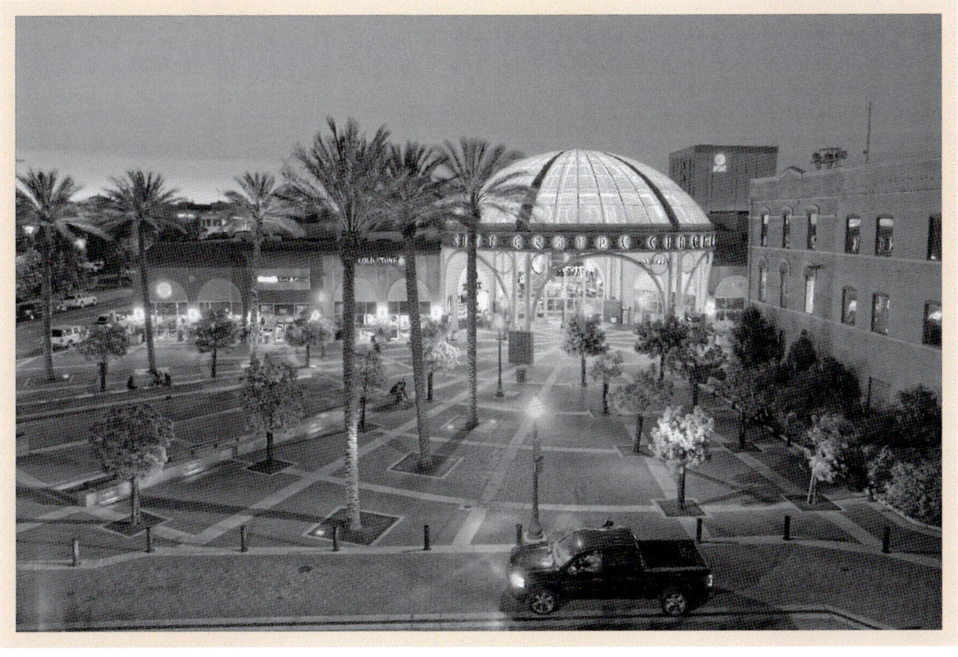

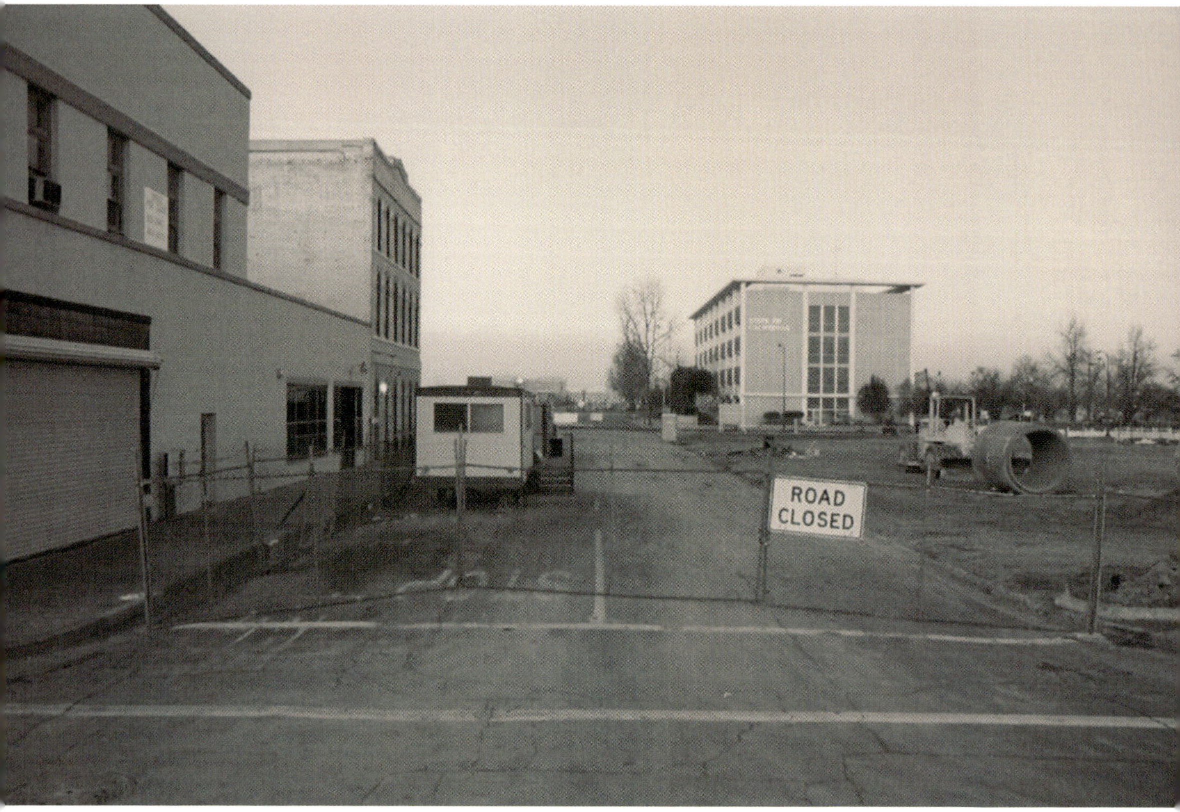

The redevelopment of the City Center and Janet Leigh Square was designed to preserve and integrate historical buildings and produce a public environment that could accommodate a mixture of a broad range of patrons employed in the downtown region or family and friends out for entertainment and dining. The development plan razed a complete city block to achieve its goal, and Channel Street was converted to a pedestrian corridor. The plan has become a success story for Stockton. (Courtesy of Stockton Re-Photographic Survey.)

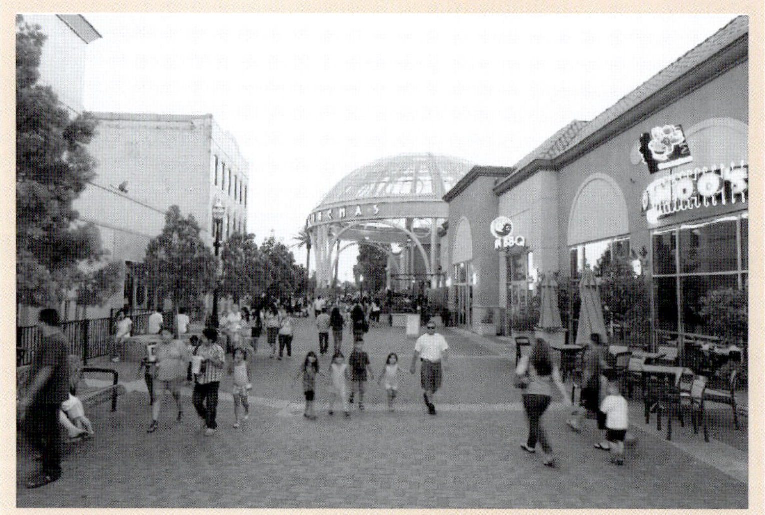

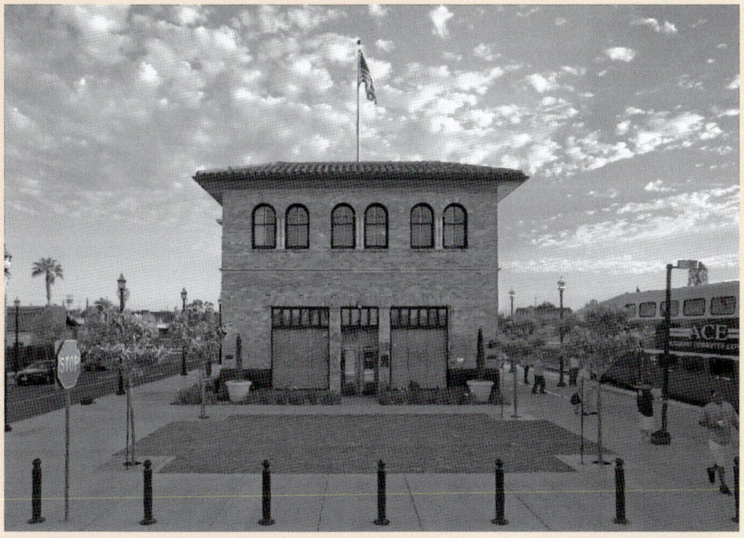

A lesser-known victory in the redevelopment of Channel Street is the renovation of the old Southern Pacific Railroad Station, located eight blocks east at Sacramento Street. The current station is the home of the Altamont Commuter Express. The renewal scheme emphasized restoration to approximate the old station's dignity. Today, the ACE train accommodates a regular schedule of commuters and travelers with destinations north to Sacramento and south to San Jose. (Courtesy of Stockton Re-Photographic Survey.)

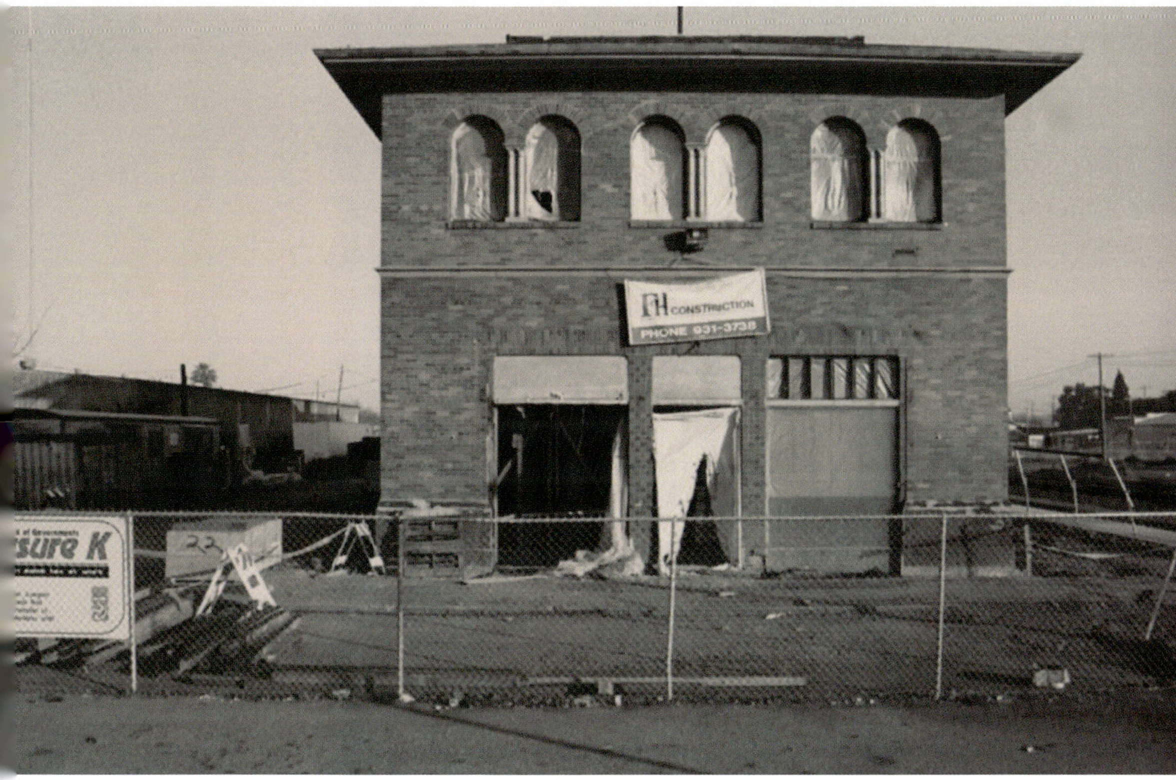

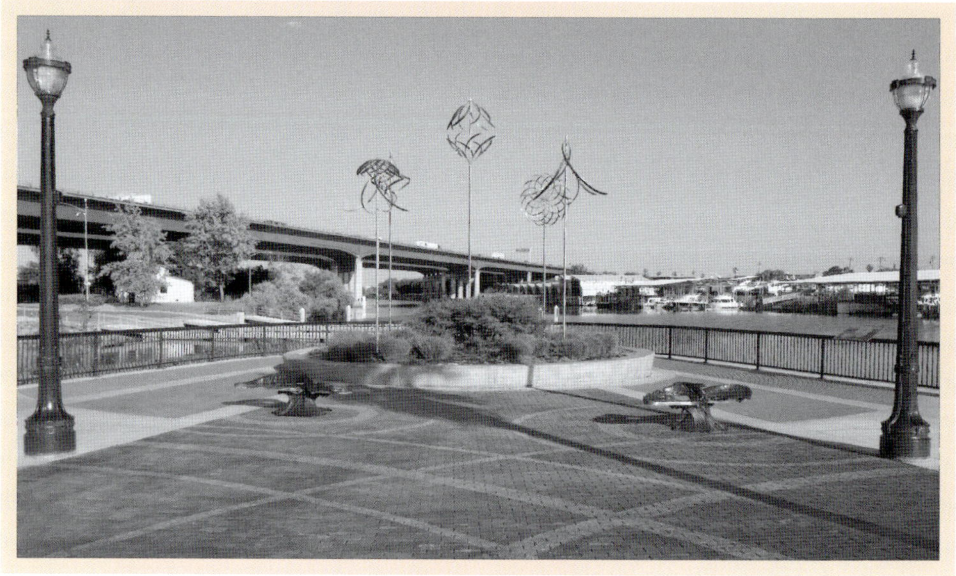

The Sacramento–San Joaquin Delta watershed includes 31,800 square miles of water and a number of marinas. The Morelli Park and Boat Launch, located on the south shore of the Stockton Channel, was reconstructed in 2008. Today, Morelli Park is connected to DeCarli Plaza via the Joan Darrah Promenade. The promenade honors Stockton's late mayor, who is fondly remembered for initiating significant downtown renewal while in office from 1990 to 1996. The promenade intersects the Stockton Marina and the Waterfront Warehouse. (Courtesy of Stockton Re-Photographic Survey.)

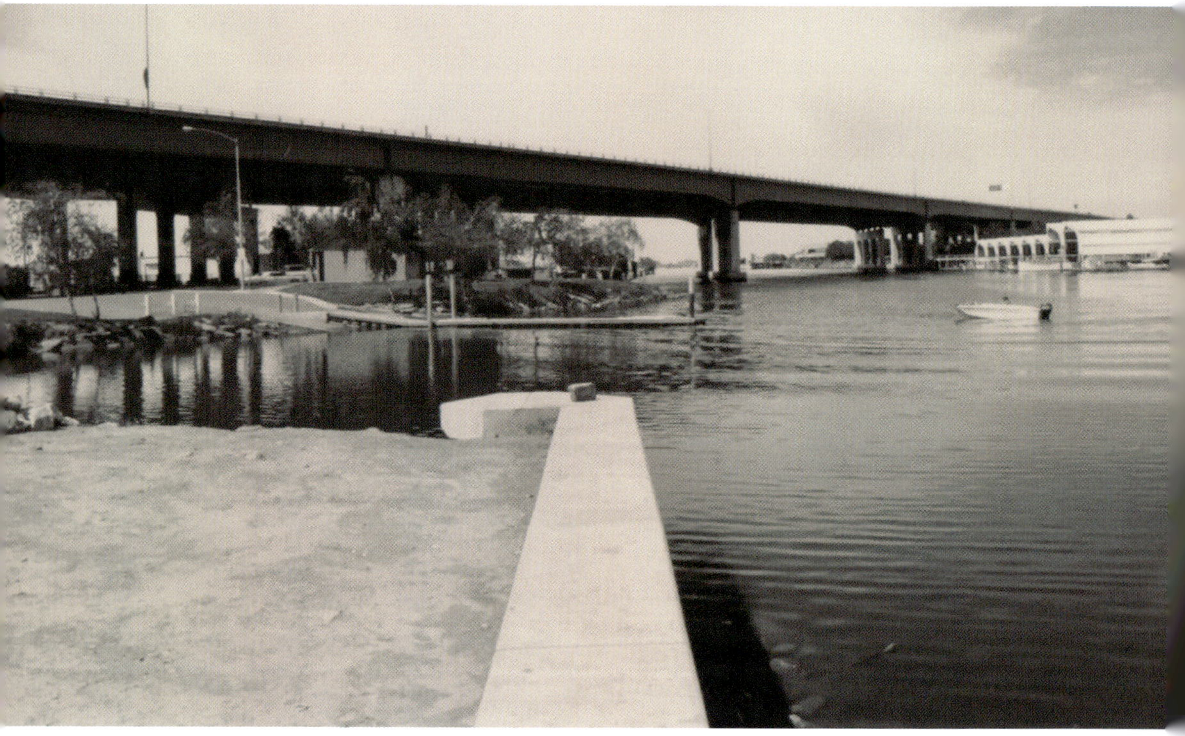

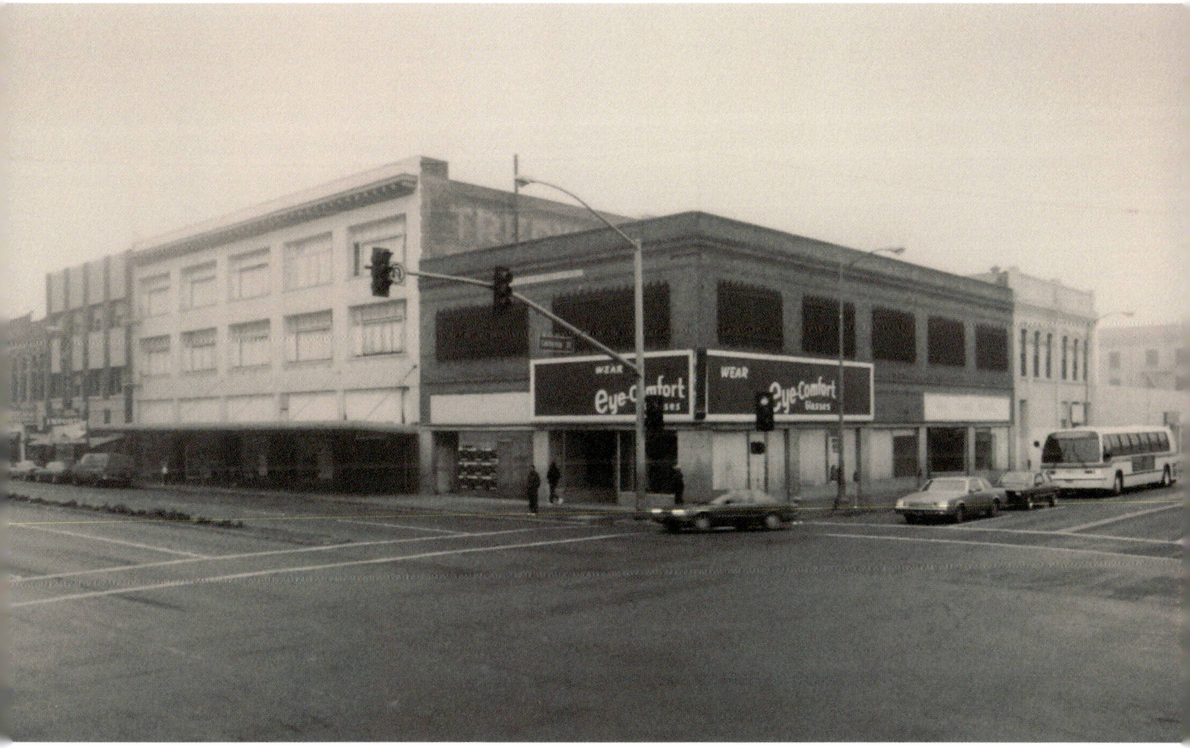

The breakdown of public transportation systems and the suburbanization of Stockton coincided with the rise in popularity of the automobile. These trends are slowly reversing, aided by a growing network of public transportation and bicycle corridors. The redevelopment of Stockton's Rapid Transit Terminal on Weber Avenue occurred in 2006 and incorporated a significant portion of the existing and historic storefronts into the renewed infrastructure required for quality service and economically efficient operations. (Courtesy of Stockton Re-Photographic Survey.)

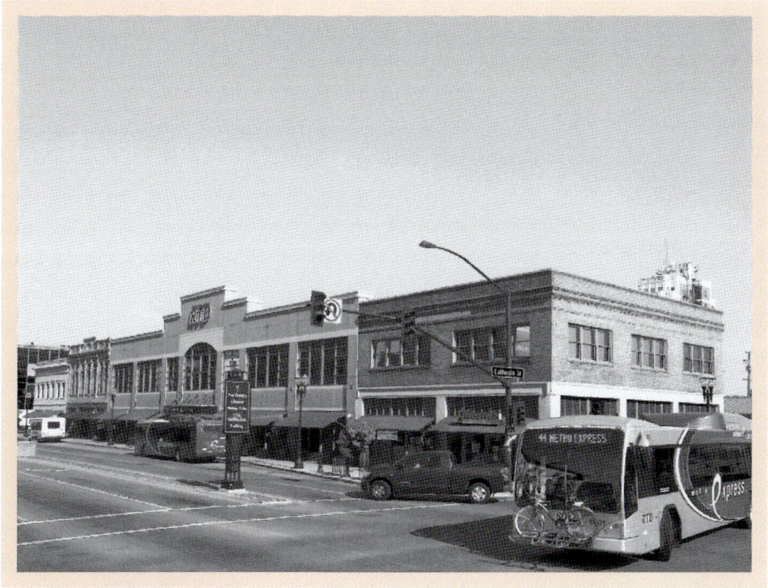

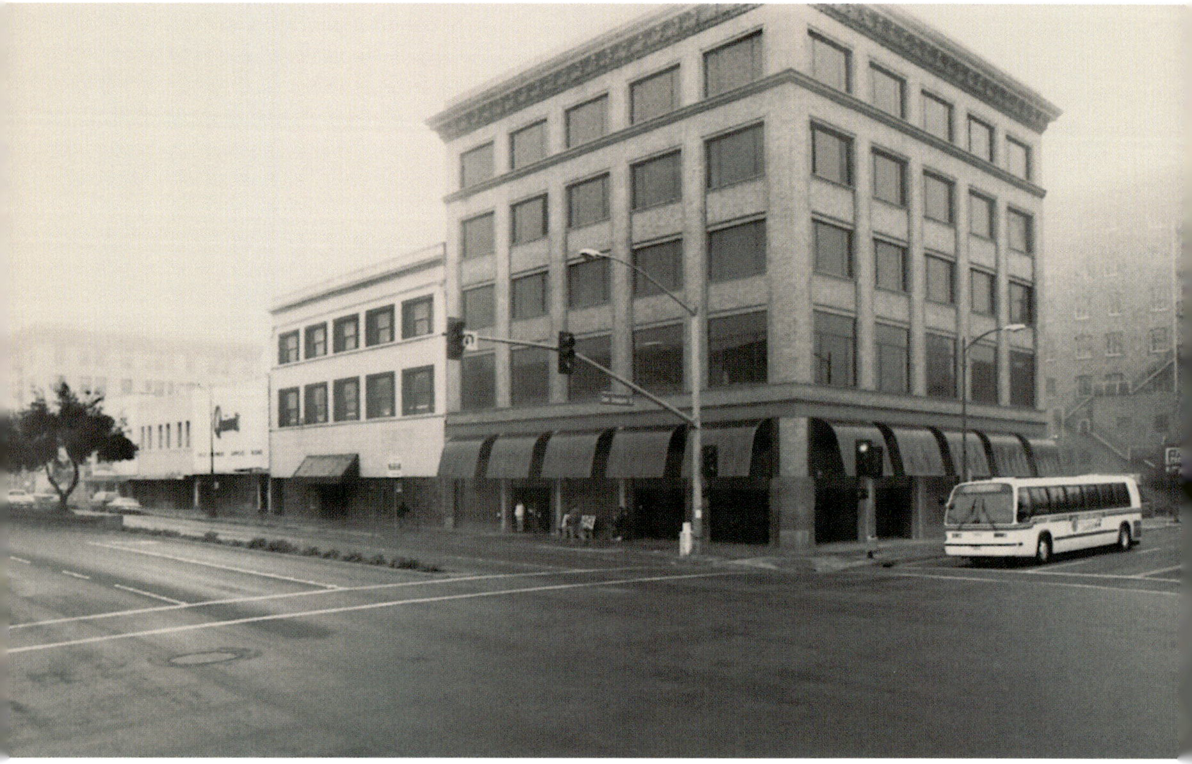

The most recent addition to the Stockton skyline is the new County Administrative Building, located at the intersection of Weber Avenue and San Joaquin Street. Fentress Architecture of Denver, Colorado, designed the building. In addition to its bold contribution to the urban textures of downtown, its unique interior design (inspired by the patterns and relationships between county farmland, rivers, and delta) provides spaces for viewing the work of contemporary artists of regional and international significance. (Courtesy of Stockton Re-Photographic Survey.)

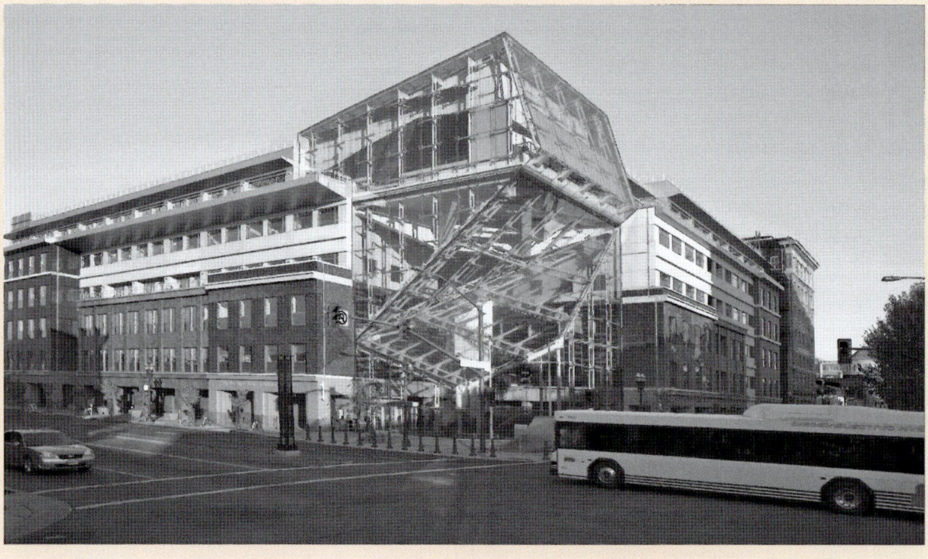

Bibliography

Barnett, Roger Thomas. "Suburban Subdivision: The morphogenesis of housing in Stockton, 1850–1950." PhD diss., University of California, Berkeley, 1973.

Beauregard, Robert A. *When America Became Suburban.* Minneapolis: University of Minnesota Press, 2006.

Berman, Marshall. *All That is Solid Melts Into Air: The Experience of Modernity.* New York: Simon & Schuster, 1982.

Cosgrove, Denis. *Geography and Vision: Seeing, Imagining and Representing the World.* New York: I.B. Tauris, 2008.

Gratz, Roberta Brandes, and Norman Mintz. *Cities Back From the Edge: A New Life for Downtown.* New York: John Wiley & Sons, 1998.

Jackson, John Brinckerhoff. *American Space: The Centennial Years, 1865–1876.* New York: W.W. Norton, 1972.

Kasser, Daniel. *Downtown Stockton.* Charleston, SC: Arcadia Publishing, 2005.

Martin, V. Covert, R. Coke Wood, and Leon Bush. *Stockton Album: Through the Years.* Woburn, MA: Simard, 1959.

McManus, Ruth, and Philip J. Ethington. "Suburbs in Transition: New Approaches to Suburban History." *Urban History* 34, no. 2 (2007): 317–337.

Meinig, Donald W., ed. *The Interpretation of Ordinary Landscapes: Geographical Essays.* New York: Oxford University Press, 1979.

Payne, Walter A., ed. *Benjamin Holt: The Story of the Caterpillar Tractor.* Stockton, CA: Holt-Atherton Pacific Center for Western Studies, University of the Pacific, 1982.

Van Ommeren, Alice. *Stockton in Vintage Postcards.* Charleston, SC: Arcadia Publishing, 2004.

Wood, R. Coke, and Leonard Covello. *Stockton Memories: A Pictorial History of Stockton, California.* Fresno: Valley Publishers, 1977.